The Club

The Club

CHRISTY O'CONNOR

PENGUIN IRELAND

PENGUIN IRELAND

Published by the Penguin Group
Penguin Ireland, 25 St Stephen's Green, Dublin 2, Ireland (a division of Penguin Books Ltd)
Penguin Books Ltd, 80 Strand, London WC2R 0RL, England
Penguin Group (USA) Inc., 375 Hudson Street, New York, New York 10014, USA
Penguin Group (Australia), 250 Camberwell Road, Camberwell, Victoria 3124, Australia
(a division of Pearson Australia Group Pty Ltd)
Penguin Group (Canada), 90 Eglinton Avenue East, Suite 700, Toronto, Ontario, Canada M4P 2Y3
(a division of Pearson Penguin Canada Inc.)
Penguin Books India Pvt Ltd, 11 Community Centre, Panchsheel Park, New Delhi – 110 017, India
Penguin Group (NZ), 67 Apollo Drive, Rosedale, Auckland 0632, New Zealand
(a division of Pearson New Zealand Ltd)
Penguin Books (South Africa) (Pty) Ltd, 24 Sturdee Avenue, Rosebank, Johannesburg 2196, South Africa

Penguin Books Ltd, Registered Offices: 80 Strand, London WC2R 0RL, England

www.penguin.com

First published 2010
5

Set in 12/14.75 Bembo Book MT Std
Typeset by Jouve (UK), Milton Keynes
Printed in Great Britain by Clays Ltd, St Ives plc

A CIP catalogue record for this book is available from the British Library

ISBN: 978–1–844–88252–6

www.greenpenguin.co.uk

Penguin Books is committed to a sustainable future
for our business, our readers and our planet.
The book in your hands is made from paper
certified by the Forest Stewardship Council.

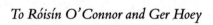

To Róisín O'Connor and Ger Hoey

Contents

1. Doubts

From 70 metres away, even against the blinding rays of the sun, I can see their midfielder arch his body back on the turn. He is leaning so heavily on his right leg that it's almost possible to observe a pirouette in the manner of his address. I know that his attempt at a score from that distance isn't going to have the legs to carry over the bar. He gets a clean strike, but the ball has a lower trajectory than normal and it's drifting, hanging, teasing in the air. That means one thing: danger.

Their corner-forward has got goal-side of our corner-back and is tracking the flight path of the ball like a hawk closing in on its prey. I'm fully focused on the ball but I can see him out of the corner of my eye, and now I can hear him charging like a rhinoceros, which further heightens my awareness of the threat. I know I'm probably outside the square, which removes any protection I might get from the referee or umpire, so that leaves only a split second to decide how to deal with this situation.

I'm already on a yellow card for railroading the same player in the first minute when he was straight through on goal, but I don't have time now for my brain to compute the ramifications of another reckless challenge. I can only worry about the ball, because there's nobody else behind me. I should probably bat the ball away to limit the danger but I'm confident in my handling and my mind is made up in a millisecond. I decide I'll take it at its highest point by out-jumping the forward and fielding the ball over his head and above his reach.

Bad decision. The ball loops that bit lower than I anticipated and he gets the gentlest of caresses on it. I don't know whether it has glanced off his hurley or his arm, but it's not in my hand. I don't need to look behind me to know where the ball has ended up because I can hear the forward's shriek of elation before the roar rises up from the belly of the crowd. The ball has just crept beyond the line and is nestled in the bottom right-hand corner. Another half a foot and it would have been outside the post, which is almost like another slap in the face.

Frantically, I opt for Plan B, something every goalkeeper has in his bag. 'SQUARE BALL! Ah, come on, umpire, he was definitely inside in the square. He was all over me.'

The umpire doesn't entertain my plea for a second. He's already reaching for the green flag. But this is more than just a goal. It's like a dagger in our hearts, a mortal blow to whatever chance we had in this game.

The timing is critical. As soon as I puck out the ball, the referee blows the half-time whistle. I glance up at the scoreboard behind me and there is the harsh reality, staring at me in big bold letters and numbers:

Newmarket-on-Fergus 1-8

St Joseph's Doora-Barefield 0-2.

As I pick up my hurleys and bag from the side of the net, the agony of the goal is tearing up my mind and I silently and angrily mutter words that seem vulgar, obscene and selfish in the context of a hurling match: 'Jesus Christ, why did you do this to me?'

It makes no sense – but right now nothing seems to make sense.

They've scored 1-8, and we've had to save a penalty and survive some manic goal-line scrambling. They've decoded our puckout strategy and have gone a long way to shutting it down. Our defence has played some heroic stuff but it's being slowly suffocated by the pressure originating higher up the field where our midfield and half-forward line are being annihilated. And on a dry and sunny October Sunday, in a county senior hurling semi-final, before a crowd of around 6,000, we've managed to score just two points in 32 minutes. This is embarrassing. This is wrong. All wrong.

Trailing by just six points at the break might have given us some hope to cling to, but the goal has killed any optimism. Our legs are weak and we've been stumbling. All through the half, we knew we were just one haymaker away from hitting the canvas. And now, they've just landed it on our chin.

The dressing room is mayhem. Guys roaring and shouting at one another, leaving little or no opportunity for critical assessment as to how we can somehow retrieve this situation. I walk through the shower area and into the adjoining dressing room to change my under-armour garment and to try and clear my head. Our corner-back, Marty O'Regan, follows me in. He doesn't seem to know where he's going.

'Are you all right, Marty?' I inquire.

'I'm seeing double,' he responds.

He's been our best defender all year but he's just been destroyed by their corner-forward, Colin Ryan. Now it makes sense. He took a sickening hit in the first couple of minutes.

'You're concussed, man,' I tell him. 'This game is over for you.'

Marty lies upon the physio table, while I just sit down and observe him staring vacantly at the concrete ceiling that is carved out of the seat indentations from the stand above us. Normally, you can hear the hum of the crowd and the Irish music playing from the tannoy, but today there doesn't seem to be any sound. It's almost as if this nightmare is happening while we're suspended under water.

As our physio, Eugene Moynihan, tends to Marty, I can hear more roaring and shouting in the next room. As I make my way back in, two of our substitutes, Fergal O'Sullivan and Eoin Conroy, have taken over the floor.

'What had we spoken about beforehand?' roars Sull. 'We said we'd get in their faces and drag them into the trenches for a battle. And we're just letting them walk all over us.'

Conny was more personal. Their full-back and centre-back have been dominating, so he takes aim at Noel Brodie and Seánie McMahon, our centre-forward and full-forward.

'Will ye at least stand down on top of those two fuckers. They're outside there doing what they like. Walk down on top of them. Start a fucking brawl if ye have to. Grab one of them by the throat, but do something to stop them waltzing out with ball after ball. AND GET INTO THE FUCKING GAME.'

Our management, though, seem to have just accepted the inevitable. 'Whatever about the result now, I want ye to go back out and at least show some pride in the second half,' says our coach, Seán Chaplin. 'What we've shown is just not good enough. We need to go back out there and not lie down like we have done in that last 30 minutes.'

Those words don't appear to have reached us, but I doubt if any words can pierce the layer of doom that has enveloped the room. Then Seánie McMahon stands up and begins to talk loudly and assertively, spittle almost splattering from his lips. This is a man who effectively launched the Clare hurling revolution in 1995. With Clare trailing by two points to Cork deep in injury time of the Munster semi-final, McMahon, withered from pain after breaking his collarbone, somehow engineered the sideline cut which led to Clare's match-winning goal.

To him, nothing is impossible. 'Fuck that shit about going out and fighting for pride. I'm going out in the second half to win this game. We're nine points down but we haven't even started to hurl yet. We've been asleep for 30 minutes, but if we wake up, this game is still there for us. If we get a goal, we'll put them under pressure. And if we get a run on them, these boys will fucking collapse.'

Seánie's voice has jolted us from our seats and got us back up on our feet. This is a time to see who cares and how deeply this all matters. Time for all of us to give something.

But as we gather in a huddle, arms wrapped tightly around one another, the soundtrack still doesn't seem convincing. Looking around the huddle, there is enthusiasm and hope, but you know it's false. There are too many blank stares and stooped shoulders, too many faces mirroring anxiety and confusion and an unmistakable vulnerability. You can sense the doubt, almost feel the fear.

We know. We just know. We can feel it. A forest fire of aggression won't be enough to burn Newmarket because they're playing at a level way above us. Half-time has only been a respite from the barrage they have already hit us with and it's inevitable that the agony will soon start again. In hurling, nine points can be erased with three pucks of a ball, but doubt appears to have taken a crippling hold of our collective consciousness.

They hit us hard again just after the break. Bang, bang, bang. We respond with a goal, but their scores are coming more frequently now. Each score is now like an accurate jab which thuds home even harder than the last.

We have no real history with Newmarket, but they've got a real run on us and they seem to have just decided that they're going to slay us. The last ten minutes are agony. Two late goals draw some audible cheers from our supporters, but they arise from loyalty rather than from any hope or satisfaction.

Newmarket-on-Fergus 1-20

St Joseph's Doora-Barefield 3-7

The final winning margin is only seven points, but that doesn't conceal the reality that this was a total rout. Annihilation. We may have scored 3-5 in the second half, but it felt like a training run for them ahead of the county final. For Christ's sake, they gave a rake of their young subs a run in the last quarter.

As I make my way off the field, they're heading for the bottom corner to complete their warm-down. I walk straight into the middle of their pack and shake hands with as many of them as I can. Their manager, Diarmuid O'Leary, who I hurled with in St Flannan's College, seeks me out. I shake his hand, pat him on the cheek and wish him all the best for the final.

Then their coach, Ciaran O'Neill, makes his way over. Most of us played alongside O'Neill with Doora-Barefield. He was one of our great players and he even managed us for one season. But he coached Kilmaley to beat us in the 2004 county final by a point, and now he has helped another team to obliterate us. We shake hands but no words are spoken. No need for them now.

Before I make my way to the dressing room, I wait in front of the tunnel on the halfway line for their captain and goalkeeper, Kieran Devitt. He is talking to friends, but then he spots me and ambles over.

'Just one of those days,' he says. 'One of those days when nothing went right for ye.'

In the last 15 years we have played in ten Clare senior hurling semi-finals; now we've just lost our fourth. One of those defeats, against

Éire Óg in 2000, was one of the most sickening losses we ever experienced, because a vastly inferior team out-fought us to end a two-year undefeated run in Clare and Munster. That was low stuff, but this is nearly as bad because Newmarket have done more than just beat us: they've shredded the name of this team.

We really believed we could win this county title. We're short of young talent and this team doesn't have the same positive age profile associated with most emerging teams in Clare. But we felt that our physique, experience and fireproof belief might be enough to take us there. Plus, we'd been backing it up, coming into the game; in our five previous championship matches, we'd averaged a score of 1-18 and had only conceded an average of 0-12.

We came into this semi-final with perhaps a 50–50 chance of beating a young, highly talented, extremely mobile, hungry and motivated outfit. We felt that we had the men for the big day and they hadn't, and if we could drag them into a battle we'd be the only ones left standing at the end of it. Now that assessment must be subjected to serious re-evaluation.

In the dressing room before the game, the last words in our huddle were delivered by Davy Hoey. One of our best and most experienced defenders, he was out injured after almost losing a finger in a work accident four days earlier.

'My heart is broken that I can't go out there with ye,' he told us. 'I can hardly speak because I'm fighting back the tears. But I know ye'll do everything ye can to try and help me make up for the disappointment I'm feeling. The whole county is going on about Newmarket and their royalty and their place in Clare hurling. They're all saying that the Blues are back, that they're going to start dominating Clare hurling again. Well, fuck the Blues. We'll show them what championship hurling is all about. We'll fucking eat them alive.'

Those words seem hollow now. They physically dominated us and they got the scores whenever they wanted, safe in the knowledge that we were incapable of being anything more than a temporary irritant.

As a team, it's been a long time since we were a dominant force;

but we were never rolled over in senior hurling like we have just been. In the last 15 years, the heaviest defeat we ever suffered in a big championship game was an eight-point loss to Wolfe Tones in the 2005 semi-final. And they got a goal deep in injury time of a match that was still in the balance up until that point.

This was a wipe-out. We were slapped around and we went down ugly. But the most worrying aspect for the future was what I saw at half-time. Although fear is the opposite of confidence, fear can sometimes be a positive thing in a dressing room. It focuses minds, drives some players to greater lengths, makes more players obsessive in their pursuit of victory. But that wasn't the type of fear I saw in the huddle; I saw anxiety, trepidation, almost an acceptance of defeat. In 19 years as St Joseph's Doora-Barefield first-choice goalkeeper, that was something I had never witnessed in a senior dressing room before.

After a meal at the Grove bar in Roslevan, I drop Seánie McMahon home. As we make our way along the Tulla road on the way to Spancilhill, the discussion inevitably drifts back to half-time.

'Fair play to you for what you said but, Jeez, I never saw as much doubt from some fellas in a Doora-Barefield dressing room in all my life,' I say to him. 'I knew we were fucked in the second half.'

Seánie feels that the genesis of the defeat lay in training: 'We got it badly wrong. We totally over-trained. I was never as tired coming off a pitch after training on Thursday night. We should have just taken the night off and went for food. A total disaster.'

As we turn left at Spancilhill Cross, I pose the inevitable question.

'Well, is that it? Will you be back?'

Still obviously disappointed with the performance, Seánie's voice is tinged with sadness.

'I don't think so, boss. I can't see it, anyway. I'd say that's it.'

He and his wife Mary have three young boys now. Bedtime for them is normally between 8 and 9.30 p.m., which puts a real burden on Mary on the nights we train.

I have played alongside Seánie with Doora-Barefield since we were both nine years of age. The two of us have never known anything different, but there comes a time when family has to take precedence over hurling.

If today is to be our last day together as hurlers, the saddest part of the ending is that, unlike the really great days, we couldn't find an ember in our collective heart to stoke the fireplace in our souls and get it raging again. But as the boys of summer grow into the old men of winter, at least we will always have those treasured memories of when we hurled together.

Outside Seánie's house, we clasp our right hands tightly together.

'If that's it,' I tell him, 'I just want to say that they were the best years of our lives.'

'No doubt about it,' he responds. 'The best years of our lives.'

I turn the car and head for home, empty and low. Maybe today was just one of those days and we'll all come back stronger and hungrier than ever next year because of what just happened. You try and suspend that doubt and disillusionment because you don't want to admit that this show could be over.

But maybe it just is.

2. Make or Break

Before 2009 even began, the word on the ground was that we were already in danger of being ripped apart. Or even tearing ourselves apart. Two guys were going head to head for the senior management job, one of whom had two sons on the team, and the fallout could sunder our season before it even began.

At the end of November, I got a call from Tommy Duggan, the club chairman. I had been U-21 manager for the previous two seasons and he asked me about staying on for a third term, but I had to turn down the request for personal reasons. After a brief discussion about potential candidates, the name of Patsy Fahey, a recently retired player, came up.

When Duggan rang Patsy about the U-21 job a couple of days later, he also threw it out there that they might be looking for a new senior management because our coach, Seán Chaplin, was leaving us to join the Sixmilebridge management set-up. When Patsy expressed some interest, Duggan explored the possibility of him getting involved in some capacity.

As chairman, it would have been foolish of Tommy Duggan not to pursue Patsy, because he had been building an impressive CV as a coach outside the club. In 2007 he coached Corofin to a Clare county quarter-final, which was a massive achievement for that club. Then last year he took Gort to their first county senior final in Galway since 1983. They lost to Portumna, but they'd been level with them at half-time and their performance reflected a smartly coached and well-drilled side. He'd been double-jobbing all season, as he'd remained with Corofin, but he stepped down from that post after the championship. And since he hadn't been given any guarantees by Gort that he'd be going back there, the prospect of managing his own club's senior team suddenly loomed into view.

Patsy told the chairman that he'd think about it on one key condition: he didn't want to be incorporated into the existing management. If he was taking over, it was on his terms. He said that he'd be back with an answer within the week.

The possibility of removing the remainder of the management team was always bound to cause friction. They had taken us to a county semi-final just two months earlier, while Kevin Kennedy had also helped steer the club through a crisis just five weeks before the start of the 2007 championship when recruiting Chaplin as coach. Kevin was a massive clubman and he had two sons – Ken and Damien – on the panel; their allegiance was inevitably going to rest with their father. Moreover, both were extremely popular players in the club and were a central part of the senior team. In their eyes, and their father's, the only outstanding issue with regard to management was recruiting a coach, because everything else was in place.

Three days before the club AGM on 15 December, Patsy informed Tommy Duggan that he would take the job. Tommy subsequently rang Kevin, thanked him for his services, but told him that they were no longer required. Then all hell broke loose.

The following day, Eoin Conroy rang me. Ken Kennedy had just been on to him and was raging at how his father had been treated. Conny was siding with Ken. 'It's been handled badly and the boys have a right to feel aggrieved. They're not happy, and neither are some of the other players. And Ken asked me to ring you to find out where you stand on all of this.'

'Sure you know where I stand,' I said back to him. 'And Ken knows that as well.'

Patsy was a good friend of mine, and it was almost impossible for me to portray myself as neutral in this debate. But as far as I was concerned, personal relationships didn't matter here: Patsy was primarily a coach, while Kevin was a manager, and it's always far harder to get a good coach than a manager at club level.

The ideal situation would have been for the both of them to work together – which would have suited everyone – but Patsy had emphatically ruled out that possibility. As a player under Kevin's management, Patsy had history with him and had no desire to work alongside him now.

When I arrived outside Fahy Hall, a local community centre, for the club AGM that Sunday, the first person I met was Ken Kennedy, who was getting out of his jeep. 'What's gone on over the last week is a disgrace,' he said. I couldn't really engage with him because he knew that my support would be with Patsy in this debate.

The meeting was supposed to begin at 4.30 p.m., but it didn't begin until 4.45 p.m.

Kevin Kennedy wasn't present. Patsy arrived in at 4.50 p.m. and sat in the front row – you couldn't miss him because he was wearing his bright orange Denver Broncos jacket. He was sitting just feet away from the club's three executive members – Tommy Duggan, Secretary Dan O'Connor and Treasurer Martin Coffey. The only trophy the club had won last year – the U-21A football cup – was placed on their table.

When it came to the team management reports, the only one present from the senior team was Fr Michael McNamara, who'd been a selector for the previous two seasons. He hadn't anything prepared, so he just gave a brief synopsis of the year off the top of his head; then he headed off to say evening mass.

When it came to the appointment of the senior team management, Tommy Duggan said that the club had decided to ask Patsy to take over. And that he'd accepted. And then the inquisition began.

Pat Frawley, one of the club's county board delegates, asked why the previous year's management weren't considered. He highlighted the good season they'd enjoyed and he proposed that they be put back up for ratification. He was seconded by someone from the floor, and suddenly the meeting took on a totally different mood.

Tommy Duggan outlined how Seán Chaplin was not staying on as coach and how that had necessitated the trawl for a new management ticket. Marty O'Regan, corner-back on the senior team, then asked the top table about the make-up of the new management team; Patsy said he hadn't assembled it yet. He'd only decided to take on the job that week and said that he hadn't had time to approach anyone. All he knew was that if he was given the job, it would form a joint ticket with the U-21s.

Cathal O'Sullivan, the team captain, then spoke up. 'I've been speaking to the players over the last few days and we want the club to hold off on the appointment of a senior manager until both parties reveal the make-up of their backroom teams.'

Although Patsy had played with almost every player present in the room, it was obvious that he didn't have universal support among his peers. That was hammered home by Damien Kennedy, Kevin's son. 'The club dropped a bombshell on Thursday night and it's not acceptable the way it was done,' he said. He thought the players needed time to absorb what had happened.

The chairman was clearly annoyed with Damien's response. 'There was no bombshell dropped on Thursday night and there was nothing underhand about how it was done,' he replied. 'We've all seen in the past how hard it is to get a good coach. We have an excellent coach on our doorstep and I felt I had to act quickly to try and get him for the senior team. I felt if I hadn't, Patsy might have been snapped up by another club, and we'd be trawling the county for a coach. And we've seen in the past how hard that can be and how long it can take.'

But Tommy was still on the back foot and there was clear support for Kevin all over the room. No one had offered a single show of support for Patsy. I decided to speak up.

'Look,' I said, 'as far as I'm concerned at the moment, the Under-21s are the most important appointment we're going to make here this evening because their campaign is beginning in March and we need to get that management in place. We have won one Under-21 championship game this decade and that group has to be our priority for the moment. We're not going to get a better coach than Patsy for our Under-21s, but I'm just wondering – if Patsy isn't appointed as senior coach, does that mean he's not going to take the Under-21s? Forget everything else for a moment; that needs to be clarified straight away.'

Patsy addressed it immediately.

'I haven't my mind made up yet but I probably won't take the Under-21s if I'm not over the senior team. I've heard a couple of rumours that another club [in Clare] were going to approach me. And if I'm not with Doora-Barefield, and am with another club, I'll probably take their Under-21 team as well. That's what I did with Corofin because it provides a good link between the Under-21 and senior teams. And if I'm with another Under-21 team, I can't really take the Doora-Barefield Under-21 job.'

You could have argued that Patsy was using the U-21s as a weapon but that's not his style, and his point was valid. Because if he wasn't with us, he was definitely going to be snapped up by some other club in Clare. Either way, it was clear that any decision on appointing a manager couldn't be taken this evening.

After another ten minutes' debate on the subject, it was decided that both candidates – Kevin and Patsy – would assemble their management teams over the next three weeks and the club would convene again on 5 January, when the managerial appointment would be decided by a vote.

After the meeting, I approached Cathal O'Sullivan, the team captain, in the car park. 'When you were articulating your view, which I respect, you said that you had been discussing the issue with the players,' I said to him. 'Well, you didn't say anything to me.'

'I thought Ken had contacted you,' he responded.

'No, he didn't.'

It was obvious already that a split was developing in the panel. We'd been down that road before, in 2003, when Kevin went for the job against Ciaran O'Neill, who had only retired as a player at the end of the 2002 season. Half the players wanted Kevin, while the other half wanted O'Neill. At the AGM, Kevin was proposed and seconded by Mikey McNamara and Ollie Baker, two highly respected figures in the club, and he won the vote.

We didn't get out of the group that year, and the following season Kilmaley beat us in the county final with a team coached by O'Neill. To this day, there's still some bad blood in the club over that split. The last thing we needed now was more division. We were fragile enough. Another split could finish the team.

★

The GAA has a complicated, umbilical relationship with the community around it, and the club is a forum for magnifying the experiences of local life. It is largely a coalition of friends, neighbours, blow-ins and recruits, but sometimes the club is a magnet for resentments and arguments.

My relationship with Kevin Kennedy goes back a long way. I played with him on the club's first team when I was only starting out and he was coming to the end of his career. I always had great regard for him because he was an unbelievably genuine hurling man. He played the game for as long as he was able to, and he finally packed it up in 1996 only after he had fulfilled a long-held ambition of playing alongside his son, Ken. A year later he managed the Clare minors to the 1997 All-Ireland title, and when he went for the club senior job at the end of that season I voted for him in a head-to-head with Michael Clohessy. Claw went on to become the most successful manager in the history of the club.

Louis Mulqueen, who trained us to the 1999 All-Ireland club title, had been recruited by Kevin in 1997. Even when he wasn't involved during the glory years that followed, Kevin was still heavily linked to the team and he never wanted anything but the best for us. He'd be there, carrying hurleys or water bottles, always offering us support and advice. At the end of the 1999 All-Ireland club semi-final against Athenry, he was the first man I met on the field after the final whistle because he was down behind the goal with a batch of sticks. If you look at the video, you can see the two of us rolling around Thurles, him on top and me hardly able to breathe with the weight from his large frame.

He had an excellent record as an underage manager and he managed us to the Clare Cup (league) title in 2003. We had a load of injuries that season but I still felt that we needed to change direction afterwards. It was nothing personal, just hard-headed business. At a players' meeting at the end of that season, I stood up and said that he should go. It was an extremely difficult decision, especially with his two sons on the team, and I wonder if the lads have ever really forgiven me for it. Sometimes, the pursuit of success can be blind and damaging, but I was prepared to accept the pain at the time in the hope of the pleasure of success down the line with a new manager.

We've consistently had our differences ever since. After last year's group game against Tubber, we exchanged words. There was a cooling-off period between us for two weeks before the quarter-final. Then after we whipped Inagh-Kilnamona in the quarter-final, he came over and shook my hand in the dressing room and I just smiled at him.

Ten days later, the man proved that he'd do anything for you. The Tuesday before we played Newmarket in the 2008 county semi-final, my puckout hurley was stolen during a training session in Roslevan under lights. I left it down on the side of the pitch and a few young lads from the town made off with it. Paul Hallinan, one of our young hurley carriers, knew one of them, but he wasn't sure if he had taken it. I was like a lunatic: a goalkeeper often sees a puckout hurley like a favourite snooker cue and I needed mine back. Kevin is a detective in Ennis Garda Station and he was the obvious man to go to.

'I need that stick back,' I said to him.

'Leave it with me; I'll see what I can do.'

The following day, I got a call from a private number around 4 p.m. It was Kevin. 'Good news. I've got your hurley.'

He probably had the forensic squad out looking for it all day. 'I owe you one big-time,' I said to him.

His response summed him up. 'All I want is a win on Sunday.'

Kevin has massive experience from managing Clare minor, U-21 and intermediate teams and he is a hugely popular figure, both inside and outside Clare. Many people within the club wanted him to get the job because of his huge historical connection to St Joseph's. His two grand-uncles played hurling for the parish team in the early part of the last century. In 1970, Kevin won a Junior League medal with the club as a 16-year-old alongside some members of the St Joseph's county title-winning team from 1958. Before he retired, he had also played alongside many of the players who won the club's next county title, in 1998. That's how strong his link is with the club. Fr McNamara, a selector in 2008, has also committed to joining Kevin's team in 2009, further strengthening his candidacy. With all of that going for him, there's no doubt that he's going to get a lot of votes on 5 January. Conny and I were in town just before New Year and we ran into a clubman, Justin O'Driscoll, in the Temple Gate Hotel. He said that Patsy would be better off not turning up because he felt Kevin already had it wrapped up.

Meanwhile, Patsy was gradually putting a decent package together. Brian O'Reilly, a respected fitness coach, had agreed to join him as physical trainer, while John Carmody, who had managed Kilmaley to the 2004 county final, was also part of his ticket. So was Steve Whyte, a former player.

It didn't seem to be enough, though. Even though the manager's job was set to be democratically decided, there were rumours floating around that if Patsy won the vote, four or five players were not going to play under him in protest. I didn't know if those rumours were true, or if they were just released as a scaremongering tactic to sway some floating voters, but it was a concern. It didn't matter who won the vote, we couldn't afford to allow that kind of insidious negativity to grab us by the throats and choke the life out of the spirit we'd built up in 2008.

Over that weekend before the vote, moves were made behind the scenes to get Patsy and Kevin to team up together. Kevin was prepared to go with it, but Patsy wasn't prepared to work with Kevin. And anyway, he had expended enough time and energy in assembling his backroom team – he had asked 14 people before getting his first positive response – and he wasn't prepared to let those people down, now that they'd committed to him.

On the Sunday night, Tommy Duggan rang Kevin to ask if he'd finalized his backroom team, and Kevin said that all would be revealed the following evening. That was a concern to the club executive, because they weren't sure if Kevin was recruiting a coach. And if he was, would that coach be looking for expenses?

At 6.15 the following evening – the meeting was due to begin at 8 p.m. – Cathal O'Sullivan, the team captain, rang me. He said that

Kevin had got a coach. He was a very respectable name who had huge experience. It was a positive move for Kevin, but I wanted to broach a totally different issue with Cathal.

'Look,' I said to him, 'it doesn't matter who gets the job, but I'm sure you've heard these rumours about some lads not playing if Patsy gets the job. That's pure bullshit. No matter who gets the job, we all have to row in together. If we don't, we're totally fucked. And you'd better call every player together before we go into the meeting tonight and re-emphasize that point.'

I'd been elected vice-chairman at the AGM, but only to allow me to head up a new committee to look for an underage coach for the club. I made it clear that I'd no interest in getting involved in administration or politics and that I'd be going back to coaching underage teams next year. Given our poor underage record in recent years, getting a qualified coach into the schools was something that I'd been pushing for years. And at the AGM, it finally seemed to be getting the green light.

Because of my new position, I had to be at the Auburn Lodge Hotel at 7.30 for a meeting of the club executive before the main event. In the bar of the hotel, eight members of the executive were sitting on stools around two small tables, debating what might unfold within the hour. The club had more or less committed to financially backing the part-time appointment of a new underage coach, which would seriously impact upon its ability to pay a coach expenses for the senior team. Patsy had informed the club that he wouldn't be looking for expenses to coach the team, but no one was sure if Kevin had discussed any arrangements with his prospective backroom team.

Joe McNamara, the club's registrar, reminded everyone how strong the support was for Kevin within the parish. And no matter what happened now, the club would have to back him if he won the vote. Yet since Kevin was primarily running as a manager, he needed a coach. And if the club couldn't afford a coach's expenses, the knock-on effects were going to be huge for the players. Players rarely have any difficulty with a manager once they're treated properly and the coaching is enjoyable and challenging. If it's not, then the red flags go up.

We were sitting beneath the large TV in the bar and, just as the meeting finished, Sam Allardyce, whose Blackburn Rovers side were taking on Blythe Spartans in the third round of the FA Cup, was being interviewed on Sky Sports.

'I wonder, would Big Sam do the job for us if we approached him,' said Martin Coffey, the club treasurer.

'He might be worth a try,' I said to Martin. 'But I think he'd be slightly out of our reach.'

By the time I made it to the lobby of the hotel, a sizeable group of players had gathered. They knew beforehand that some kind of meeting had been called and most of the players started looking at me to kick it off. I just nodded over to Cathal. 'Lads,' he said, 'whatever decision is taken here tonight, we've all got to row in behind it.'

The room was packed once we got inside. There were about 50 chairs laid out in eight rows, but there was double the crowd that had attended the AGM, and some people were standing at the back. Tommy Duggan opened the meeting and he got straight down to business. He asked Kevin to name his backroom team.

Kevin named his coach. 'It's been a very difficult few weeks for me,' he said.

Dan O'Connor responded immediately. 'It's been a very difficult few weeks for a lot of us, especially Tommy. We didn't know what was happening with regard to you getting a coach. And that's something that can't be decided on a whim.'

'I don't know if he's going to be looking for expenses or not,' said Kevin. 'And if the club aren't in agreement with the arrangement, I'm not going to cause any trouble. I only want what's best for the club.'

Before that debate could be resolved, another subplot was emerging. The father of one of the best young players on the team got up and left the meeting. On his way out the door, he told Tommy that he had to make a phone call. When he returned two minutes later, he

sat back down and then put his hand up to speak. He informed everyone that he had just been talking to his son, who said that he wouldn't
hurl with the senior team this season if Kevin's coach was involved.
His son felt that the coach had previously deprived him of the opportunity of getting on a Clare underage team.

It was a big moment. The player in question had been our outstanding performer the previous season and there was no way we
could afford to be without his services for the season. If there were
any floating voters within the room, this news would have swung
them towards Patsy.

Then Tommy Duggan asked Patsy to name his backroom team.
Patsy had been sitting at the end of the front row, closest to the door.
When he stood up, he turned around and faced everyone to address
them. After he named his backroom team, he spoke honestly and pas-
sionately.

'Lads, it's a massive honour to be asked to manage this club and it's
something I'm very serious about. I know the club had a good season
last year and I know we can be even better again this year. If everyone
rows in behind me, I'm very confident that we can do great things
here. Ye all know that I was asked to become part of last year's management team but I just felt that I needed to come with a clean slate,
a fresh start. All I want in return is total commitment. I don't want
any expenses. I thought about it and I just said to myself, "No, it
wouldn't be right." I want to coach this group of players because a lot
of ye are my friends. This club means a lot to me and my family and
I want to win with ye. I want to win for Doora-Barefield. And I'm
sure that's what we all want.'

There's no doubting Patsy Fahey's commitment to St Joseph's
Doora-Barefield, because the club is essentially what has him in this
country. When he was only 12, his family moved to New York,
where they have strong roots – his two brothers, Mike and Tommy,
who played with the club, were already based there.

He continued to play hurling in New York, but when the family
came home for a summer holiday in 1993 when Patsy was 17, he lined
out for the club minor team. The team kept winning, and by the time

they'd reached the county final the holiday was over and Patsy refused to return to New York with his parents. His decision was already made, the deal sealed in his mind, binding like a contract. Hurling with St Joseph's was all he wanted to do. Nothing else really mattered.

So at 17, he moved back into the family home on his own and began his new life. The culture change must have been massive, because he went from living among the close, sheltered Irish community in the Bronx to running a home on the extreme periphery of the parish in Doora. He hadn't finished high school, so he got a job in a local factory and cycled to work every day, no matter what the conditions.

When the U-21 team began training for the championship at the beginning of the following season, he would strap his gear-bag to the back of the bike, pack some food into a bag, and carry his two hurleys across the crossbars to attend the weekday sessions. He still hadn't turned 18 and was nowhere near the team but, after work, when he'd still have a couple of hours to kill, he'd go to the field early and use the time to practise his skills. And when training had finished, often in the pitch dark, he'd cycle home again, arriving into the house 16 hours after his day had begun.

Although he made his senior debut in 1996, it wasn't until 2001 that Patsy really established himself as a first-team player. Yet he was always regarded as one of the central characters within the panel, mainly because he had a charisma that few people possess.

One story sums him up best. Back in 1998, he entered a competition on the Ian Dempsey breakfast show on 2FM. Each competitor was asked to mimic commentary on a horse race using the names of actors and actresses, and Patsy had the nation in raptures. 'Tom Cruise is coming hard on the outside and Wesley Snipes has just edged through the pack with his sheepskin noseband. Madonna, who is liable to do anything, is coming strong but Frank Sinatra is making a break for it. Demi Moore is right on his back but Sinatra, who was nearly put down last year, is now in the clear and he's striding for the line. SINATRA IS GOING FOR IT, HE'S NEARLY THERE. AND SINATRA HAS IT!'

When some of the lads, who were driving to work, heard him, they nearly went in over a ditch. The prize was a three-day trip to the Cheltenham festival for two, with £500 spending money. Before Ian Dempsey announced the winner on Friday morning, the whole factory where Patsy worked more or less shut down to listen to the result. When Dempsey said that there 'was only one real winner – and it had to be Patsy', the place exploded.

That's the type of warm, feel-good factor that Patsy creates, a charisma that enables him to bring people along with him. But most importantly, he was coming on board more as a coach than as a manager.

Before the vote took place, I wanted to have my say, particularly to people who hadn't been at the AGM. 'I'm vice-chairman now and the only reason I took that job was because the club have decided to look into appointing a part-time underage coach,' I said. 'The lack of coaching done in the schools really concerns me. Our poor underage record in recent years also concerns me. As far as I'm concerned, appointing a coach for the schools and our underage academy is more important than anything else. And that is going to cost money. Serious money. So I can see where the club are coming from when they're concerned that maybe having to pay expenses to an outside coach could be detrimental to that process. The long term is always more important than the short term, particularly where we're coming from at the moment. When my son grows up, please God, I hope that he will play hurling and that he'll be playing with a great club here. That he can aspire to All-Irelands, and win them, like we did. And if we plan and do things right, I'm sure we'll get back to those great days again.

'The one thing that really worries me at the moment, though, are these rumours that I'm hearing. And I'm sure that ye've all heard them. That four or five lads are not going to play this year if one candidate gets the job. That's the greatest load of bullshit I've ever heard in my life and it's an insult to this club. Look, no one in this room has had more run-ins with Kevin than me. But nobody in this room respects Kevin more than I do either. And if he gets the job here tonight, I'll back him 100 per cent. If Patsy gets the job, I'll do the same for him. But if guys start taking sides and start looking to settle old scores, we can forget about it, because we'll be on the road to nowhere.

'Look around the room. Look at the players that are here. None of us are getting any younger. Time is running out for us to win another county title, and if we are divided after tonight, it will be a long time before we win one again. It will wreck this club. Whoever gets the job here tonight, we back that man. No matter what, we have to stick together.'

Darragh O'Driscoll, who had played on the team for the last ten years, was sitting beside me and he began talking as soon as I had finished: 'I want to reiterate everything Christy has said. We have to stick together. And if some guys are talking about not playing this year, well then I don't know my teammates.'

Before the vote began, Tommy Duggan said that neither he nor the secretary, Dan O'Connor, would be casting their vote but that they would both fully support the successful candidate. Tommy also said that only paid-up members of the club could vote and that Joe McNamara, the registrar, had a full list of that membership in front of him. If you weren't on it, you didn't get a white slip of paper to cast your vote. That immediately removed about 15 people, although that didn't stop one of them down the back from trying to swipe a ballot.

After the votes were cast and counted, the result was passed to Tommy. 'OK, lads, here is the result. Kevin 14, Patsy 25.'

Tommy thanked Kevin for his service, and a minute later Patsy stood up and was magnanimous in victory. Kevin said nothing. And with that, the meeting broke up and everyone went outside into the cold January air.

No GAA club in the country is unstained by politics at some level, because the ecosystem is always bound by loyalty, friendship, family history and club tradition. The geography of a parish as big as Doora-Barefield will always place minor socio-political distinctions at the root of any conflict or difficult decision. At club level, that much is inevitable.

But much of our season now would depend on how we reacted to what had happened over the past few weeks. On how well we could separate politics from the absolute necessity of being true to ourselves. And that could make or break us.

3. Róisín and Ger

The hardest game I ever had to play was against Sixmilebridge in the 2008 championship. The day before, my wife Olivia and I found out that our unborn baby daughter was not going to survive outside the womb. She had a terminal condition. It was the most devastating news I had ever received. I wanted to explode afterwards. I drove up to the pitch in Roslevan, the place where I had spent most of my childhood, to try and let it all out, to unleash the dam of anger and desolation. But I didn't. Because we had a match the next day, I felt I had to keep my emotions in check. To tranquillize the fear. To try and keep focused. Sometimes, hurling just doesn't make any sense.

I tried to battle it out, to suppress the terror raging inside me. The anxiety of not knowing what the future would hold. Of having that projected future suddenly ripped apart. I took a sleeping tablet that night and still couldn't sleep. The day of the game was miserable. It was wet and cold and windy, and it was the last place I wanted to be. I just put the head down and got on with it. Told nobody. We won. Won well. But winning didn't matter. Hurling didn't matter. I felt nothing. I drove home on my own and went to bed.

How do you prepare for your daughter's death? You can't. I could not take it in, but you just try and get on with life as best you can. Keep to the routine. Keep hurling. A week later, we played Cratloe in the second round of the championship. We won again. Won well again. We were suddenly on a roll for the first time in four years. We felt we had a chance to win a county title because we'd taken apart two of the best teams in the championship. The emotion deep down inside of me would remain suppressed, coated over with layers of hope and promise through hurling. That was the best place to keep it. And hurling would eventually bring it out of me.

But it doesn't work like that. The hurling season always ends. And then dealing with the impending grief becomes unavoidable. The baby gets bigger. The kicks get stronger. Yet there is no future outside the womb. It's all a slow march to inevitable grief. Almost madness.

People congratulate us on the expected new life. You nod and try not to engage with them. Do ye know if it's a boy or a girl? Have ye chosen a name? There are other priorities. Purchasing a white coffin. And a grave plot. Making prior funeral arrangements. By that stage, hope has long faded into anguish and it becomes harder to hide it.

Róisín was born on 26 January 2009. A beautiful baby girl who only survived for five minutes. Olivia got to hold Róisín for two of those precious minutes before she died in the midwife's arms. She had fought a heroic battle to stay alive for as long as she did, but her little heart just gave up and she slipped away.

All along, I had tried to prepare for that moment with the mindset of a hurler getting ready for battle. It seems almost vulgar and selfish to make a comparison between hurling and a daughter's impending death, but that was all I had to draw on. You become conditioned to steeling your mind, getting ready to deal with whatever is thrown at you. But you soon realize that it's only wet sand against the tide of reality and the trauma of death.

It's difficult to lose your child, but it's an unnatural act for a mother to watch the daughter she carried, and felt so vitally inside, die in front of her. In that context, Olivia became my priority. My grief was shelved. I could express it later, in my own time.

When you lose someone you love, yet never even got the chance to know or protect, there is a horrible surrealism to the daily routine. There was a sense of dread for so long and Olivia was in so much physical discomfort in the final weeks that the events of the initial days after Róisín's passing brought us along with their own momentum. Life goes on, but initially you feel disgusted that the sun has the gall to rise, time appals you with its passing and every moment and experience seems to have the nerve to take your loved one further away from you. We had absolutely no concept about how to move forward, and certainly we thought life could not get any worse. And then life dealt another devastating blow.

My brother James called to our house that Tuesday evening, 3 February, five days after Róisín was buried. I was in the kitchen, but Olivia was sitting in the front room and, about 30 seconds later, I heard her crying. I ran in immediately. James told me that Ger Hoey had died about an hour earlier.

I didn't believe it – didn't want to believe it. Ger Hoey always seemed irrepressible, indestructible almost. How could he be gone? Was it really true? Yet James had just come from the hospital, where Ger lay, and the sense of shock and bewilderment that we felt was corroborated by the devastation reflected on his face and the sense of disbelief that came through in his body language. 'I had planned on playing golf with that man and enjoying his company for the next 30 years,' he said. 'And now he's gone.'

Ger was our former teammate, but mostly he was our friend. On the St Joseph's team which won the All-Ireland club title ten years ago, he was effectively the side's spiritual leader. Despite the fact that that team was spearheaded by three of Clare's greatest players, and three of the best hurlers of modern times, Ger was still regarded as the most inspirational member of the group, especially among the younger players. That was the status and respect he commanded. Unequalled.

After Ciaran O'Neill, Ger was the oldest player on that panel, but he had the ability to connect with people, no matter what age they were. That was a recurring theme of his character: he always valued the quality of the person, the quality of their future. He was our leader and, while we took the same path, nobody ever filled the space like Ger did. And even now, with the reality slowly beginning to hit that he is dead, nobody will ever repair the hole that his parting leaves. How could they?

It seems wrong that the man with the huge heart was claimed by a heart attack. Ger was training for the Ballycotton 10-kilometre road race in Cork, which he'd run the previous few years for charity, when he collapsed on the side of the road and died instantly. As soon as the horrendous news began to spread, everyone flocked to the hospital. Most people ended up in the chapel along with the family, trying to lend any kind of support, somehow trying to help the Hoeys come to terms with the unimaginable grief.

This certainly wasn't supposed to be how his journey ended. Only 11 months earlier, when we gathered in the Shibeen bar in Doora, where his wife Siobhán had arranged his surprise 40th birthday party, we had largely come to celebrate the return of Ger into our embrace. For the previous 20 years, work had taken him away from Doora-Barefield; but a recent promotion meant he was finally returning home. Home to his family. Home to his club. Home to where his heart was.

That ordinariness, that sense of who he was and where he had come from, was essential to understanding Ger Hoey. Ger was only 11 when he played corner-back on St Joseph's U-14C team that won the 1979 county title, the club's first underage title of any description for 21 years. When St Joseph's finally reached the pinnacle of club hurling 20 years later, Ciaran O'Neill and Ger Hoey were still playing. They were the embodiment of Doora-Barefield's ultimate journey.

Although the team from the 1950s, which won the club's first two county titles in 1954 and 1958, produced legendary Clare players such as Mick Hayes and Matt Nugent, O'Neill and Hoey were the ground-breakers for the new generation of young players in the club. They were the first players in our time to regularly appear on Clare under-age teams. Ger captained the Clare minors and played for the county U-21s for four seasons. Probably one of the greatest memories for James and me was watching O'Neill and Hoey play out of their skins on the same half-back line on the Clare U-21 team that went down to Cork in an epic Munster semi-final in Kilmallock in 1988.

That year, Ger moved to Portlaoise, when he began working there with the AIB. He didn't have a car at the time, only a bike, and a friend would drive him from Portlaoise to Roslevan and back, twice a week, for club training. Without a car, though, the effort was unsustainable and Ger joined Portlaoise the following year. In 1989, he won his first county medal after Portlaoise beat Camross in the replayed Laois senior final.

In 1991, Ger got a transfer to the AIB branch in Patrick Street in Limerick and he immediately moved back to St Joseph's. The following year, he and Siobhán bought a house in Caherdavin, less than a mile from the Clare border. He was back where he belonged. In 1993 he captained the club to the intermediate title, breaking down in tears during his acceptance speech afterwards on the field in Tulla. A year later, he captained the club to its first county senior final appearance in nearly 40 years.

Outside of work, all he did revolved around Doora-Barefield, and when the club finally began to enjoy success towards the end of his career he absolutely revelled in it. Although he had three young kids, he was still probably the most committed member of that squad. He set immense standards. He radiated positivity and was a man of massive self-belief.

'I'm going to be man-of-the-match today,' he told us in the dressing-room huddle before the 2001 county final against Sixmilebridge. 'And I defy any man here to be better than me.' He had that unwavering conviction in his own ability, but he was also challenging everyone else to try and surpass the standards he had set for himself.

That 2001 county final was his second-last game for the club because, the following January, Ger and Siobhán and the family moved to Baltimore in the USA, where Ger took up a new position with AIB. Twelve months later, he was promoted to manager of the AIB branch in Carrigaline in Cork.

He continued his playing career with Carrigaline, where he won his last hurling medal, a South East Cork junior title, in 2003. The Hoeys lived five happy years in Cork until he got news that a vacancy had arisen for manager of AIB Ennis. The conversation with Siobhán about the prospect didn't last long. They were coming home. Ger started work in April, while Siobhán and the girls moved up in July. They rented a house in Ennis and then bought a site in Doora-Barefield because Ger wouldn't live anywhere else. The plans were being drawn up for the new house when he passed away.

Ger's working life had almost come full circle since he joined the AIB when leaving college. The zeal which he carried on the hurling field sustained him during his professional career. He became a branch bank manager at 30, a grade two manager at 34 and a grade one bank manager at the age of 40. Yet everywhere he went, his Doora-Barefield identity still defined him.

After he was initially promoted to branch manager in Patrick Street in Limerick, his manager, Denis Brosnan, suggested to him that he might need to take down the framed photograph of the 1999 All-Ireland club-winning side from his office wall in the middle of Limerick City. Ger politely told him that the photograph would not be coming down. The person he had become had been partially shaped by the people on the wall staring down at him.

The impact of his death cannot possibly be explained in terms of accumulated nostalgia. Ger Hoey was the type of guy who had values and ethics that you would want your own children to adhere to. He was so assiduous in his manners and his remembrance of duty, so faithful to the person he was reared to be, so loving and committed to his family, that it is almost impossible to appreciate fully the magnitude of what he achieved during his short life.

The night before Ger was waked in his parents' home in Roslevan, a group of us went to the house together: James, Seánie McMahon, Donal Cahill and myself. Ger's sister Maeve was sitting outside the back door as we made our way in. 'The hurlers are here,' she said quietly. 'The hurlers are here.'

We embraced Ger's brother Davy, who was in the kitchen, before tentatively making our way through the hall and into the front room where Ger was laid out. It was an unbelievable shock to see him in his black suit. But he looked graceful, almost like he was smiling up at us. It was a surreal image, and it was impossible to fully grasp that he was gone. One of his old hurleys was resting against the coffin, his St Joseph's jersey was draped across its base.

After we offered our condolences to Siobhán and the family, we waited in the corridor for about half an hour. Nobody was talking.

Nobody was doing anything. We didn't know what to do or where to go. It was like we were suspended in a vacuum of denial and disbelief.

When we returned for the removal the following evening, the club had arranged for a guard of honour outside the house, and then along the route between the first roundabout heading into Barefield village and the church. Players and officials from the club were lined up on both sides of the driveway, two human chains snaking from the front door to the front gate. After Ger's coffin was carried to the hearse, Davy pulled Ger's car around from the back and Siobhán and her three daughters got in. Siobhán was in the passenger seat and she smiled at Davy, before the two of them embraced.

Maeve Hoey was standing in front of me, just beside the gate. 'David had always wanted to drive Ger's car and he would never let him near it,' she said. 'I'm sure Ger would never have believed that David would be driving his car at such a slow pace.'

By the time we made our way to Barefield, the air was biting and raw. As we waited for the funeral cortège to arrive, the numbers for the guard of honour had swelled with the arrival of nine people from Portlaoise, including former Laois players Pat Critchley and Niall Rigney. They all had their green-and-white jerseys draped across their shoulders, their tribute to a man who had won a county title with them 20 years earlier. Less than ten minutes later, the numbers had grown bigger again when a group from Carrigaline joined the line. After the coffin was carried into the church by some of Ger's colleagues from AIB, four jerseys – St Joseph's, Portlaoise, Carrigaline and Clare – were draped across it.

The funeral mass the following day was said by the parish priest, Fr Michael McNamara. During his homily, he told an anecdote from the moment he found out about Ger's passing and how it triggered a dream he had that night. On the evening Ger passed away, Fr Mac was coming out of Doora church after a parish meeting when he met Lorcan Hassett, who captained the club to the 1999 All-Ireland club title. He told Fr Mac the tragic news and that he was going into the church to say a prayer for Ger.

'I didn't sleep much that night, and at one stage I had a vision,' said

Fr Mac. 'There was this big empty room, with a chandelier in the middle. Certain things were reflected from the chandelier and I saw this image of myself and Ger and Lorcan. It was from after the 1999 county final, when I presented the cup to Ger – when I was county board chairman – and then Lorcan made the speech because he was still captain.

'There were other things also reflected from the chandelier. At one stage, I saw this man who has since passed away. At one stage, he was experiencing difficulties and Ger had really helped him. Ger helped a lot of people because that was his nature. They were the primary images from my vision. Of Ger playing hurling and how much he gave to people. It summed him up.'

Fr Mac also mentioned how Ger sang certain songs – 'Spancilhill' and 'My Lovely Rose of Clare' – and that he was also learning the words of 'Slievanamon', which Siobhán had taught him. Siobhán hailed from Clogheen and her loyalty to Tipperary was unquestioned, but when Ger's brother John spoke on the altar afterwards he said that he could 'categorically deny that Ger ever sang "Slievanamon"'. The Clare blood in him just wouldn't allow it.

Mostly, though, John tried to articulate the essence of Ger as best he could. How he always stood for 'courage, honesty and integrity'. When John struggled to get the final words out, David and Maeve joined him and assisted him. 'He was a great father, brother and son. A special person who we will never, ever forget.'

On the last leg of his journey to his final resting place in Templemaley cemetery, the family had decided that four groups would carry him home: a group of Ger's friends, some of his former Carrigaline teammates and friends, and two groups of his former St Joseph's teammates.

I was part of the second-last leg of Doora-Barefield players. With the grave looming into view, we passed Ger over to his closest St Joseph's teammates: Jamesie, Seánie, Donal Cahill, Ciaran O'Neill, Lorcan Hassett and Joe Considine. In a beautiful corner of the cemetery, beneath a large tree, with speckles of early spring sun breaking through the branches, Ger was laid to rest.

His brother David put three of the jerseys – Portlaoise, Carrigaline and Clare – into the grave. The St Joseph's jersey had been rolled up by Donal Cahill and given to Siobhán, who was holding on to it tightly. She didn't want to let it go.

After everyone had moved on, a group of us remained in the corner, talking, for almost half an hour. Then the lads began filling in the grave, each one taking turns, each shovel of earth acting as a thudding confirmation of the finality of it all.

When all the earth had been moved and the flowers were placed on top, the funeral undertaker Joe Daly gathered us around him and we said three Hail Marys.

With Ger finally gone, we all slowly walked up the hill, staring into the bright spring sunshine, but with the darkest shade imaginable lodged in our souls.

There is no easy way to define death and its impact, but it often feels like larceny. It has a habit of breaking in on us and stealing the irreplaceable. Now that Ger has gone, you wonder: will life in the St Joseph's Doora-Barefield club ever be the same again? Will hurling even mean anything to us this year? Yet that misses the point. The void which Ger leaves behind reflects the sort of person he was and his understanding of the true perspective in which to view the game he loved and played.

After the Tyrone footballer Cormac McAnallen passed away in 2004, the legendary sportswriter Tom Humphries elegantly wrote about the impact of his death and the magnitude of mourning which greeted it. Humphries rightly acknowledged that the sport which Cormac McAnallen loved and devoted himself to wouldn't shrink in importance because he was gone; that it wouldn't be unseemly for football to be played again and for Tyrone people to lose themselves in the passion of it. It would be fitting and welcome.

'The glory of an All-Ireland does not stay long,' wrote Humphries. 'The glory of an honest, robust life is the community's glory. What made the difference was a full and passionate existence. The best commemoration of a passionate life is passion itself.'

It doesn't feel like that now, but as the season unfolds we hope that daily life of the St Joseph's club will become more vigorous and more visceral than ever before. That the pitches in Gurteen will be singing with kids' voices and the air will be full of hope and promise. There will be rows and scrapes and good days and bad days, but it will all be fuelled by passion and energy and drive. That's what Ger Hoey was all about. That's exactly what he would have wanted.

The club will be our refuge. Our sanctuary. After Róisín was buried, I didn't leave the house for three days. When I finally ventured out, the first place I went to was Gurteen. To the hurling wall. A hurley and a sliotar and a wall was all that seemed normal at that time. It was the only place where I could clear my head. Where I could find some peace. No separation.

The last time I met Ger Hoey was in Drumcliffe cemetery, just five days before he passed away. He was the last person I spoke to before we left the graveyard that day, just after we'd buried Róisín. When I think of the two of them now, I hope they're in a better place. And if they are, I know that there's nobody who I could rely on more to keep an eye out for Róisín than Ger.

4. Down to Business

On Friday night, 13 February, the senior panel met the new management for the first time. The meeting had originally been planned for the previous week but was cancelled owing to Ger Hoey's funeral. So in a small function room upstairs in the Auburn Lodge Hotel, a top table had been set up, with a maroon cloth – the club's colours – draped across it.

Behind the table, Patsy Fahey was flanked by Brian O'Reilly, the physical trainer on his new management ticket, and John Carmody, who was effectively coming on board as manager. Patsy couldn't tout Carmody in that capacity before the AGM because Carmody had worked closely with Ciaran O'Neill in the past, and some players might have assumed that he'd recruit O'Neill as part of a new backroom team. O'Neill had managed the team in 2006 and some players on the panel didn't want him back now. Two more selectors, Vinny Sheedy and Steve Whyte, were sitting on either side of Carmody and O'Reilly. The five lads looked full of ambition, but the player turnout didn't exactly reflect that zeal. Only 20 players were present, including ten of last year's starting team, plus four U-21s.

The club chairman, Tommy Duggan, who was sitting in the front row of the assembled line of chairs, got up to speak just after the meeting was supposed to begin at 8 p.m. He wished the new management team all the best for the season, but his contribution inevitably focused on the tragedy of the previous week and what Ger Hoey had meant to St Joseph's Doora-Barefield.

'Sometime later in the year, we'll honour Ger's memory,' he said. 'At the start of a new year, we all have great hopes and intentions. But maybe carry the thought with ye all season that this is the year to really bring the county title back in honour of Ger.'

Before Patsy spoke, a sheet detailing the schedule and timetable for club senior hurling and football league and championship games was handed out. The league agenda nearly always remains the same, but the championship schedule is dependent on how the Clare hurlers fare in the Munster and All-Ireland championships. Darragh O'Driscoll just gave a wry smile when he looked at the sheet. Adhering to the timetable last year, he booked a holiday in August but missed the championship match against Corofin and lost his place for the next game.

Patsy spoke next. 'I'm looking forward to starting,' he said. 'I know ye as my friends, former teammates and men with great character. I'm just so looking forward to working with ye. I haven't seen some of ye for a few years but most of ye know how enthusiastic I am. I had great enthusiasm when I managed Corofin and Gort and if I was jumping up and down the line with those teams, what am I going to be like with Joseph's? This is a dream job for me. It's an honour.

'There are just a few things I want to outline from the start. One of my pet hates is bad timekeeping so I don't want to see any lads coming late to training. My philosophy on training is that we train for one hour fifteen minutes, no more. We train at top speed and with full intensity for that one hour and fifteen minutes and that's it, we're gone home. We won't be keeping lads for over two hours, but we'll be working on whatever aspects of our game we feel we need to address. From ground hurling, to winning aerial possession, to hand-passing. The sessions will be varied and enjoyable, but we want to see leaders emerging at training every night. We want to see guys constantly improving and we want to see infectious enthusiasm. They say that a team should be a mirror image of their coach and that's what I want.'

Then he went through his backroom team, introducing each one of them individually. Brian O'Reilly, a former Kilrush Shamrocks footballer living in Doora, had trained numerous teams over the years and was last involved with St Joseph's in 1996 when he was on board as physical trainer early in the season. Brian's arrangement would be broadly similar again this time around.

'Brian was delighted to be asked and delighted to be asked by one

of his own,' said Patsy. 'He will work on our fitness for the next few
months and then he'll slip away when the hurling begins. And then
he'll come back every so often to top up our fitness.'

Vinny Sheedy was a former player and a close friend of Patsy's.

'He's already with the juniors, so he will be a good link for me to
have between both squads,' Patsy said. 'I respect his opinion on hurling and you need guys who are going to be around the whole time.
And I can guarantee everyone here that Vinny Sheedy will not miss a
single training session this year.'

Steve Whyte wouldn't be able to match that 100 per cent commitment, simply because of his job. 'Steve is a farmer and he has to go to
the mart every Thursday evening,' said Patsy. 'He won't be at training on those evenings but he will be here for every other session.'

When John Carmody managed Kilmaley to the 2004 county final,
recruiting Ciaran O'Neill as his trainer was deemed the masterstroke.
O'Neill was an excellent trainer but, when he took us over in 2006,
the move just never worked out. After we lost our opening group
match to Éire Óg by a point, having surrendered a six-point lead
with 15 minutes remaining and having failed to score for the remainder of the game, I felt O'Neill panicked. He believed that we weren't
physically or mentally strong enough, so we trained like animals over
a long and inactive summer without championship games and we
were burned out by the business end of the season. O'Neill walked
away after we lost a play-off to Newmarket by one point, when
one player – Bernard Gaffney – scored Newmarket's entire total of
just 0-10.

We could so easily have won a county title that season, but there
was still an undercurrent of tension from 2003 when some of the
younger players had backed Kevin Kennedy ahead of O'Neill. It
seemed to me that O'Neill never fully trusted some of those players
who, he believed, hadn't always shown the intense commitment
which he demanded.

So a man who would die for Doora-Barefield departed the job in a
more acrimonious manner than he deserved.

O'Neill had coached Newmarket to hammer us in last year's

semi-final, but nobody doubted his loyalty to Doora-Barefield or his closeness to John Carmody. There were concerns from some players that O'Neill would also be signing up with Carmody. That was never a runner, but in that context Patsy originally had to dilute the impact of the role he saw Carmody fulfilling.

'John has managed a team to a county title and he knows what it takes,' said Patsy. 'But I need an outsider. I know some of ye very well, maybe too well that I might be too nice to ye at times and let ye away with things when I shouldn't. John isn't close with anyone here and he will nip any of that stuff in the bud. I couldn't say it at the AGM but he is really coming on board in a managerial capacity. He will be the manager of this team.'

Before he concluded, Patsy said that eight players had contacted him with legitimate excuses for not attending tonight, and he also addressed the issue surrounding the possible retirement of two of our biggest names – Seánie McMahon and Davy Hoey. Seánie hadn't made any decision yet but was contemplating coming back for one more season, while Patsy obviously hadn't spoken with Davy yet about hurling but said he was 'hopeful' that he would return.

In any case, we needed to drive on with what we had. Last year, we began training on 16 January, so we were already a month behind to prepare for a championship that was going to close in fast. With the Clare senior hurlers not playing in the championship until 21 June, the two championship matches provisionally fixed for May would definitely be going ahead.

'We need to hit the ground running,' Patsy said. 'We need to get those two wins in the bag. If we do, then we can ease off the gas a bit and build it right back up again when we need to. But we're really going for this. The club needs a massive lift this season. Everybody in the parish needs it. And our ultimate goal is to win the Canon Hamilton [Trophy] so we can finally put smiles back on people's faces in October.'

Patsy then handed the floor over to Carmody, who proposed a minute's silence for Ger. You could have heard a pin drop in the room during the 60 seconds. Given the poignancy and heartbreak of the previous few weeks, Carmody's gesture was a very simple but hugely positive start.

Then Carmody addressed the group. 'When Patsy contacted me and asked me to get involved, he told me to take a few days to think about it. I got back to him the following evening and said I would do it. There were two reasons. The first was Ciaran O'Neill. That man gave me and Kilmaley everything and I felt that I owed it, not to Ciaran O'Neill, but to St Joseph's to give something back now in return.

'Secondly, my wife is from this parish and so is my uncle, and I have massive respect for this club. I would have always seen ye as nearly the top club in this county, definitely one of the best. Most people in this county would nearly feel that whoever finishes ahead of Joseph's every year will win the county title. In Kilmaley anyway, we would have always seen ye as one of our main threats to winning a county title.

'That's how highly ye are rated from the outside – and make no mistake about the talent that's here. I know some of the older lads from coming up against ye, and ye are still some of the top players in this county. There is great talent among the younger players as well. I know ye only have one player on the Clare senior panel, but I really believe that there are about five or six of ye just one step away from making that panel.

'What we're looking for now is to merge all of that experience and talent together and to create a real team, a real panel. I will be going to games at every level – minor, Under-21, junior – and everyone will get an opportunity to play. If you get a jersey in the Clare Cup [league], hold on to it. I don't care what age a player is, if you're good enough, you'll play. If guys of 17 and 18 haven't the ambition to play senior hurling, you're going nowhere. And if some guys on the senior panel think they are above playing junior, think again. We can only play 20 in a Clare Cup game so you need to be showing us something to get a chance.

'We will need every man available. We will need 26 for every championship game – ten defenders, ten forwards, four midfielders and two goalkeepers. The challenge for everyone is to get on that first 26. The crowd who won it last year [Clonlara] did it with only about 19 or 20 players. But those 19 or 20 would have gone through a wall. We need guys like that, players who will just refuse to be beaten.

'Talk is cheap but we need guys who are just prepared to go that extra mile. Look, lads, I wouldn't have come here if I didn't think ye could win a county title. Patsy wants to train ye to a senior championship and I want to help ye to achieve that goal as well. And I can promise ye one thing: I'm a Kilmaley man, but I'll be more of a St Joseph's man than some of ye by the end of the year. There's a great history of managers in this club, from Kevin Kennedy to Michael Clohessy, so I have a serious standard to upkeep. And I have absolutely no intention of dropping those standards.'

Patsy's and Carmody's words hit the mark. There was no need for table-thumping or firing out expletives to try and motivate players. It was still only springtime and everybody wanted the same thing: to end the year with silverware, and the feeling that success was the start of even greater things for the club. But deep down, we didn't need to be told that this season was about more than just that now. Before Carmody finished, he touched on the subject that Tommy Duggan initially raised.

'Lads, we all know what Ger Hoey gave to the St Joseph's jersey,' he said. 'And all I'll ask is that ye give the jersey what Ger would have given it.'

There was no need to say any more.

At our first training the following Tuesday night, the conditions were perfect. The temperature was 2°C, the air was fresh, the numbers were high and the vibes were good. There's always a sense of trepidation on the first night back, caused primarily by the dread of the projected traditional slog and its finger-drumming monotony; but it came less of a shock to the system than expected.

Maybe that was because some guys had gym work done or because the pack was loaded with young gazelles from the U-21 squad who were bounding over the patch of soft ground behind the goals, sparsely lit from the dim lamps positioned high on two poles. Or maybe it was just because the session lasted only 50 minutes under Brian O'Reilly.

Everyone pushed himself hard – stamina runs, sprints, push-ups, sit-ups, star-jumps – an easy evocation of hurling's toil. It's hard to imagine the long evenings of summer in the dark of winter, but that's what always keeps you going: the stretched evenings when the hurling goes on and on and on. The nights that capture the lovely madness of hurling and feeling part of a group sharing the same goal.

Sport at its most moving and visceral doesn't have to involve cups or medals. It has to do with a group coming together and sharing experiences until such time as those shared experiences turn them into something else. We want this year to be special, and tonight you can feel that desire to make it happen.

Every club, though, has more immediate aims, and there is no getting away from the knowledge that just keeping the show on the road is an arduous business. After training finished, and after I'd washed the sweat off my body, I made my way into the small anteroom off dressing room number two. Most players have no interest in the affairs of committee rooms, but the club executive had their first meeting of the year and, as vice-chairman, this was the world that I now had to enter.

Nine people squeezed into the small room, no bigger than a small utility room and warmed by a small heater.

What goes on at these meetings? The chairman began by offering sympathies to recently bereaved families. Then the secretary, Dan O'Connor, read out recent correspondence, which ranged from a concrete company in Limerick advertising their rates on the construction of affordable hurling walls, to the upcoming U-21 hurling championship draw, to a race-night to generate funds. The secretary also read out a directive from Croke Park, whereby clubs claiming physiotherapy costs from Croke Park's injury scheme could now claim only for using chartered physiotherapists. That was a huge financial blow to many clubs who were using physical therapists. Our physio, Eugene Moynihan, was a physical therapist; he was also a recent European Masters cross-country champion, and was excellent at his job.

Being a dual senior club, with 50 teams at all levels in hurling, football, camogie and ladies, requires huge financial planning, but the club is in a pretty good place, particularly when compared to other clubs. In 2000 the club bought land in Gurteen on the Quin road and turned a stretch of lunar surface into one of the most impressive grounds in the county. The money was borrowed from the bank, but the scheme was primarily powered from a fund-raising drive in which club members and people around the parish signed up to five-year direct-debit commitments. Some members paid €5,000 over the five years.

Our original home was in Roslevan, which the club decided to sell in 2005 after an Extraordinary General Meeting in the old clubhouse. It was a modest ground, with just one pitch, a small warm-up area behind the goal, two dressing rooms and a small clubhouse. The reason the land was initially bought in Gurteen was because the club had just outgrown Roslevan and couldn't cater any longer for its huge needs. There was nowhere left for expansion because housing estates were sprouting up to the east and south of the ground, and then a huge shopping centre was built in front of the grounds in 2004, which gobbled up whatever car-parking space was available.

The other problem the club now had was that it was becoming impossible to police the place. With so many new housing estates recently constructed, the stand had become a meeting place for young people and was a hive of night-time activity. Beer cans were often strewn across the pitch and used condoms regularly littered the stand. Fires were often lit under a large beech tree at the north-west end of the ground, and the chief groundsman and the club's trustees were at their wits' ends. If a serious incident or injury took place on the grounds, the club would have been liable, which was a huge concern.

Apart from the historical tug, another major difficulty with deciding to sell was that Roslevan had been re-zoned as a second town centre for Ennis, and the area now had a huge population. Selling up and moving out would remove the club's presence in the very area that was likely to be producing the most new players. But the €2 million the club received from the sale would enable them to turn Gurteen into a state-of-the-art ground, and the vote was decisive.

Now, we've got two pitches the size of Croke Park's, two underage pitches, four dressing rooms, a stand, a ball wall, and an AstroTurf facility that is rented out to platoons of five-a-side soccer teams, generating huge funds to assist the running of the club. At the start of next year, the construction of the new clubhouse, with a full-size basketball court, will begin. That will exhaust the last of the money left from the sale of our old ground.

It costs in the region of €80,000 to run a club of our size, and tonight's meeting broadened into a discussion on how to save money on the upkeep of the grounds, and how to generate further funds to keep the wheels oiled. The cost of sanding and spiking the main pitches was discussed, as was the potential purchase of a new scoreboard. New goalposts for the underage pitches were priced at a cost of €1,650. The club also required new flagpoles, and it was agreed to do a deal with a local welder to manufacture them.

Then a debate arose about enclosing the fields with some form of fencing, which might facilitate the club's chances of hosting senior club championship games, and consequently generating more revenue. We have the pitches and the car-parking facilities, but not having the pitch properly cordoned off for supporters has definitely impacted on our chances of getting big games; we hosted only one senior championship game last season.

Another concern was that the place was being used by some people as a park. Walkers (and dog-walkers) frequently used the path around the pitches, and Dan O'Connor reckoned that between 10 and 15 joggers were using the venue as a personal training track. And two weeks earlier, three cars had pulled into the car park and unloaded some electronically controlled aeroplanes, before guiding them around our airspace for the afternoon. All of this activity posed a big liability issue for the club.

It was argued that the club had spent too much money on the facilities to make them available as a public amenity and that if people wanted to use them they'd have to become members. Yet would that mean that someone from the club would have to be around to chase joggers and ask them for a membership fee? Did we really want that kind of hassle? And where do you draw the line between community spirit and reality, particularly when the club had asked so many people in the parish to contribute financially to the facilities? In the end, it was decided that a sign would be erected at the front gate, stating that dogs were not allowed inside the four walls.

What goes on at these meetings? Now I know.

The season has begun positively for us. Training has gone really well, the effort has been excellent and the numbers have remained very steady. The only downside is the progress of our U-21s. They've been doing most of their training with the senior panel, but the turnout, attitude and application so far has been abysmal.

The U-21s have drawn Inagh-Kilnamona – one of the best teams in the competition – in the first round, and the players seem to have already made up their minds on their chances. All panels have continued to train together and on Thursday evening, 12 March, five days before their game against Inagh-Kilnamona, I took the stretch and warm-up. Just before we began the session, I called everyone into a huddle.

'I'm only going to talk for 30 seconds, lads,' I said. 'The effort has been great so far and let's keep it up. But as far as I'm concerned, the priority now is the Under-21s. There's a lot of talk going around the place that Inagh-Kilnamona are going to wipe us out. Well, this club doesn't back down from anybody, so get that into yere heads now. I want to see the Under-21s setting the agenda tonight. I want to see ye driving the session and setting the standard for the rest of us to follow.'

To be honest, I felt hollow saying it. I counted only eight U-21s in the pack and the writing was on the wall. A couple of weeks ago, a challenge game organized against Corofin had to be cancelled on the day when only seven showed up. Patsy went wild afterwards but it doesn't seem to have made any difference.

'We just can't get them out,' Vinny Sheedy, who is also part of the U-21 management, said to me during a water-break. 'It's the same seven or eight lads who are training the whole time. There's nothing we can do. We can't force them to train if they don't want to.'

During one of the drills, I had a quick chat with Declan Meehan, one of the most committed U-21 players.

'What's the story, Deccie, where the hell are guys five days before the championship?'

'There's just no effort being made,' he said. 'Lads are making no effort to come home from college to make training.'

At times, it's easy to feel that St Joseph's Doora-Barefield are a big club only in name. Most of us would like to believe that we stand for respect, pride and honour, and yet it seems to be getting harder and harder to transmit that code to some young players.

In the last ten years, the club has won just one U-21 championship match, and there has definitely been a correlation between our demise as a real force at senior level and our terrible record at U-21 level.

The championship traditionally begins on St Patrick's Day and concludes at the end of April or early May. Getting beaten consistently so early in the competition seems to have provided a sense of finality to some young players; many go back to college, cut their links with the club until the exams are over, and then seem to feel that it's too late to resume playing with a team they have little or no connection with. Others just head off travelling for the summer and won't pick up a hurley again until the U-21 championship rolls around again next season. Their hurling development is consequently stunted, which leaves many of them with little or no chance of becoming senior hurlers. When that reality hits home, it's always easier to go off playing football.

Although Doora won a senior football championship in 1898, and Faughs (an amalgamation between Éire Óg and St Joseph's Doora-Barefield) won a senior title in 1994, the club has always been dominated by hurling. But the excellent work at underage level in the last decade has seen us become a real force at football. Last year, the club won the U-21A title for the first time, beating the powerhouse of Clare football, Kilmurry-Ibrickane, who were going for six titles in a row.

Most of the best young hurlers are also the best footballers, and the club has had a huge presence on Clare U-21 football squads over the last few years. Last year, we had five guys starting on the team. That is a huge honour for the club, but the real difficulty it annually presents is that the Munster U-21 football championship always runs at the same time as the domestic U-21 hurling championship. Which means that our best U-21 hurlers rarely train with the team.

Last year was a huge disappointment for our U-21s. I was manager and we had an excellent backroom team in place – Seánie McMahon, Ken Kennedy, Fergal O'Sullivan and Mikey Cullinan – all senior players, who were 100 per cent committed to getting the most out of the group. I had previously been manager of the same group at minor level when they were narrowly beaten in a semi-final by Clooney-Quin, and it was obvious that the talent was there to go places. More importantly, we saw the group as the future St Joseph's senior team.

We began training in December, but our first real problem arose when we discovered that the first round of the championship was fixed two days after the Munster U-21 football quarter-final against Tipperary. We felt that was unfair – almost akin to being punished for providing players for the county. The previous year, when the same club management had been in place, four of our U-21 hurlers trained hard with the Clare U-21 footballers, just two days before our first-round U-21 hurling defeat to Crusheen-Tubber, and it definitely had an impact on the performance of some of those players on the day.

After our request to have the game brought forward a week was granted, the five Clare U-21 footballers requested a meeting with management. A couple of them were unhappy because they had a training weekend planned that weekend and were concerned that it was impacting on their preparation for their game against Tipperary. They said it wasn't fair on them; we said that the other option wasn't fair on the other 20 players who had been training since December.

We subsequently hammered Éire Óg in the championship – our

first win in the competition since 2000 — but we never saw our five Clare U-21 footballers until a couple of days before the quarter-final. All five were playing in central positions, but their lack of hurling since the first match clearly told. It just wasn't possible for them to be up to hurling-speed or to have the sharpness required for a sticky pitch in March. We lost by three points.

This year's U-21 side face more or less the same difficulties. We have three guys starting on the Clare U-21 football team that is due to play Limerick next week. All three are probably our best hurlers but they've been able to attend only a handful of hurling sessions. Moreover, two of those three are selected to play with the Clare seniors in the national football league on Sunday against Kilkenny, just two days before the U-21 hurling game.

'We haven't seen the footballers at all in the last few weeks and we won't see them now until the day of the game,' said Patsy after training. 'No disrespect to Kilkenny, but one of our boys will probably be marking the bus driver. He'll probably end up marking J. J. Kavanagh [the bus operator].'

Last year, the club supported a motion to play the U-21 club championship later in the year, so as to allow the Clare minors and U-21s in both codes to prepare properly for their championships. Yet the motion was defeated at a county board meeting. If anything, that highlighted how the county is divided in terms of promoting and facilitating each code. And it's dual clubs like ours that continue to get hammered.

The reality for dual players is that hurling is always the first code to suffer, primarily because hurling involves more time-consuming skills work. Players struggle to compete if they're not specializing, and that difficulty creates untold friction within dual clubs. Whether we want to admit it or not, there are hurling people within the club who would like nothing better than to stick a knife in every football they see. And football people who would love to make firewood out of every hurley that passes through the gate.

The hurling people want success. So do the football people. Yet the club has no history of being a successful dual senior club; and with a historical hurling background it's easy to see why football people get frustrated. Back in 1998, we got to the senior football semi-final and seemed more concerned with the ramifications of winning the game than losing it. We were already in the hurling semi-final and that was our priority, especially with nine dual players starting on both teams. Lissycasey beat us in the football semi-final and they took Doonbeg to a replay in the county final. Doonbeg went on to win the Munster club football title, while we went on to win our first Munster club hurling title. Something had to give.

However, hurling no longer sits that comfortably at the altar of parish life and football has become a much more central part of the living church. The young players have developed a wining culture in football, not in hurling. In the near future, St Joseph's Doora-Barefield will be targeting winning senior football titles, not senior hurling titles. And for some people in a club so historically connected to hurling, that is a vision they're not entirely comfortable with.

Of course a dual senior club should aspire to success in both codes, but that presents huge difficulties in a club with limited numbers of senior players, and friction is inevitable. Then injuries always pour petrol on the flames. If the football and hurling managements don't work closely together, the outcome is chaos and festering resentment. With so many dual players this year, it's already easy to envisage serious problems emerging down the road. The footballers have already stated their intent this year by securing the transfer of four players from Clooney-Quin, a neighbouring senior hurling club with only a junior football team. One of those four is Declan O'Keeffe, the former Kerry goalkeeper who won two All-Irelands and two All-Stars. A player with that class and ambition isn't joining St Joseph's just to make up the numbers.

Before the U-21 hurlers played their championship match on St Patrick's Day, the club was toying with the idea of tossing with Inagh-Kilnamona for a home-and-away arrangement. The match had been fixed for Meelick, right on the Limerick border, and the U-21 management were prepared to take the risk of playing away to

Inagh-Kilnamona if they lost the toss. With the way preparations had gone anyway, they felt they'd nothing to lose.

In any case, the request was never made and the match went ahead as planned. Inagh-Kilnamona had a good side, but our lads tore into them from the start. They got a foothold in the game with an early goal and then they dug in for a battle. In a team loaded with minors, they showed fantastic spirit and were level with less than two minutes remaining. But then they ran out of gas and Inagh-Kilnamona blitzed them with a late 1-2.

The secretary, Dan O'Connor, said in the dressing room afterwards that it was one of the best fighting displays he'd ever seen from a St Joseph's team. Most of the players were really disappointed, which showed that it meant something to them. It was a huge performance, really encouraging for the senior team, but it was still laced with frustration, regret and anger.

Not that they'd lost. But Jeez, how could they have done if they'd trained properly?

5. When We Were Kings

As far back as March 2008, we had begun planning a ten-year reunion trip for the St Joseph's Doora-Barefield squad that won the 1999 All-Ireland club title. When we properly mobilized towards the end of the year, we established a five-man organizing committee: Ger Hoey, Seánie McMahon, Noel Brodie, Lorcan Hassett and me. We decided on a weekend away in Kilkenny, with golf and drink and plenty of opportunities to rekindle old memories.

Ger took over as chairman of the committee and everything was planned with military precision. He set up a direct debit account in the AIB for anyone who wanted to pay the €230 cost of the trip over a period of time. The date was set for the weekend of 27–29 March. Golf in Gowran Park was booked for the Friday, while a host of activities, ranging from archery to clay-pigeon shooting, was laid on for Saturday – if you had the head for it. We arranged a meal for Saturday evening and were booked into Hotel Kilkenny for both nights, where Liam Griffin had cut us a fantastic deal.

After Ger passed away, Seánie received the planning folder Ger had assembled for the trip from his brother John. We seriously considered cancelling the whole event, coming as soon as it would after Ger's passing. But John and the Hoey family had encouraged us to go ahead with the trip. They said it was what Ger would have wanted.

So on Friday, 27 March, we took off to Kilkenny. Some of the lads had tee'd off in Gowran Park golf club at noon and the guys who were working followed them down. We all met in Hotel Kilkenny that evening. We had planned to spend that evening together in a local pub, so Seánie had rung Kilkenny hurler Martin Comerford, and he'd suggested Sham O'Hara's pub in Thomastown. We had a bus organized to take us there.

Late in the evening, about ten of us gathered around the warm fire,

and a debate began as to the merits of Portumna's emphatic All-Ireland
final success the previous week. Portumna had certainly earned the
right to be considered the greatest club hurling team of all time: the
first club to win three All-Irelands in such a short time span (four
years); a record final winning margin; the highest scoring total ever
recorded in a club final over 60 minutes. A Munster club team had
never previously lost an All-Ireland final by more than six points, but
De La Salle were skewered by 19 points – and Portumna could have
won by more if they'd really wanted to.

Then the debate heated up: how would the St Joseph's Doora-
Barefield team of 1999–2000 have fared against Portumna? It's impossible
to compare teams from past and present, but such comparisons are at
the heart of sporting discourse. A thousand pub conversations would
otherwise die in the throat.

Personally, I felt we wouldn't have beaten Portumna, primarily
because of the telepathy and pace of their forwards and the threat of
Joe Canning. Lorcan Hassett was thinking along the same lines. But
that's where the agreement stopped.

'[Ollie] Baker and [Joe] Considine would have eaten alive their
midfield pairing of Eoin Lynch and Leo Smyth,' said Jamesie O'Connor.
Fair point. Physically, Baker and Considine were massively imposing
and they had an infectious lack of respect for reputations. In his
prime, Baker was one of the most powerful midfielders ever to play
the game, and yet Considine was still our outstanding player in many
of our big matches. They were our tone-setters, too; some of Athenry's big guns tried to start a scrap early in the 1999 All-Ireland semi-final,
but the two boys finished it pretty quickly with a couple of right
good slaps.

'We'd have had the big guns to shut down their key men up front,'
said Eoin Conroy. Very valid argument. Seánie would have gobbled
up Kevin 'Chunky' Hayes and Donal Cahill was a brilliant club full-
back. Eugene Cloonan told the physio Colum Flynn one time that
Cahill was his most difficult opponent. After Brian Lohan, Cahill was
the best full-back in Clare for a decade. He was so mentally strong
that he'd have relished a crack at Joe Canning.

'Physically, we'd have been able to stand up to them,' said Seánie. Absolutely, because the physicality of some of the top clubs has really dropped in recent years and nobody has really stood up to Portumna physically in the last couple of seasons. That Athenry side that we ran into, and which won three All-Ireland club titles, were a physically awesome side. Huge men, real enforcers: Joe Rabbitte, Brian Feeney, Brian Hanley, Gerry Keane, Paul Hardiman, Brendan Keogh, Cloonan. When the teams met in 1999 and 2000, some of the hits were as ferocious as I've ever seen on a hurling pitch. Athenry may not have had the pace or class of Portumna, but they were a real warrior side who would have fronted up to Portumna. They certainly wouldn't have allowed them to consistently dominate games like they do now.

Portumna are a scoring machine, but our game was built on a superb defence and they wouldn't have railroaded through us like they do against most teams in the country. We conceded the second lowest score in an All-Ireland club final against Rathnure in 1999. Of the nine Munster and All-Ireland club championship games we played between 1998 and 2000, we kept six clean sheets. Every member of that back seven played for the Clare seniors at some stage.

Portumna are an exceptional side, but not having to negotiate a tough provincial campaign is a huge advantage in peaking for an All-Ireland semi-final and final. In our three years competing in the Munster club championship, we never once had a home draw. Some of those away games were like entering a cauldron: Mount Sion in Dungarvan in 1998, when the sulphur from the replayed Clare–Waterford Munster final was still hanging in the air; against Toomevara in Thurles in 1999, when the Clare–Tipperary rivalry was at its poisonous apex. That club game was almost seen as an extension of the ongoing inter-county battle, as reflected in the crowd of 15,000.

As we entered the dressing room at half-time that day, some young lads spat at us. Inside the dressing room, we turned the mood into an engagement between Clare and Tipperary. Jamesie had his arm broken in that year's replayed Munster semi-final, while Ken Kennedy and Darragh O'Driscoll had been part of the Clare U-21 squad which lost that year's Munster U-21 final to Tipp when there was a mass

brawl after the final whistle. Baker used it all as fuel to ignite the bon-
fire. 'Tipp shit down on you, you and you over the summer,' he said
to Jamesie, Ken and Darragh, pointing at each of them in turn with
that mad look in his eyes. 'And now we're going to do something
about it.'

Then Jamesie had the last word before we left the dressing room.
'For ourselves,' he said. 'And for the Banner.'

There were some serious teams knocking around the Munster club
championship ten years ago: Toomevara, Ballygunner, Mount Sion,
Ahane, Blackrock. And yet the hardest struggle was getting out of
Clare. Clare clubs won six successive Munster club titles between
1995 and 2000. During all those years, the county championship was
run on a knockout basis, so if you weren't 100 per cent prepared for
every game, you'd walk into a haymaker.

The standard of Clare club hurling now is light years behind what
it was a decade ago. The overall quality of club hurling around the
country has definitely dropped in the last decade, with the exception
of the Kilkenny championship.

'Look,' said Ciaran O'Neill, 'we'd have beaten Portumna by ten
points.' There was probably an element of drink and pride associated
with that assessment; but the discussion brought home just how special that team was and how good those times really were.

It also probably demonstrated that we didn't fully appreciate that
fact at the time and that our ambition didn't always match our potential. There is still a lingering sense of regret that the team
underachieved, especially within Clare, and a degree of disappointment that we didn't win the second All-Ireland.

The team was driven by three of the best and most important hurlers to play the game over the last 20 years. The Friday night before we
won our first Munster club title in 1998, Jamesie O'Connor, Seánie
McMahon and Ollie Baker won All-Stars. They had also managed
the same feat in 1995.

When Brian Lohan ran into Wexford and Rathnure's Rod Guiney
a couple of weeks before the 1999 All-Ireland club final, Guiney asked
Lohan for a synopsis on Doora-Barefield. 'Twelve very good hurlers,'

said Lohan. 'Where are the three weak links?' inquired Guiney. 'Weak links?' responded Lohan. 'The other three are All-Stars.'

Failing to win successive All-Ireland club titles cost us our place in the pantheon of great club teams, but we still have a lot to be proud of because we're the only Munster club to reach successive All-Ireland club hurling finals. All the other great clubs in Munster — Thurles Sarsfields, Mount Sion, Ahane, Newtownshandrum, Glen Rovers, St Finbarr's, Toomevara, Patrickswell, Ballygunner, Sixmilebridge, Clarecastle, Newmarket — failed to match that feat. The legendary Blackrock team of 1978–9 — perhaps the greatest club team of all time, because they included a combined total of 28 inter-county All-Ireland senior medal winners — are the only other club to win successive Munster club titles. When you consider those statistics, there's no doubting what our team achieved. And it's even more striking when you consider where we came from.

When I first started playing with the club in the early 1980s, we were only a junior outfit. We won a junior A title in 1983 and an intermediate title in 1985 to take us back into the senior grade for the first time in decades. We lasted three years up there before we were sent packing again with our tails between our legs. The relegation final against Newmarket-on-Fergus in 1988 was played on our own pitch in Roslevan and I remember thinking we were a complete joke. We barely had a team, we switched goalkeepers at half-time, and we ended up getting beaten by a side that seemed more interested than us. I was only a young fella, but the lack of ambition still hit me in the face.

The following year was my first season on the panel and we reached the intermediate semi-final, which we lost to Clonlara. Smith O'Brien's beat us in a quarter-final in 1990 before we reached the final in 1991. That team contained five minors and Corofin just rolled over us. My outstanding memory from that game was of an auld fella from Corofin on the line with a woolly hat; every time Corofin got a score in the second half, he banged the hurley against the ground and roared: 'Sew it into the bastards.'

Still, we knew we were coming strong. We won a minor A title in

1990, the club's first in 30 years, and that team provided the bedrock for the club's maiden U-21A success in 1993. We finally won back the intermediate title that season, and we retained our U-21 title the following year. Although it was our first year back up senior in 1994, we went straight into the final, which we lost to Clarecastle by three points.

That defeat marked the beginning of a period during which we remained under Clarecastle's thumb. They beat us by a point in the first round in 1995 and by two points in the quarter-final in 1996. In the showers after that match, Jamesie said, 'The wheel will turn, it always does.' We expected it to turn the following year but it didn't; they beat us in the 1997 final by six points.

By that stage, people within Clare had a certain perception of us: a nice team with some really good players but who weren't able to cut it at the top. Clarecastle on the other hand saw it in more crude terms. They labelled us as a 'poo-poo' team and they weren't shy in proclaiming it around the county: that basically we shit ourselves every time we met them. It absolutely galled us and we never believed it for a second. But we still couldn't crack them.

That Clarecastle team was packed with hardened and experienced campaigners. They saw us as a crowd of young lads who were there to be bullied. When Joe Considine made his senior debut in 1996, he was almost excited to be in the exalted company of players like Anthony Daly, who was marking him. At one stage of the second half, the two of them were jostling after the ball and Daly saw it as a perfect opportunity to lay down a marker; he clocked Joe with the butt of the hurley into the jaw.

Considine is originally from Cooraclare in west Clare but he had gone to school in St Flannan's College as a boarder. Cooraclare didn't have a hurling club and Considine didn't have a hurling background but, like a lot of young boarders in Flannan's, he spent his evenings honing his hurling skills in the ball alleys. Considine made the Dean Ryan team (U-16½) but wasn't good enough to make the Harty squad. His hurling days looked numbered after he left Flannan's because he wasn't affiliated with any hurling club. Since he was good friends with Ben Conroy and me, he joined our club while he was still a minor.

It was a massive achievement for Considine to play senior hurling within three years, but this was a whole new level of reality. He was nearly in shock after Daly's introductory lesson and now he had to listen to a host more Clarecastle players calling him a hillbilly and telling him to 'fuck off back to west Clare' where he belonged.

The two of us were out on the town that night and Considine was still reeling from the events of the day.

'I thought Daly was a nice guy,' he said to me.

'He is,' I told him. 'But these fuckers would take your life on the field to beat you. Wake up, Joe, this is the reality of senior hurling.'

Joe was offended by what he'd been called on the field, but I assured him that that was mild. Word came back to us later that evening of how they had referred to us in the dressing room before the game: neo-townie scum. They didn't give a damn about any of us and they would have cut our throats once they crossed that white line. Seánie had soldiered beside Daly and Stephen Sheedy with Clare for years, but when he moved up to centre-forward in the closing stages of the 1997 county final, Daly and Sheedy tore into him. They told Seánie that he had no business up their side of the field and to 'fuck off back down to where you belong'. It was never our style to go sledging or mouthing on the pitch, but they had us under their thumb and they'd been giving us a lesson in the ruthless edge we needed to adopt if we were going to live with them.

After four years of Clarecastle oppression, we were absolutely ravenous in 1998. Jamesie returned from his honeymoon after only six days, and on the day he got back we trained in Roslevan at 4 p.m. because we wanted to maximize the session on a cold Wednesday in early November. He said that day that he had come back for one reason: that we owed it to ourselves and to two men in particular – Ciaran O'Neill and Ger Hoey – to do everything we could to win that county title.

When we played so poorly to defeat Kilmaley in that county final, our first title in 40 years, the overbearing pressure told in the performance. In truth, it felt like an anticlimax. But we were liberated afterwards, and that spirit was evident the following week in Dungarvan when we mowed Mount Sion down like roadkill. The suppressed emotion and satisfaction burst out like a geyser and the feeling in that dressing room afterwards has never been matched since.

By then, we had the belief to chase real history. At a training session in Cusack Park the day before we played Mount Sion, Jamesie said if we beat the Waterford champions that we'd win the All-Ireland club title. After beating Mount Sion, it almost felt that we were on a mission of destiny.

Some of the hurling we played in the first half of the Munster final against Toomevara – on a muddy and sticky pitch in the Gaelic Grounds – was the best we ever produced. Physically, we had also developed into a massively imposing side. Once we defeated Athenry in the All-Ireland semi-final, nothing was going to stop us. We beat Rathnure in the final by 12 points.

There was still one caveat, though. We never ran into Clarecastle during the 1998 campaign because Éire Óg had taken them out in the first round after a replay. In their eyes, we weren't the real All-Ireland champions because we hadn't beaten them. Johnny Callinan, the former Clare player, said as much in his column in the local newspaper, *The County Express*.

We knew we were in line to meet them in 1999, but we were almost derailed by Ogonnelloe in the quarter-final. The game was fixed for Broadford, in the heart of east Clare, on a really wet Saturday. A massive east Clare crowd were at the game, baying for blood. There was no stand or proper crowd-policing policy, and it was pure mayhem. Jamesie went on a solo run down the line at one stage of the second half and the crowd had veered so far out on to the pitch that he was weaving in and out through the bodies.

We were chasing the game all the way through, and when they got a point with a minute remaining to push them ahead by four the show looked over. From the puckout, Ollie Baker, who had been moved to full-forward, scrambled home a goal. Deep in injury time, we were awarded a free from about 100 yards. Seánie, as you'd expect, slotted it to take us to a replay, which we won by six points.

Clarecastle felt that the wheels were coming off our wagon and they were primed for us. Despite all the huge games we'd played in the previous 12 months, the 1999 county semi-final honestly felt like the biggest game we'd ever played. It was all on the line: not so much our county, Munster and All-Ireland titles, but our reputation and our quest for true respect. We knew that the only way Clarecastle would ever respect us was by beating them.

Before a huge crowd – 12,000 – we blew them away in the first half and led by 0-10 to 0-2 coming up to the break. They got a goal to give them a real lifeline in the game, but we were physically standing up to them and they knew it.

The usual abuse towards Joe Considine had been flying in the first half, primarily from their substitutes bench. At one stage, one of their mentors came in to give advice to one of their players and Considine buried him with a shoulder. The message was very simple: for years Clarecastle had been dealing with boys; now they were dealing with men. And this was a group of players who were prepared to finish them as a team.

'The onslaught will come now,' said Jamesie to us in the dressing room just before we went back out for the second half. 'And we're going to meet it head on.'

We banged in two goals in the space of 90 seconds after the break and they spent the second half chasing us. Anthony Daly single-handedly kept them in the game and they won a penalty with ten minutes remaining with only four points between the sides. Before the penalty was taken, some Clarecastle supporters were singing an old tune.

'Ye have them, lads. They're going to shit themselves again.'

Those days were long over, though. We saved the penalty and won by four points. We'd been the dominant team and the deal had been closed. We were not only officially the best team in the country, but we'd also finally earned our true respect in Clare. Clarecastle couldn't deny that any longer and Daly acknowledged as much afterwards. He stood at the entrance to our dressing room and shook every St Joseph's player's hand on the way in.

★

Respect was always what it was about for us because we worked so hard to earn it. On the night we won the All-Ireland title in 1999, we were welcomed back into the bosom of our people in Roslevan. Jamesie made a great speech which really underlined how the team had been shaped and defined along the journey. He told a story from a challenge game we'd played against Clarinbridge in Galway three years earlier.

The game was on in Clarinbridge on a Sunday evening and we arrived with a full squad. They only had 13 players and we ended up giving them two players to make up the numbers. They were a young side with a raft of players on county minor and U-21 teams, but we still felt that they had shown us a serious lack of respect that evening. As Jamesie recalled that story he finished with the line: 'Now that we have achieved what we have, no club will ever disrespect us like that again.'

We went on to win another county and Munster title in 1999 before being beaten by Athenry by four points in the 2000 All-Ireland final. We took out Clarecastle in the first round of that year's championship but got sucker-punched by Éire Óg in a low-scoring dogfight semi-final. That game was part of a double-header semi-final on a Saturday evening and there must have been over 12,000 people at it, even though the weather conditions were dire. After Éire Óg got ahead, the crowd smelt blood. Every score they got and clearance they made was greeted with a crescendo of noise.

Éire Óg were probably one of the poorest teams we'd met, but they were the first Munster team to beat us in over two seasons. They deserved the win and they celebrated it afterwards almost like a county title. Some of their substitutes were trash-talking as we were coming off the pitch. We later heard more loose comments about our worth as a team flying around from some of their players and supporters. They were delighted with themselves, and then Sixmilebridge came along two weeks later and wiped them out in the final.

When we were growing up, Éire Óg had always been our main rivals because we'd gone to school with most of their players in Ennis. They'd never really regarded us as a threat, but they were forced to

review that attitude after we beat them in the 1990 minor final, hammered them in the 1993 U-21 final and took them out in the senior
semi-final a year later. After that, Clarecastle assumed the status of
our archrivals.

When 2001 arrived, we were like men possessed. When we beat
Clarecastle in the county quarter-final, the prize was another shot at
Éire Óg in the semi-final. We thought they'd disrespected us the previous year and we were refuelled by a desire for retribution. In our
eyes that day, every club in the country respected us – except Éire
Óg. 'Even Clarecastle respect us,' said Jamesie in the dressing-room
huddle before that 2001 semi-final. 'Well, today we're going to teach
respect.' We annihilated them by 24 points.

We beat Sixmilebridge in the county final before narrowly losing
the Munster quarter-final to Ballygunner in Walsh Park. Since then
we have failed to win any more county titles; our last final appearance was in 2004, when we lost to Kilmaley by a point, with the
second-last puck of the match. That team still had the core-group of
bodies from the All-Ireland winning side, but more and more of
those players have slipped away in recent years and we've never really
replaced them. The aura around St Joseph's Doora-Barefield has been
stripped away, layer by layer, with each passing season. That aura is
what we've all been struggling to rediscover over the last few years.
Ten years on, ambitions of winning another All-Ireland club title
exist only in a parallel universe. That is our reality now.

As the chat continued around the fire in Thomastown, a few of us
got talking about how fortunate we were to have played with some
of hurling's greatest players of the last 20 years – Jamesie, Seánie,
Ollie. But to many of us in Doora-Barefield, Ger Hoey more than
anyone else stood for everything we believed in: respect, honour and
dignity. He was the player who everyone really looked up to, who
always carried people with him through the immense force of his
character and personality. It was fitting that the last 12 people to carry
his coffin in Templemaley cemetery on that fresh February morning
were all former St Joseph's teammates.

One of the defining moments for that team came at half-time in the 1999 All-Ireland semi-final against Athenry. Six points up, but having to play into a near-hurricane in the second half, we knew we were going to face the ultimate test of character, belief and spirit. The side was full of leaders, but the true warrior stepped forward and set the tone. 'I can guarantee ye, this game will be level with 15 minutes to go,' said Ger Hoey. 'And then we'll see who the real men are.'

Ten years on, for those of us fortunate enough to have been on that team, the real sense of satisfaction and pride was knowing that you were surrounded by great men. Really great men.

6. The Future

The sweetest victory I ever tasted was our minor A win in 1990. The final whistle was absolutely beautiful; the explosion of emotion, the kinetic charge of elation as myself and Seánie McMahon hugged each other in the goalmouth, and the absolute purity of the satisfaction which followed. Beating our archrivals, Éire Óg, enhanced the sensation because we'd been listening to their players in school for the previous two weeks telling us by how much they were going to beat us. They were reigning champions and hot favourites, but we won an epic match by a point.

There's no doubt about it but that win was effectively the launch-pad for our All-Ireland club success nine years later: eight players from that minor panel in 1990 started the 1999 All-Ireland club final. It was the club's first minor title in 30 years and it heralded the beginning of a great odyssey for many Doora-Barefield players, none more so than Seánie McMahon.

He couldn't make that team and the only reason he played in that 1990 minor final was because our full-back, Donal Cahill, cried off with illness that morning. Seánie never seemed destined to become a good player, never mind possibly the greatest centre-back in hurling history. In his early teens he was a light, timid player. That could possibly be traced back to when he was 12 and he got all his front teeth smashed in during a schools match, an incident which probably set him back about four years.

When Seánie was 16, there were 60 players called for a Clare U-16 trial and his name wasn't among them. That devastated him, but he couldn't claim to have been a victim of injustice when he couldn't make the Doora-Barefield minor team a year later. He only got his chance through the misfortune of someone else, but he played well in that final and he always spoke afterwards about the huge level of confidence he gained from it. We all did.

We never had a culture of underage success, but winning that minor title infused us with the belief that we could go on to greater things. Three years later, we won our first U-21A title, hammering Éire Óg in the final. The night before that game, our trainer, Tony Kelly, told us that Doora-Barefield were going to play a huge part in the future success of Clare hurling. Clare hurling was at an all-time low at the time, but Kelly could already see the bigger picture through the talent in our panel. Anyone in Clare will tell you that the county would not have won All-Ireland titles in 1995 and 1997 without the influence of Jamesie O'Connor, Seánie McMahon and Ollie Baker – all members of the 1990 minor panel.

We haven't won a minor title since. We continued to reach minor finals over the next decade – we narrowly lost five finals between 1992 and 2001 – but we haven't even been back to one since then. We won our last U-21A title in 1994, and our record in the competition over the last decade has been one long horror-story.

In our club there is absolutely no culture of underage hurling success between the ages of 15 and 21 any longer, and the rate of player fall-off in those age groups has nearly been at haemorrhage level. We haven't had success at U-15A since 1994 or at U-16A since 1995, while we've won only three more underage A hurling titles in the meantime.

On the other hand, we've developed into a real underage football powerhouse, winning 17 A titles in the last two decades. In the last three seasons alone, we've contested six A finals in football (including one Feile final) and not one in hurling. It's always much harder to win underage hurling titles, especially when most of the dominant underage hurling clubs concentrate solely on hurling. In order to remain competitive at hurling, a dual club like ours has almost to double its efforts at underage hurling coaching because the skills development of young hurlers requires a much more concentrated investment than for footballers.

We have had some fantastic people working with our underage teams over the last decade, but we made the same mistakes that the county board made after Clare won All-Ireland titles in 1995 and 1997: we rested on our laurels.

That was the time the club needed to really push the underage development, yet one parent once told me that his son didn't bring his hurley to school for six months after we won that All-Ireland. At the time, that kid was an enthusiastic ten-year-old, and the club shouldn't have just left it up to the school to foster his development. When he and his friends – the kids who brimmed with excitement and vigour when the All-Ireland trophy was brought around to the schools – played at U-14 level four years later, they were competing in the B grade. The club has to stand indicted for allowing that to happen.

In our defence, we had just bought the land in Gurteen and most of the energy from the people in the club was poured into that development. But we still took our eye off the ball.

When I wrote an article for the club yearbook in 2003 entitled 'Time for Action', I interviewed Joey Carton, who was then, and still is, Provincial Games Manager for Munster. He had been at the heart of the De La Salle underage revolution in Waterford city. When Carton first got involved in the club, De La Salle were on the floor and they'd seriously discussed winding up the club at an AGM in the 1970s. They were an intermediate team without prospects. By the early 1980s, they couldn't field a minor team, and the only way was to start again, from the bottom. A juvenile committee was formed with teenagers such as Carton on board, and that's where the long climb to the summit began. In the last decade, they've won half a dozen U-16 county titles, five U-14s and a minor crown. Last month, they reached an All-Ireland club senior final.

Talking to me for that article in 2003, Carton emphasized the importance of nurturing hurling skills development between the ages of six and ten. At the heart of it was the setting up of an underage development committee to cater for those age groups. 'That committee seems like the most unimportant in the club but it is the most important,' said Carton in 2003. 'The club can have its finger on the pulse there and can see what's coming. You cannot understate how crucial that is to a club.'

Carton's comments always made perfect sense. If kids can manage to execute the basic skills at that age group, they have a far better chance of progressing as underage hurlers. Moreover, they will be far more confident and will get far more enjoyment out of hurling, which consequently makes it far easier for the club to hold on to those players. Hurling is such a technical game that it's almost impossible to eradicate bad habits from a 14- or 15-year-old.

In that article, Carton had also spoken about the importance of continuing that coaching in the schools. That was always a no-brainer, because whatever coaching is done in the club would inevitably break down if it wasn't maintained in the schools. No hurler – no matter what age – can drop a hurley for a sustained period of time and then expect to be at the same level when he next picks it up. Hurling just doesn't work like that. For years, the schools filled that gap, but coaching hurling in the schools is no longer a priority for principals and teachers who face increasing demands from school life. And the club needed to acknowledge that.

For years, some of us had been raising those points at AGMs, but nothing was ever done about it. Finally, at a meeting in July 2008 to draw up the plans for our new state-of-the-art clubhouse, I couldn't take it any more. 'I'm sick of all this talk about the development in Gurteen. When are we going to realize that we need to start pumping money into our underage structures? The way we're going, we'll have the best facilities in the county and we'll have no players.'

The club had been sending people into the schools over the years, but it was only a sporadic exercise. There was no structure to the policy, and what we were doing clearly wasn't working. When I raised the point again at the AGM about the necessity of employing a part-time coach, I was backed up by the minor chairman, Anthony O'Halloran. He had his folder on his lap and he detailed the figures the minor club had to cater for and the subsequent recruitment drive for mentors which that entailed. Apart from the difficulties involved in coaching young kids, recruiting 54 mentors in hurling and football for 240 kids was the sole responsibility of the minor chairman. He clearly needed assistance.

The club agreed in principle at the AGM to explore the possibility of hiring a part-time coach, and the only reason I agreed to become vice-chairman was so I could try and assist in the development. Once a committee was then set up, the first person I contacted was Joey Carton.

In February, we met in a hotel outside Limerick to discuss what the whole process would entail. The meeting was the first real indication of how hard the economic recession had hit. The lobby was dimly lit and freezing, the kitchen was closed and the hotel seemed to be functioning only to cater for its gym members, who were filing in and out at an impressive rate.

Joey was asking me about the identity of some of the local club tracksuits worn by some members, and when we eventually got down to discussing the detail of our meeting, there were two obvious starting points. Firstly, hiring a coach was going to require a huge financial commitment from the club. Secondly, before we could even look at employing somebody, we needed to devise an overall underage coaching plan because the club needed to be adequately structured to benefit from any extra activity in the local schools.

Joey gave me a questionnaire, which I subsequently forwarded to our minor club chairman and secretary, Anthony O'Halloran and Bernie Hallinan. There were 28 questions, which probed some key areas:

How many active qualified coaches have you?
How do you recruit your new players – and what about players not in schools in the parish?
How do you recruit mentors?
Have you a specialized group looking after the 6 to 10 age group?
Do all of your players receive a proper programme of games?
How receptive are principals and staff to regular visits during school hours?
Have you a club/school liaison officer?
Have you a club notice board in the schools?

The last question of the questionnaire focused on how the club would have to be conditioned to adapt to change. When the questionnaire was returned to Joey Carton by Bernie Hallinan, his answer to that question touched on a hugely important issue. 'We as a club need to be very careful to ensure that the employment of a coach does not have a negative effect on the huge voluntary pool of people who give freely and generously of their time working in the club in all capacities.'

The hiring of a coach – whether part-time or full-time – should primarily assist and complement the volunteers, not replace them. The coach could not be seen as a panacea to all the coaching ills, where other members might back off and subsequently think that all the bases were now covered. That was a hugely important message to transmit.

Finally, a critical decision had to be made with regard to defining the coach's working brief. When the topic was raised at the AGM, one club member – Seánie Lyons – said that since we were a dual club, he assumed that a new coach would cater for both hurling and football. However, since the club was leaning towards hiring somebody on a part-time basis, and hurling needed far more time investment than football, it was decided that the new coach would be for hurling only.

The decision was taken with all those reasons in mind, but it would have been easy for the football people in the club to perceive it as a politically motivated drive to promote hurling at the expense of football. However, Seánie Lyons was also a member of the minor club executive and, once he saw the reasoning behind it, we didn't feel there was any reason to explain the decision to anyone else.

When Joey Carton arrived to Gurteen on the last Wednesday in March, all of those topics were discussed at a meeting between him and the committee. He advised us on the best means of drawing up an overall coaching plan and he agreed to sit on the panel when we began interviewing for the job. His central theme, though, was the importance of the underage academy (U-6 to U-10) and the obsessive perseverance it takes to drive it.

The meeting was hugely positive, but there was a lot of work to be done and the new coach probably wouldn't be in place until September, when the schools would be starting back. But we couldn't wait that long to begin up-skilling our underage coaches; Joey said he would return on 23 April to take a coaching workshop in the club. After waiting for so long, we're now a club in a hurry.

On the warmest day of the year so far – Saturday, 18 April – the senior team produced probably the coldest display in our history. Terrible stuff, absolutely dire. In the third round of the Clare Cup against Tulla, on a fast surface and on a perfect evening for hurling, we managed to score just five points. And we failed to score at all in the second half.

Tulla only managed 1-6, but they could have had at least 20 scores if they'd showed a bit more composure, because they had all the possession. We hadn't trained all week because we played Burgess from Tipperary in a challenge under lights on Wednesday night, when we performed really well against a side that had contested the north Tipperary final the previous year. Maybe we thought we'd reproduce the same kind of form now, but we were flat and the performance was nothing short of embarrassing.

When he met us on the first night, Patsy said that he wanted this team to mirror him as a coach. The reflection staring back at him this evening was an embarrassment. 'Jeez, lads, maybe there was a party on last night that I didn't know about,' he said. 'Maybe I have to take some of the blame for having the challenge game on midweek and not training on Tuesday and Thursday night. But that still wasn't good enough. Lads, we need to start asking ourselves some serious questions.'

Davy Hoey was sitting in the corner with his shirt off, drying the sweat off his body. As he put the towel to his face to wipe his brow, he suddenly felt the urge to speak. 'Maybe I'm a bit emotional, but what the fuck was that all about? We were all terrible, myself included. When are we going to start getting it together? This is hard east-Clare hurling territory and we just didn't want to know about it tonight. Well, we better get used to it because that's what we're going to be facing in the championship.'

Darragh O'Driscoll, one of the team's most experienced players, then got up off the bench and moved towards the centre of the dressing room. 'That performance was scandalous. Five points? No score in the second half? Mother of God, we're playing championship this day four weeks and we go out and produce that kind of shit.

'It just won't happen for us. We've got to start making it happen. Fast. Young lads here might be thinking that ye have loads of time – ye haven't. I've been injured for the last two years and you never know what's around the corner. Before you come training now on Tuesday night, drink water, stretch, do whatever you have to do to get yourself right. But come on Tuesday night prepared for hard work.'

The showers were hammering water off the tiles but nobody was standing under them. The sunlight was dipping in through the narrow window panes but the mood was still dark and sombre.

Before he left the dressing room, Patsy tried to alter the picture. 'Maybe we need something to spark us into life,' he said. 'And the good news is that Seánie McMahon is coming back to training with us on Tuesday night.'

With the way we're going, though, we'd need our Lord to return to snap us out of this vat of desperate form. I texted Seánie on the way home. 'Hail the Messiah. We'll have the red carpet out for you on Tuesday night.'

He rang me back the following day.

'I'll have to get a new pair of togs anyway,' he said.

'Well at least you'll bring the average age of the team back up again and I won't feel like an auld lad,' I said to him.

'Well I still won't be the oldest there and you know who that is,' he responded.

'Not by much,' I retorted. (I'm just two months older than him.)

We talked about Saturday's performance. The only positive I could take from it was through making a comparison with a league game against Sixmilebridge the previous year when they whacked us around the place, and then we came along five weeks later in the championship and knocked them out cold.

'Yeah, but it's that inconsistency which has been killing us,' said Seánie. He was dead right.

At least Seánie's return will be a boon. If he never even hit a ball, his presence alone in the dressing room would be an immediate advantage because the man is an institution. He's still some way off decent fitness but he's been running to keep himself in some shape and, more importantly, he's fuelled by a raw emotion that will push him to the limit. He was always likely to come back, but the passing of Ger Hoey more or less copper-fastened the decision in his mind.

Seánie was as close to Ger as anyone. The second the final whistle went in the 2001 county final, Seánie made straight for Ger because he knew it was the last time they'd play together in Clare as Ger was moving to work in the USA later that year. That embrace encapsulated the respect that great players reserve for each other when they know an ending is in sight.

On Tuesday night, there was no red carpet laid out for Seánie because he walked back into a wall of fire. Patsy had left the dressing room on Saturday evening in a rage and there were still plumes of smoke billowing from his ears three days later. After he instructed us to complete an eight-minute warm-up, he called everyone back into the dressing room.

Patsy had a sheet of paper in his hand, which was clearly labelled with a number of bullet points, and he expanded on each point calculatedly and coldly. He said he wasn't prepared to let Saturday's game go without addressing the issue and that he wouldn't be doing his job properly if he did. He described our use of the ball as 'willy-nilly' and referred to our worrying inconsistency from game to game. We'd been flat for our opening game against Clooney-Quin, really up for our second game against Newmarket (which we also narrowly lost) and then flat again against Tulla. We had a crucial league game against Crusheen in 11 days' time and Patsy had no doubt that we'd be geared for a big performance. But then we'd Ballyea in our first championship games two weeks later. Were we going to be off the boil again for that game?

Patsy had known bad defeats before and he wouldn't have spared himself in the tribunals of inquiry that followed. But there was some public shelter in not being the manager, or not being from that particular club; after the Tulla game there was none. This was the inevitable moment when Patsy was crossing the threshold from close friend to ruthless manager. His affiliation and loyalty to some players had been holding him back, but that umbilical cord was now emphatically being severed. 'From now on, there's no more Mr Nice Guy from me. Guys are getting away with too much and I'm not fucking standing for it any more. If guys aren't putting in the effort and names have to be named, they'll be named. I don't care any more.'

Just before he finished his speech, he said our performance had been a 'disgrace' to the St Joseph's jersey – and all the more so in light of how much this season is supposed to mean to us. 'I know you're here, Davy, and I'm reluctant to bring it up,' said Patsy, looking over at Ger's brother. 'But I'm going to. Ger Hoey may have been beaten on the pitch but he was never once beaten for heart, passion and commitment, and what went on on Saturday was an insult to everything he stood for. The parish needs a lift. Everyone needs a lift. So let's get our fucking act together.'

It was a very productive session, but the turnout – there were 14 present – wasn't really acceptable after what had happened on Saturday. As we were completing our stretching at the very end, John Carmody stepped in. 'It's up to everyone here, not just us, to get the players out who are supposed to be here,' he said. 'We're just sick of chasing guys.'

Who was he talking about? For a start, some of the senior footballers were missing. Caimin O'Connor said that some of them were training with the senior football squad in Lees Road, a venue across town. Patsy was clearly annoyed, as the deal seemed to have been that they would train with us tonight and then with the footballers on Thursday night.

By the time I got to Gurteen at 6.30 p.m. on Thursday to meet Joey to prepare for the coaching seminar that night, he'd already set up his PowerPoint presentation in dressing room number four. He was going to speak with the coaches for roughly half an hour before moving outside for some practical coaching. He had asked me to book the AstroTurf because it was far easier to go through the basic technicalities on that surface than on a soggy pitch, especially if it was raining. He was spot on, because the rain was spilling from the sky all evening.

By the time Joey began at 7 p.m., 16 coaches had gathered, all of whom worked with U-6s to U-10s. That number included Jamesie O'Connor and Seánie McMahon, along with four women, one of whom – Therese Wall – is one of the outstanding young coaches in the club. Some of the other coaches were rookies, parents with no background in hurling who were eager to learn and get stuck in.

Most coaches, at that level anyway, were starting from scratch, and Seánie was the perfect example. He had coached U-21s in the club but he hadn't a clue of the specifics needed for young kids. In that regard, Joey was absolutely perfect: he had been instrumental in helping to draw up the Go-Games coaching package, which is the basic underage coaching model implemented by Croke Park. More importantly, though, he could also speak to the group as a parent. Along with one other person, he still co-ordinates the underage coaching programme in De La Salle, where his kids also play. So he went through basic stuff that is of fundamental importance to starting kids off right: how to hold a hurley; how to stand; how to turn the nose of the hurley.

By the time we went out to the AstroTurf, the rain was coming down even harder, but it didn't have any impact on the collective enthusiasm. At one stage we were learning drills and I was in a line with Seánie, who was shielding the rain from his little notebook with his left hand while he scribbled down notes and drew diagrams with his right hand.

Seánie remained on, but I only stayed for 35 minutes because we were training at 7.45 p.m. On the way to the dressing room, I met James Hanrahan and Justin O'Driscoll from the senior football management. After training on Tuesday night, Patsy had asked me to ring Keith Whelan – one of our talented U-21 dual players – to find out if he would come to senior hurling training. I had enjoyed a good relationship with Keith when I'd coached him at minor and U-21, and the senior management thought my intervention would be beneficial.

So I rang Keith on Wednesday night and said that I'd clear it with the football management for him to come to hurling training on Thursday night. The football manager, John Halpin, had no problem with that, so I just informed Hanrahan and O'Driscoll that Keith Whelan would be training with the hurlers this evening. Then the two lads told me that he wouldn't be training with the hurlers and neither would the rest of the senior hurlers.

When I got into the dressing room, I sat down beside Cathal O'Sullivan and Greg Lyons – two of our best dual players – and asked them who they were training with. They didn't know. They asked me what the story was and I said I hadn't a clue. All I knew was that the footballers had a league match on Saturday, but I assumed that since some of them had trained with the footballers on Tuesday night they'd be expected to train with the hurlers tonight. Looking around at the numbers in the dressing room, there would have been only nine hurlers at our session if the dual players went with the footballers. After Tuesday night, Patsy clearly wasn't going to allow that to happen.

By the time I made it on to the pitch, Greg Lyons told me that there had already been an altercation between Patsy and Hanrahan and O'Driscoll. Both managements were fighting their own corner but Patsy just insisted that the dual players train with us. I counted five dual players in our group, but there were two more on the bottom field with the footballers. It was obvious now that there was tension between both managements, and that would inevitably lead to more conflict down the line.

With three defeats from our first three league games, we desperately needed a result against Crusheen in round four. We needed to arrest a slide, especially just two weeks before our opening championship match. We set the week up like a championship run-in: a hard training session on Monday and then a light session on Thursday. Everyone had been well forewarned about the importance of hydration and fuel-intake because the game had been fixed for 12 noon on Saturday, to facilitate anyone who wanted to watch the Heineken Cup semi-final between Munster and Leinster in Croke Park.

In the dressing room beforehand, you just knew the mood was at the right pitch. The only concern was that we were a bit too hyped up, which can affect performance. We had aimed to play on the edge, but we went very close to overstepping it after only two minutes. Our corner-back Marty O'Regan got involved in an altercation with their corner-forward and Marty turned around and dropped him. The Crusheen player was on the ground for about four minutes while he received attention. I hadn't seen the incident and neither had the umpires but I had heard the belt and Marty was lucky to have got away with it. After I caught his eye, I just tapped my index finger against my temple. We needed to be more clear-headed.

Still, our performance was really positive in the opening half. We dominated possession, but they were far more economical with the ball against the breeze. We shot ten wides to their two and were only two points up at the break. Ken Kennedy laid into Kevin Dilleen, Greg Lyons and Conor Hassett for going for their own scores instead of playing more ball into the full-forward line. 'This game would be over now if ye looked up and used yere heads.'

Then our full-forward Deccie Malone weighed in with his observation. 'They know exactly what ye are going to do,' he said, in a pointed reference to the same players. 'They surround ye with three or four bodies because they know ye are going to run with the ball. And if that happens, there must be some of our players free.'

Patsy remained positive, but he stressed the need to control their corner-forward Gearóid O'Donnell, who had been the most effective player on the field in the opening half. He had scored three points from play from only about four possessions.

A couple of minutes into the second half, O'Donnell won a ball out in the half-forward line, turned and headed straight for goal. Marty

O'Regan went to meet him and just as O'Donnell offloaded the ball, Marty buried him head-on. He was committed to the challenge, but O'Donnell collapsed in a heap and the ball was cleared down the field.

Their players were roaring at the referee and then they turned their attention towards the umpires because blood was spilling from their teammate's forehead. I told one of the umpires that I thought Marty couldn't pull out of the challenge because both of them were going at full pace. The umpire agreed and that was the message conveyed to the referee when he came in to consult with his officials a minute later. O'Donnell was carried off and by the time he returned, around fifteen minutes later, his head was bandaged up and the game was really in the melting pot.

A goal had given us some breathing space but Crusheen had charged at us midway through the half and they had all the momentum with the stiff breeze. We had been holding on, but they got a well-worked goal with just four minutes remaining which put them ahead for the first time in the match.

It looked like another disappointing day, but we kept going and put a decent move together in a final attempt to save the match. I played a quick free to Kevin Dilleen near the far sideline and he quickly switched the play back across the goal to stretch their blanket cover. The ball ended up in the square and was scrambled across the line by Damien Kennedy. Seconds later, the final whistle blew and we were ahead by a point on a scoreline of 2-12 to 1-14.

Jeez, we hadn't felt this good after a league match in years. But this was more than just a win and two points finally in the bag; it was a performance that reflected honesty, integrity and work rate, qualities that we hadn't really shown to date. And we'd just proved to ourselves that we can be a match for any team in the county when we produce those qualities. As we gathered in a huddle in the middle of the pitch afterwards, the vibe was excellent.

'Great result, lads, wonderful character, that's what this team is all about,' said Patsy as we circled around him. 'Since it's a Bank Holiday weekend, I have no problems with guys going out tonight and tomorrow night. But that's it then, no more fuck-acting between tomorrow night and championship. The real serious stuff starts from Tuesday on.'

Before we broke up, I just wanted to make one quick point. I didn't want to dampen the mood but I felt that Patsy had made a really important point to us 11 days earlier. And that it was now time to reiterate it.

'Patsy identified a trend, and we have to be really aware of it. After a poor performance, we've then delivered a positive performance next time out. And then we've been poor again. We can't allow that to happen now after this good performance. Especially when everyone is going to be telling us over the next few weeks that we'll definitely beat Ballyea in the first round of the championship.

'Well, they relegated Éire Óg to intermediate last year, just five weeks after Éire Óg had drawn with Clarecastle in the championship. We can't afford to be flat against them because they are dangerous. [Tony] Griffin is sure to be looking for some form to bring into the championship with Clare and if he gets it into his head, he could go to town on us. We need to really tune into these boys now for two weeks and not be thinking about the big one against the 'Bridge [Sixmilebridge] at the end of the month.'

By the time we made it to the dressing room, Noel Brodie was slagging Seánie about the impact his '18 stone' frame had made in Damien Kennedy's pushover goal. But as we emerged from the showers, water still dripping off us, Pat Frawley arrived in to alert us to the stormclouds gathering outside. He said that Crusheen weren't happy about the O'Donnell incident and that a group of them were waiting outside for a showdown. He said that they were blaming Ken Kennedy.

With that, I looked over to Ken, who was already dressed and making for the door. 'Hey, where are you going?' I asked him. 'Wait up for the rest of us.'

'What for?'

'We'll all go out together in case there's any hassle.'

'I couldn't care less,' he responded. 'I didn't go near him.'

With that, he took off straight out the door, turning right in the direction where the Crusheen players were supposedly gathered.

Most of us hadn't a stitch of clothes on, so Eoin Conroy, who hadn't showered and was heading for the gym, ran out after him. As the rest of us tried to get dressed in a panic, Seánie looked out the window and spotted Ken getting into his jeep, unscathed.

7. Let's Get It On

The Clare senior club hurling championship has become a bear-pit. Prior to 2007, eight clubs had shared the title over the previous 40 years, and each of those four decades was dominated by one of the three big powerhouses: Newmarket, Clarecastle and Sixmilebridge. When Clare club hurling was at its peak in the 1990s, winning six successive Munster club titles, there were only four realistic contenders: Clarecastle, Sixmilebridge, Wolfe Tones and ourselves. Now? Twenty clubs enter the championship and at least 12 feel they can win it.

The Clare championship has no regard for reputation or tradition any more. Tulla narrowly lost a Munster club final in 2007 and managed to win only one championship game out of four in 2008. Wolfe Tones, champions in 2006, also failed to emerge from that same group as Tulla in 2008. Inagh-Kilnamona topped that group and surfed into the quarter-final on a huge tide of optimism until we beat them by eight points.

Nobody is untouchable. And if you're really unlucky, you could end up in a group of death. One group this year contains Newmarket, Clarecastle, Wolfe Tones, Cratloe and Tubber. The first four have serious ambitions of winning the title, and yet only two can make it to the quarter-finals. Tubber won't win a county title but they're an emerging side who beat us and Sixmilebridge last year and they've developed a reputation as big-game slayers.

On the opening weekend of the championship in the middle of May, Tubber were at it again, beating Clarecastle by eight points. A result like that in the past would have sent shock waves around the county and Tubber would have celebrated it like an All-Ireland. At the final whistle, their players just casually accepted the congratulations and walked off the field like it was any other game. The rest of the county just shrugged its shoulders.

Our first game the following day, Sunday, 17 May, was a treacherous fixture. Ballyea had gone well in Division Two of the league and their side, packed with young players, had just won the U-21B title. Our form had been poor and, between exams, football and injury, the starting 15 had never played together before. But we're not complaining because at least we're beginning our championship in summer. And not in autumn.

Last year was a joke. A complete joke. We started training on 16 January and didn't play our first championship match until 15 August. There was a round of games played in early June, but we'd a bye that weekend. We were supposed to play our first game on Friday, 27 June, but the Clare hurling manager, Mike McNamara, went into a county board meeting the previous evening and requested that all club games be pulled that weekend. He didn't want any disruption to Clare's preparations before their Munster final against Tipperary on 13 July.

That was understandable and we were made aware of McNamara's intentions. But we still trained that evening, fully primed to play 24 hours later, because we'd believed that, as a compromise, the games involving the four clubs who had received a bye in the first round would be allowed to go ahead. We were due to play Sixmilebridge and, since there were only three players on the Clare panel between the two clubs, we couldn't see any reason why the match shouldn't go ahead. We had been preparing for the game for months, but just as we were warming down and going through our game plan, we received news that all the games had been called off.

It was a sickening feeling, but it wasn't anything new to us. In 2005 there was a five-week break between the National League final and Clare's Munster hurling semi-final, but the club delegates chose not to play the championship in that time frame. Our first-round championship match was then fixed for midweek, ten days before Clare were due to play Wexford in the All-Ireland quarter-final. The county hurling management were unhappy with that arrangement and they requested a meeting with the county board less than 24 hours before the game was scheduled. At 9 p.m. that evening, just after training, we were informed that the match had been postponed.

Eoin Conroy was halfway back from Dublin when he got word. He had already taken the following day off work. In 2006, we played our first championship match on 7 May and our second on 29 August – a 112-day lay-off. We ended up in a play-off, and by October we were still slugging it out in a group that had begun in May; by that stage, guys were just burned out and fed up. In 2007, we didn't play a championship match in July or August.

It's no wonder so many players walk away from their clubs each year: they just can't handle the hassle. It's almost as if county boards assume that club players don't have jobs, they don't take holidays, they don't have family commitments, they all still live at home with their parents and there's no such thing as divorce. The ordinary club player often exists on a week-to-week basis, not knowing when or if the county board has decided to fix a game.

We've become conditioned to feeling like second-class citizens.

Constant training with no matches is soul-destroying – and often damaging to a club's ambitions. In 2004, the Clare hurlers didn't play between 16 May and 26 June, but there were no club hurling games played in that time span. Clare were annihilated by Waterford in the Munster quarter-final and I remember Seánie saying to me afterwards that going back to the club for a few weeks would have been the perfect valve-release for many of the players, as opposed to continuously training with Clare. The championship didn't begin until August and we eventually ended up playing five matches in six weeks in September and October. We lost the county final by a point.

The constant grind eventually caught up with us. The week before that county final, we picked up a couple of serious injuries and guys had no time to recover. Injury is one serious issue with regard to condensing championships. If a player breaks an arm in, say, May, he'll still probably be back in good time for the championship. If another player gets injured in September, he'll probably miss the business end of the championship.

The same principle applies to suspensions and travel. A player could get suspended in May for three months and he won't be affected. Another player could get sent off towards the end of the season and end up missing three matches while serving a one-month suspension. Similarly, a student can go to the USA for the whole summer and not miss any games, while one of his teammates could book a one-week holiday, the county board changes the proposed structure of matches, and he ends up missing a key game. Or if he chooses to stay, his decision has wider ramifications on his personal life. That instability puts a constant strain on relationships. I know because I've been there.

Six months before Olivia and I got engaged, we broke up for a week. I was minor coach and we had a minor championship quarter-final against Clarecastle the same day that we were supposed to attend a wedding in Mayo. I had promised Olivia that I would go to the wedding, but the match was rescheduled at short notice and something had to give. Jeez, we were playing Clarecastle. Anyway, my non-appearance at the wedding was the last straw from a summer of serial disappointments and cancellations.

If you were to think about it for just a second, how could you rationalize it? You risk your future with your loved one because of a match? A match you're not even playing? For a crowd of young lads, some of whom might not even bother to show up? You must be mad. But that's just the pull that the club has over you. It consumes you.

The commitment of inter-county players, and their wives and partners, is absolutely massive and it far outweighs that of club players. Given the nature of the inter-county championship, and its unpredictability over the summer, it's often impossible for county boards to define a structured championship. Yet it is very wrong when the tail, which comprises the 4 per cent of players who play senior inter-county, wags the big dog, composed of the 96 per cent of players who don't.

In the last decade, the landscape of the inter-county championships has changed radically to accommodate the need for more matches, and the strain has been felt at club level. The treatment of club players has been a scandal in an organization that prides itself on amateur status and the equality of all members. The club player is repeatedly held to ransom by the interminable postponements and the now accepted imposition of asking club players to play midweek or under lights, regardless of work commitments or travel. He is often made to feel that he just doesn't matter.

The inter-county championships now are populated by players who think, behave and perform like elite athletes. By any reasonable understanding of the term, top-class GAA players ceased to be amateurs years ago. They deserve to be treated as the elite. Yet the reality is that such elite preparation also exists at club level. In an interview earlier this year, Portumna's Damien Hayes said that 'things are so professional here that we're like a county team'. There's no doubting that Portumna would beat any inter-county hurling team outside the top ten – and, on a good day, maybe the top eight. So would Ballyhale Shamrocks. Given their experience and style of play, Crossmaglen Rangers would beat at least six inter-county football teams, maybe more.

Club players can reach exceptional standards without the structured apparatus that assists inter-county players. Club players don't receive player grants or bursaries, while the vast majority of them don't get travel expenses or meals after training. Many club players don't even claim physiotherapy expenses, which leaves them out of pocket. And all they really want in return is to be treated properly by the county board.

A decade ago, the report of a Club Fixtures Work Group recommended a modest target of 20 matches a season for club players. The group found just one county reaching that figure. Half of the counties were providing 12 matches or fewer and 27 per cent of club players were getting fewer than ten matches. At the time, GAA Director General Liam Mulvihill described the provision of fixtures for clubs as 'shameful'. Revisiting the issue in 2004, Mulvihill said that there was 'no evidence that the provision of regular games for the average club player has been improved in the 75 per cent of the counties in which this was rated a serious problem'.

As things stand in Clare now, senior club players are guaranteed just 14 games per season – nine league and five championship matches. That number can increase with a better league and championship run, but the majority of senior players play an average of 15 games per season – still five games short of what was recommended ten years ago. Yet the central issue does not concern the number of games a club has in any given year – just when they are played.

Of course, the problems derive from the GAA's unique playing structure. The county team is the primary focus of county players for most of the year. Yet players are expected – and for the most part want – to play for their clubs as well. But that's not all. Some counties have divisional teams and championships; most have dual clubs fielding hurling and football sides. Then there are underage and colleges competitions, which can place a desperate burden on some talented young players. New regulations regarding player burnout have been in place for the past two seasons, but all teams still need to be accommodated within the competitive structures.

The problem has intensified since the advent of the All-Ireland qualifiers, which introduced a new level of uncertainty into the calendar. Increasingly, county managers look to have club activity frozen for the duration of a team's involvement in the provincial or All-Ireland championships.

The GAA authorities need to adopt a more interventionist approach to ensure that club players are not left on ice all summer. The whole mindset at local level has to change. County boards must ensure that matches go ahead within a certain time frame and clubs must realize that they can't delay games because of injuries or suspensions. More importantly, Croke Park must issue a directive that inter-county players and managers cannot dictate to county boards.

Much of what is wrong with the system is caused by the clubs themselves. Clubs pander to county boards because they want to ensure decent ticket allocations for inter-county matches, or because they may need a game switched. They are reluctant to play without their inter-county players, and as a result ordinary players' schedules suffer. We've seen our inter-county players support a decision by their manager to call off a club game.

With the competition among the three main sports (Gaelic games, rugby and soccer) more intense at grass-roots level than ever before, the inability of the GAA to plan their games properly at local level will cause more and more players to defect. Some rural clubs are haemorrhaging players to such a degree that they're in danger of being wiped out.

In 2006, Croke Park announced two new windows of opportunity for club matches to be played during any given season. Even the delegates present at the time couldn't pretend that this time wouldn't be eaten up by insecure county managers greedy for more time with their players. We've only got our window now because the Clare hurlers don't play in the championship until 21 June. But if Clare go on a winning run over the summer, the timetable will just be ripped up all over again.

When you begin training at the outset of every year, the promise of long summer evenings and the thrill of championship matches on a hard summer sod are invariably the stimulants that keep propelling you through the muck and dirt. You just assume that your first championship match in early summer will be played on a dry pitch with a fast ball.

But the weather was absolutely desperate for our match with Ballyea. As we went through our warm-up in Gurteen beforehand, torrential rain was drenching us, the dampness and cold soaking into our bones. As we did one warm-up striking drill, sliotars were consistently getting slow-tracked in the saturated grass or becoming lodged in surface water.

Before the team was named, we gathered in a huddle to do a stretch. As we did a back stretch, lifting our upper backs and necks with our prone bodies propped up by our elbows, the water was flowing so heavily from my hair that I could barely see in front of me. 'Cool heads the whole time but we see what's ahead of us,' I said to the group as we got up to loosen out our arms. 'This is going to be a fucking war in the trenches. And we better be ready to go over the top to drive these fuckers back.'

Driving to the game in Clareabbey was like going through a ride at a water-park. When we got to Clareabbey, it was too wet to walk the pitch: it was like a paddy-field.

The dressing room was busy and cluttered. Bad weather means more gear, extra pairs of boots and less space. There was no space left on the benches by the time I got in so that I had to tog off on the floor against the back wall, with my hurleys leaning up against the physio table.

The conditions were going to affect our game plan on short puckouts so I called the half-backs, midfielders and forwards into the shower area. 'It's just too risky today to go short. I'll hit the odd one but we can't afford it to break down on a pitch as bad as this. Just make the space out the field and I'll try and find you.'

Championship-day dressing rooms are always different. There's no real roaring or shouting, just guys trying to find the optimum state of mind amid the nervous energy and tension. Before we got ready to go out, Patsy walked to the centre of the floor.

'OK, lads, anyone here with a county medal, I want ye to stand up.' Seven of us got up on our feet. 'Look around now,' said Patsy. 'I'm sick of these same guys doing it every year for Doora-Barefield. It's about time the guys sitting down started doing it for them. And it's about time ye got yere hands on a county medal. Next year, Seánie, Christy and Ken could be gone and it's time now that more guys started to stand up and drive this team forward. We deal with what we have to and we only focus on what's ahead of us. But I just want ye all to remember that we need to do everything we can this year to get our hands on that county medal.'

Darragh O'Driscoll, our captain, had the last word in the huddle before we left the dressing room: 'Total focus. Take nothing for granted. Some people might think these guys are minnows. Well, there are no minnows in Clare hurling any more. Look at Tubber last night. Be ready for anything out here. Anything.'

By the time the game began, the rain had stopped falling and the sun was trying to peek out from behind the clouds. But the pitch conditions were just desperate, almost dangerous. The first high ball dropped in on top of me after about 90 seconds and, as I focused on it, I could see the moisture spinning off it. One slip and the consequences could be deadly in a game like this.

Ballyea were on top early. They had the first two points on the board and then their right corner-forward ghosted in for a goal after six minutes. A shot from out the field was topped and he was running across the angle inside the 13-metre line as the ball dropped. As soon as he caught it, I came to meet him but he got the shot off quickly and I couldn't get my body in front of it. As the ball hit the back of the net, Darragh O'Driscoll was running back in as cover. 'Who the fuck is supposed to be marking that guy?' he said to me.

It was Niall White, one of three young players making his championship debut. 'Whitey,' I called out to him, 'keep your head up now, stay positive and forget about that goal. But don't be ball-watching, make sure you know where your man is at all times.'

Ballyea were really going for it. The early scores had given them a huge confidence boost and on ten minutes they had another goal chance, which I saved. Afterwards, Patsy came down behind the goal and I was impressed with how cool he was. There was no need for panic and that was the message he was clearly transmitting.

We kept our heads and battled away. Conor Hassett was going well on the frees in the conditions, and we were in front on 20 minutes when Enda Lyons, another debutant, rifled a great goal through a phalanx of bodies. But their one inter-county player, Tony Griffin, was giving us huge problems. They were playing everything down his side at wing-forward and he had the physical power to dominate Darragh O'Driscoll under the dropping ball. In the first half, he scored four points from play. His dominance had ensured that we were only ahead by a point at the break on a scoreline of 1-5 to 1-4.

As I was making my way to the dressing room at half-time, T. J. Flynn, a reporter with the *Clare People* newspaper, was cutting across the pitch, dancing over the puddles of water as he went.

'God, the pitch is in some bad state,' he said to me.

'Desperate,' I replied.

'This game should hardly be going ahead at all,' he responded.

The second I got into the dressing room I sensed the kind of lethargy that I feared. I don't know what it is about our dressing room, but we've had this tendency to almost paralyse ourselves with fear when we haven't played as well as we know we can. Nobody was talking, bodies were stooped low and the aura was more reflective of a team in real trouble than a side that was ahead in the game.

'Look at us again,' said Davy Hoey, who was the first to speak. 'We're fucking dead, heads down, feeling sorry for ourselves again. The same fucking shit. Well, we better pick it up because we're going out of this championship if we don't win this game. We need to pick it up now. And we need a bit more bite.'

Some of that bite we'd shown in the first half was headless stuff, which had cost us. 'Stop the fucking messing of hitting guys after the ball,' roared Ken Kennedy. 'It's a man's game, so toughen up. If you're going to hit someone, do it on the ball.'

When Patsy, who had been in consultation with his selectors outside the door, arrived in, his comments were measured but laced with a degree of annoyance. 'We're in a dogfight, just as we expected. We're up a point and we need to continue grinding it out. But we need to get a handle on Griffin. Lookit, lads, he's no Jamesie O'Connor, who could win a game on his own when he was in his prime. We're not going to be beaten by a team run by Tony Griffin. So get it fucking sorted out.'

A switch was made to try to counter Griffin's influence. Cathal O'Sullivan was stationed on him and told not to allow Griffin to catch the ball.

Although we'd been slow in dealing with the influence of their best player, at least the issue had been addressed. But there was still too much negativity permeating the dressing room. Words and phrases like 'we can't get beaten' and 'we can't afford to lose' should have been replaced with 'stay positive' and 'we will win'. Seánie McMahon, who was still suited up in his tracksuit, noticed this. 'We are better than them and we will win the game,' he said. 'We just need to keep working hard and the scores will definitely come. Just keep going, keep going. The next ball, the next ball. Nothing else matters.'

However, Eoin Conroy, who was also a substitute, felt that it was time to hammer home some of the points which had already been raised. We clearly needed something more clinical to snap us out of our torpor.

'First things first,' Conny said, 'we are winning this game. We are fitter than them and we will outlast them. But a few things need to change. I don't see that relentlessness that we promised to bring to the game. It's not there. There's no point guys feeling down in themselves or feeling sorry for themselves now. We need to go out that door and be angry, relentless animals. Fight like fucking dogs for that ball. Get angry. Davy is angry but not enough of us are. WELL, GET FUCKING ANGRY.'

As the second half progressed, we were gradually getting our best team on the pitch. Mike McNamara, who hadn't started the match due to hamstring trouble, came on and made a difference. Seánie was introduced at full-forward, while Noel Brodie came into the half-forward line, which gave us another ball-winning dimension in that sector.

We had the match-ups right and the scores began to flow more freely, but we kept conceding stupid frees. Niall White got caught on three occasions for over-exuberance and they slotted each free. After the third one, I went out to him. 'Look, they're not going to score from play off you. If he has the ball, keep him outside you and away from the goal. If you can't get the hook or block in and he throws it over the bar then, there's nothing you can do about it.'

Another Ballyea point put them ahead by one with a quarter of an hour remaining, but we replied straight from the puckout with a fine score from Conor Hassett. Damien Kennedy's excellent endeavour was helping us create the chances, but the last ten minutes turned into a nightmare because we just couldn't score. We shot six wides in succession and each one was greeted with an agonizing groan from the crowd. We just couldn't shake them off. By that stage, Ballyea had gone for broke by putting Griffin in at full-forward. They needed him out the field to get the ball in, but they were banking on him getting one chance and stitching it. They got a couple of sideline balls in dangerous positions and if one of those was hit with the right connection, and was loaded with enough spin in the wet, it literally could have ended up anywhere.

We needed something special, and Seánie helped engineer it. He won a ball in the left corner, turned and played a pinpoint pass into the hand of Enda Lyons. Without hesitation, the young debutant drove the ball hard to the roof of the net.

I just looked up to the heavens and let out a roar of elation. A game which was threatening to strangle us was finally under our control. Then Conor Hassett slotted another free in injury time to give us the result on a scoreline of 2-11 to 1-9.

When Seánie made it into the dressing room, I went over and shook his hand. 'Fair play to you. Jeez, I was never as delighted to see us score a goal in all my life. I thought we were going to blow it.'

He just shook his head with relief. 'Stop, I was thrilled to see it go in,' he responded. 'I was saying to myself, "We'll get sucker-punched now, the year will be as good as over, and that will be me definitely gone." But we didn't panic and we toughed it out. And that's the important thing.'

Winning the first game in the group stage is not always paramount, but it has always been important for us. In every year from 2005 to 2007, we lost our first group game and spent the rest of the season trying to regain momentum. In two of those three seasons, we didn't even make it out of the group.

We'd got the result, but nobody was getting carried away. And some players had already begun making critical assessments on every aspect of our performance. From players to management. That night, I got a phone call from Conny.

'Fahey was in Knox's until all hours Saturday morning,' he told me. 'That's not fucking good enough, the night before a championship match.'

'Ah, I don't know, Conny, I think you're being a bit hard on him there,' I replied. 'I thought he handled the day well. And I thought he was very clear-headed and calm on the line.'

Conny cut me off straight away: 'No, that's bullshit. That's you showing him blind loyalty. He needs to have a clear head because an

incorrect call here or there could be a disaster. And more importantly, that place is always full of Ballyea people and that was him
sending out a wrong message from us. I'm not too happy about it and
neither is Ken. Ken told me to tell you to have a word with him
about it.'

Fair enough. I need to talk to Patsy anyway about our approach at
half-time because I felt there was too much talk and not enough
information.

I'll ring him tomorrow.

8. Crossing the 'Bridge

Despite all their tradition and success, Sixmilebridge have never really been able to handle us in the championship. In the last 12 years, we've played them on eight occasions and we've beaten them six times. Big games, too: two county finals, a semi-final, a knock-out group match. They've only beaten us in one game that really mattered – a narrow win in a group decider in 2003 – because when they drilled us in a group match in 2002, both teams had already qualified for the quarter-finals.

After we beat them again in last year's championship, their manager, Paddy Meehan, came into our dressing room and told us that we'd played a brand of 'hurling that you'd aspire to and which you'd be proud to produce'. On a wet Friday evening in Shannon, we pistol-whipped them around the pitch, hitting 1-17 in the process. A late goal from a 20-metre free was all that saved them from a total flogging.

That performance was a huge endorsement of Seán Chaplin's training methods and it involved a massive sense of personal reward for him because he's a Sixmilebridge man. When they failed to qualify from the group afterwards, the 'Bridge cleaned out their whole management team and it was almost inevitable that they'd try and recruit Chaplin. When they did, he was never going to turn his back on them. And now that we're facing them in our second championship match, he can use that inside knowledge to good effect.

This is a big game for us – not a group decider, but a win will leave us in pole position in this group, which will set us up for the summer because we won't play championship again until probably August. In that context, having two wins in the bag may take the edge off us over the summer and allow carelessness to seep in, but that's not even a remote consideration at this stage. We feel that we're on a roll and it's much easier to motivate players over a lay-off when you've established a winning habit.

We're in a good place at the moment. Last Sunday evening, five days before the game, we travelled back to Quilty in west Clare to do a hurling session on the beach, just to freshen things up. The only problem was that nobody had checked the tide-times, and the tide was in. We had already arranged to have showers afterwards in the Kilmurry-Ibrickane dressing room, so we headed the short distance back up the road and trained on their sand-based training pitch, behind their main field, for over an hour. The balls were flying off the surface, our touch looked good and, with the roaring Atlantic Ocean as a backdrop across the road, the mood felt just right. Afterwards, most of us went back to the ocean for the largest ice-bath available. On the way home, we knew we were ready.

Seventy-two hours before the game, Patsy was setting the scene, alluding to our comprehensive win against Sixmilebridge last year. 'I saw ye blow them away last year and they're going to be gunning for us. They might have a slight advantage – maybe two points – in terms of them being up for it more than us. But our hurling is spot on and if we're tuned in, we'll take care of them.'

I spoke to Patsy afterwards about collating stats on the day and then I went through the template with Seán Flynn, who's recovering from a shoulder injury. In the showers afterwards, Ken Kennedy and I got talking about our approach at half-time against Ballyea in our opening championship match and he remarked on Conny's input. 'He spoke well, didn't he? He said exactly what was needed.'

'He was spot on and I said it to him afterwards,' I said. 'He mightn't be near the team but he has a big role to play with us. He can analyse a situation and address it perfectly. If he was playing, he'd probably be psyched out of his brain and he wouldn't know what would be going on.'

I was no sooner in the door after training when Conny was on to me. 'I've got my little speech ready again for Friday night,' he said. 'I've been thinking about it all day. It's a line [Ollie] Baker used before the replayed game against the Tones in 2004. "There are two types of people in life – those who bully and those who get bullied. Well, we bully."'

In 2004, we played Wolfe Tones in an epic three-game quarter-final, which we eventually won. At the end of the first drawn match, Seánie scored a free from 100 yards in injury time to put us ahead by a point. As soon as the umpire signalled the score, their keeper pucked out the ball. But at the same time, Brian Lohan was retrieving another ball from the net, which he then pucked out. Half of us were following the flight of one ball while the rest were tracing the path of the second one. Our corner-back, Cathal O'Sullivan, caught the first ball and drove it back up the field, but at the other side of the pitch Daithí O'Connell caught Lohan's ball and drove it over the bar for the equalizer. Seconds later, the referee blew the final whistle.

Lohan was only doing what he felt was best for his team and it was poor officiating that had really cost us the result, but Baker used that line, more or less telling us that Lohan had bullied us out of the result. And that it was time for us to turn into the bullies. Now, Conny feels that the phrase is perfectly applicable because of the age-profile of an emerging Sixmilebridge team; they recently won the U-21A title and have packed their squad with those players.

'We need to bully these fuckers back to the 'Bridge,' he said. 'Trample on them. Walk all over them.'

'These boys won't be easy to bully with Rusty Chaplin over them,' I replied.

Christy 'Rusty' Chaplin played with Clare in the 1994 Munster final, and although he played only one more championship match with the county he was on the panel for Clare's All-Ireland successes in 1995 and 1997 because he was the type of player that Ger Loughnane loved: hard, robust, honest, physical. If Loughnane felt some player was going soft or getting notions above himself, he'd put Rusty on him during a training match to straighten him out.

Sixmilebridge are loaded with good hurlers but they'll be a well-organized and super-fit side under Seán Chaplin. And they'll surely take their heart and honesty from their manager, Rusty Chaplin.

'We just need to be disciplined and honest,' I said to Conny. 'If we are, there's no doubt in my mind that we'll beat them. Because we're better than them.'

'Jesus, man, I'm getting goosebumps already, just thinking about it,' Conny said, his voice straining with emotion down the phone. 'Jeez, it just kills me that I can't be around home on weeks like this.'

Conny lives and works in Dublin but makes it home for training as often as he can. Then he spends half his week on the phone trying to keep up to speed on what's happening in the club and the other half checking the mood and the mindset of the players. He doesn't train with any club in Dublin because his work schedule doesn't really allow it. So he trains early every morning and then hurls on his own as many evenings as he can, his only company being a wall – the back of the stand in Parnell Park – that he beats a ball back off, or a set of goalposts on a public pitch just off the Malahide road which he drills sliotars through.

He used to have his own training unit in Dublin, because Joe Considine, Lorcan Hassett and I lived in Dublin for years. The isolation is hard for him now.

The first time we ran into Conny in Dublin was in November 2000, when Hass and I were in that fine nightclub, Copper Face Jacks, one night. Despite the loud music and the squelching sound of bodies crashing against one another, we heard our names being called out on the dance floor.

'Yeaaaaaaaaahhhh, the Doora-Barefield boys are in the house. Whaassuup, dogs?'

It was Conny, hardly able to walk. Hass and I almost ignored him. Then he told us that he wanted to come training with us the following season. That's when we knew he was totally inebriated from drink, so we just basically walked away from him.

Although he was one of our biggest supporters, Conny hadn't hurled in years by that stage. He'd been preoccupied by college, work placement in London and summers abroad. But he was keen to go back and play a bit of junior hurling, and since Joe Considine was playing with the Clare senior footballers that season, Conny fitted neatly into our training programme.

Even though there were only three bodies, our attitude was to train like absolute dogs. No science, just sweat. One man in the middle of a drill for 90 seconds or a minute, annihilate yourself, then go back out and let the next man in. You'd just have recovered when it was time to go back into the middle again and torture yourself once more. The shooting drills were even more frantic. Bang, bang, bang.

At the outset, Conny just wasn't able for that relentless pace. The constant weekly trail to Copper Face Jacks had taken his fitness, and the years away from hurling had claimed his first touch. At times, Hass couldn't handle him at all. The man at the end of the line was supposed to have three or four balls so that he could keep feeding the man in the middle with sliotars. Yet Conny would be off like a pet rabbit chasing balls that had already gone flying past him. And Hass would be standing in the middle, the drill having completely broken down, roaring at him like a lunatic.

'Where the hell are you going?'

Then Hass would turn around to me. 'Is he gone home?'

At the outset, Conny couldn't hurl spuds to ducks but he gradually tuned in to what was required and the training really began to pay off for him. By the summer, he'd forged his way on to the senior panel.

He'd also bought into the discipline that was required. One Friday night in the summer of 2001, the three of us ended up in another fine Dublin nightclub, Break for the Border, because Hass was chasing this gorgeous girl called Diane.

As soon as we got inside the door, Conny took one look at Diane and turned to me. 'Hass hasn't a hope, he's only wasting our time here.' I don't know whether Hass wanted us there for moral support or back-up, but we were warned to be on our best behaviour and none of us were drinking. We didn't leave the place until 2.15 a.m., but the three of us were still back in Clare that morning for training at 9 a.m. That was the resilience and commitment that the team demanded that time and that secured us a county title that summer. And three years later, Hass married Diane.

By the middle of the summer, after the Clare footballers had been beaten in the qualifiers by Laois, Joe Considine rejoined our pack. By that stage, Conny had got cocky about assuming Joe's position in the group, so Joe decided to take him for 'a trot' one evening. The two boys went on a 5-kilometre run and Joe ran him into the ground.

Conny never lost the run of himself again, and any time he hinted at doing so, Hass would keep him in check. In August 2002, the three of us went out in Dublin one Friday night. We'd arranged to train in Fairview Park the following day at noon, and Hass and I went home at a respectable hour, but Conny pushed the night into the real early hours and was in the horrors by the end of it.

The following day was baking hot and the sweat was coming out of Conny before we even began the session. He must have been seeing three balls because his first touch was non-existent. After about 20 minutes, Hass couldn't take it any more. He called the two of us into the huddle and lambasted Conny. And then sent him home.

Before I'd even realized what had happened, Conny was traipsing off Fairview Park with his tail between his legs. And Hass and I just continued the session.

Apart from linking up with St Vincent's – who were brilliant to us – for a couple of months in early 2003, we never trained with a club while we were in Dublin. We just felt that we could control and regulate our own sessions better and push ourselves that bit harder. At that time, some former inter-county players had organized a training camp for country-based players, where you paid a small fee to take part in a well-drilled session. But we still wanted to maintain our own identity as St Joseph's Doora-Barefield players.

One of the main difficulties with that approach was getting someplace to train. We were like nomads and we trained everywhere: Fairview Park, the Phoenix Park, Bushy Park in Terenure, the back field in Scoil Uí Chonaill, Dollymount Strand, Clonliffe College. The back field in Scoil Uí Chonaill would be partially lit from the floodlights of a tennis club; the bullring on the Clontarf road had plenty of space and really good street lights; the field adjacent to the long-term car park in Dublin Airport was always lit up well enough for ball drills.

We were like private detectives trying to locate these places around

Dublin. We trained on the grounds of a convent in Clontarf for a while until a nun ran us out of the place. When we chanced it again a few weeks later, she threatened the cops on us.

We had to continually improvise. If the huge space in Fairview Park was covered by a blanket of local soccer games, we'd use the timber hoardings that sealed off the works on the Port Tunnel as a ball wall. We used the huge Railway Wall at the corner of the Nally End and the Hogan Stand in Croke Park for the same purpose. One evening outside Croker, Hass made a suggestion.

'Come on, we'll break in, get some goal-shooting done and be gone before anyone spots us.'

'Have you gone completely nuts?' I asked him. 'You'd get locked up for that kind of a stunt. We'd end up out in Mountjoy for a night sharing a cell with a crowd of drug-addicts.'

'Fair enough,' said Hass. 'But Jeez, it would still be nearly worth it.'

Hass is one of the most intelligent people I know, but the man was almost possessed when it came to hurling. He pushed himself to the limit, and the harder, the more miserable, the more excruciating training was, the more he loved it. He used to come up with these small grid-drills where the three of us would just basically leather the shit out of one another. A friend of Conny's – a former All-Ireland U-21 medallist – came out training with us one evening, and Conny had to come between Hass and myself from going at one another's throats. We were training on the field beside the airport car park, just days after the place had been ploughed to ribbons from staging a cross-country race. It was impossible to strike the ball along the deck, but during one striking drill Hass told me to 'do it right or fuck off home'. Conny's buddy must have thought we were totally mad because he never came near us again.

We built up a really strong bond, which will always be there. When we lost to Ballygunner in the 2001 Munster club quarter-final, it was probably Hass's greatest hour. He scored 1-5 from play in the 1999 All-Ireland club final against Rathnure, but that day against Ballygunner he delivered the most honest performance I ever saw from a Doora-Barefield player. Joe Considine had been harshly sent off after eight minutes and it was Hass who rolled up his sleeves and put in a double work-shift. The man literally ran himself into the ground. Watching him during the match that day, I knew where his drive was coming from: the nomadic training trek around Dublin during the dark winter.

Hass collapsed with disappointment on the pitch afterwards, and he was so shattered he never made it to the team meal in the Granville Hotel on the quays in Waterford. He went across the road on his own for a walk and was so broken-looking that a woman approached him and asked him if he was all right. She thought he looked suicidal and was about to jump into the river. And then a text message beeped through on his phone. 'You were immense today – an epic display. At times, I just wanted to pick up my hurley and go out and carry you on my back.' It was from Conny.

At times, we felt closer to each other than we probably would have done if we lived together at home. We needed one another in Dublin. And that intensity made us better players. Before the 2004 county semi-final against Clarecastle, Hass pulled his hamstring and couldn't really run on it in the lead-up to the game. Ten days beforehand, he and Conny went training in Bushy Park and Hass concocted an acclimatization drill for Conny. It was a shooting exercise which basically entailed Hass hitting a ball at Conny and then Hass belting him with the hurley as he passed him.

'What are you trying to do to me, kill me?' Conny asked him after the first assault.

'I'm only trying to toughen you up,' responded Hass. 'Because this is what the Magpies [Clarecastle] will do to you.'

So on a lovely balmy autumn evening in a south Dublin park, with kids playing near by, old couples out for a leisurely stroll and more people walking their dogs, they were greeted by a vision of a demented lunatic chasing after someone with a stick. When Conny got home an hour later and took off his clothes for a shower, he had welts and red marks all down his back and legs. It was like someone had given him 30 lashes with a horsewhip.

Winning with the club had just consumed Hass, as it had all of us.

When we were in Dublin, that camaraderie and those training sessions were often all that kept us going. As young people in a vibrant capital city, we probably didn't make the most of life up there, primarily because we came home every weekend for training or matches. Dublin was just where we worked, because our lives were in Clare and with St Joseph's Doora-Barefield. And that's what ultimately brought Hass and me back to Clare. Although Conny is still in Dublin, his heart is 150 miles away. And always will be. He has been courted by several clubs in Dublin but he just can't turn away from St Joseph's.

One of my sweetest memories in hurling was after the 2004 county semi-final win against Clarecastle when Conny, Hass and I embraced tightly at the final whistle. Four years earlier, Conny couldn't make our third team; that day, he was one of our best players. And the journey we had all taken together just added to the purity of the moment.

On Friday evening, 29 May, after we completed our puck-around in Gurteen before making our way to Clarecastle to take on Sixmile-bridge, Conny stepped into the middle of the huddle and set the tone for what lay ahead.

'The match the last day only began at half-time because we were bullied by Ballyea. Well, there are two types of people in life: the guy who bullies and the guy who gets bullied. Well, we're the fucking bully today and we lay down the law from the first ball. We hit them with everything we have, we dominate them from the first ball. A crowd of fucking young lads aren't going to come up here and dictate to us. We make it into a battle and then we'll swallow them up.'

It was a beautiful summer's evening, perfect for hurling. I had a chat with Patsy beforehand about the way we'd play. The sun was high in the sky but was glaring straight down the pitch from the west and was going to dip lower in the second half, which can make it a nightmare for a goalkeeper. But the wind was also blowing in that direction and I said that we should play with it in the first half: 'Let's get on top of these boys early and knock whatever optimism they have straight out of them.'

The dressing room was busy: guys stretching, getting taped up and rubbed down, some players hopping a ball off some part of the wall they had claimed for themselves. Ken Kennedy and I talked to the backs in the showers before Seánie and Conny addressed the forwards in the same space we'd just vacated. The mood was nervous and edgy. But positive. Really positive.

'It's a fucking disgrace that this club is waiting eight years for a championship and we want to have two feet in a county quarter-final this evening,' said John Carmody. 'That's what's at stake here now.'

All week, we'd been driven on by the lash of Patsy's tongue. Now, he was preparing to hunt us out of the dressing room by the sharp stick of his insight. A year earlier, as coach of Corofin, he had been in exactly the same position that the Sixmilebridge coach, Seán Chaplin, was in now. Facing down his old crew.

'All I'm hearing about all week is Chaplin and his inside knowledge on us. That he knows us inside out. Well, what did I know about ye last year? What inside knowledge did I have? I knew everything about ye and it made fuck-all difference. It made fuck-all difference because yere heads were right. When I met ye the previous year, yere heads weren't right. Greg [Lyons], you broke my heart last year and there was absolutely nothing I could do with you. You ran the game on your own. There was nothing I could do with any of ye because yere heads were just right. And if yere heads are right today, what Chaplin knows about us will mean fuck-all. Well, are the heads right?'

'YEEEAAAAAAH.'

We gathered in a huddle to the familiar big-game pose: arms wrapped tightly around one another. The words said at that moment often don't register; the real truth is in the body language or behind the eyes of the men staring back at you, who nod to confirm the mental readiness of the group.

The last words we hear before we hit the field are delivered in bullet-point format.

- Cool heads.
- Composure on the ball.

- Discipline.
- Workrate.
- Savage intensity.

And then somebody roars: 'Let's give them fucking hell.'

The 'Bridge waited in their dressing room until just before the whistle. Then they won the toss and elected to play with the breeze, clearly looking to take the game to us from the first whistle. Their goalkeeper was booming his puckouts over the head of our centre-back, Davy Hoey, but our cover defence was coping well with the tactic and we soon got a foothold in the game.

We were three points up after the first quarter and had extended that lead to five points by the 25th minute. They had completely restructured their attack by that stage and had switched Niall Gilligan to free-taking duties after Caimin Morey had missed three frees. They surged back into the game before half-time, but that was more to do with our indiscipline than their creativity. In a three-minute rush before the break, Gilligan slotted three frees to leave us ahead at the interval by 0-8 to 0-6.

The dressing room was calm and measured. It was sticky and humid, even for a goalkeeper, and after towelling down I went over to Seánie. He hadn't started but was sure to be coming on. 'If you're inside in the full-forward line,' I said to him, 'be on your toes the whole time because that ball is flying through the half-back line with the breeze and the hard ground. It could bounce literally anywhere.'

'I'm going in now,' he said to me. Deccie Malone was coming off with an injury.

I hit Seánie a dunt into the chest. 'Boss those fuckers around the place, use all your experience. Dictate the play in there for us.'

When our puckout stats came through, I wasn't that disappointed with how poor they'd been, because the wind was so strong that it was often a matter of just trying to clear our half-back line. It was more important now that we used our heads on our own puckout in the second half.

'I'm going to be able to reach the full-forward line but the half-forward line can't get dragged down the field and allow them to condense it inside,' I said to the group. 'If their half-back line go back, make the run and I'll pop it in front of you. But our midfielders have to come down the field and the half-back has to hold the line. If you're free, I'll find you.'

We were on our statistical target for our hooks-blocks-tackles category, but there was clearly one area where we were falling behind. 'How many scoreable frees have we conceded?' I inquired.

I heard somebody say nine.

'Too fucking many, lads. We're killing ourselves. We've got to stop diving in and we've got to get our timing better.'

Then Damien Kennedy made a basic but important point. 'Look, they didn't do any shooting from distance and they've had no wides from out the field with that breeze. They used their heads for a lot of that half and we need to do the same now. No stupid stuff with the ball.'

Some guys still had their jerseys off and everyone was loading up on fluids. As we all got to our feet and got ready to go again, Ken Kennedy had the final words. 'We were in exactly the same position against this crowd last year at half-time and we went out and won the game in the ten minutes after half-time. We fucking buried them. Now let's go out and bury them again.'

Against the breeze, they were the ones who had clearly upped their work rate. They had the first score in the 33rd minute and nearly had a goal two minutes later, but it was tipped over for a point. By the 40th minute they were back in front with another Gilligan point, which was their sixth without reply. They should have gone further ahead two minutes later when they had a clear point which was waved wide.

To be honest, it was just inside the post. I knew it was over but I was roaring 'Wide ball!' and the umpire waved it wide. The 'Bridge full-forward, Brian Culbert, roared at him for getting the call wrong and, after I took the subsequent puckout, the same umpire asked me if that ball was a point. 'No,' I told him. 'Wide ball. Good call.'

Honestly, this is something I have a slight moral dilemma over. It's dishonest and I sometimes feel like a total hypocrite, especially because I often write about the importance of honesty and integrity in GAA. The prevailing culture in our games is to push the limits of fairness, to see what you can get away with. Trying to influence an umpire isn't the same as cynical play or verbally abusing a referee, but it's still wrong. It's hard to defend or explain it, but in the heat of a championship battle, when the game could go either way on a marginal call, you just become conditioned to battling for those calls. It's hard to describe it but you almost do it without thinking. It's an inbuilt mechanism that you hit to survive. And anyway, with the speed the ball travels, you can often be on the wrong end of those marginal calls. We lost a championship match to Éire Óg in 2006 by a point with the last puck of the game. The ball was at least a foot wide and the umpires, who clearly didn't see it, panicked and put up the white flag. And that defeat effectively wrecked our season.

Anyway, with this game slipping from us, we needed to find some spark, and we finally did. Seánie had begun to exert his influence up front and four points in five minutes from Seánie, Conor Hassett, Damien Kennedy and Kevin Dilleen pushed us three back in front, heading into the final quarter.

Then, I nearly blew that lead with ten minutes remaining. On a free-out ten metres from our own goal, I tried to pick out Kevin Dilleen with a short pass and never saw Gilligan drifting across my line. He launched the ball back into the square and, after a mad scramble when it broke, I had no choice but to throw myself on it to ensure it stayed out of the net.

Seconds later, Patsy came down and abused me for not driving the free longer. So did half the back line. When one of the selectors, Steve Whyte, then came down the line from the other side of the field to have his say, I lost it with him.

'I was trying to do the right thing. So will you ever just clear off and don't be annoying me.'

The game was still in the balance, heading into the last five minutes, when we finally broke their resistance. Seánie laid the ball on a plate for Conor Hassett, who broke through the cover of the full-back line. The goalkeeper came out and Hassett took it around him and slipped it into the net.

I looked out at Ken and pumped my fist. This game was as good as nailed down.

Hassett quickly scored a point to push us six clear. They responded with two late points, but the referee only played nine seconds of injury time – you could see it on the electronic clock – and we were winners on a scoreline of 1-13 to 0-12.

By the time I made it down to the bottom goal, just in front of the dressing room, Seán Chaplin was standing on the edge of the pitch, having shaken hands with all our players. 'Well done,' he said as we shook hands.

'Hopefully, we'll see ye again,' I responded.

A couple of minutes later, both he and Rusty Chaplin entered our dressing room to extend their congratulations on our win.

'I said it to ye before that there is a championship in this team,' said Seán Chaplin. 'And I still believe there is. But there is a long way to go and hopefully we can regroup now and we might meet ye down the line.'

The mood in the dressing room was electric. There's nothing like winning a championship match on a beautiful summer's evening. With such a giddy atmosphere, Patsy decided to announce details of our bonding weekend.

'We've a few Clare Cup games still to play, but we're going to the Aran Islands on the weekend of the 4th of July. Try and keep that date free.'

After congratulating everyone on the performance, John Carmody then took a more circumspect tone. 'We haven't even started yet. We have 30 sessions and ten matches played, but we're going to train like madmen now for the summer. So be ready for it. Just remember what I said before the game – do whatever it takes this year to bring that Canon Hamilton back to the parish. Make the commitment now that we're going to do it.'

It's already looking positive for us. One of the most satisfying aspects of this evening's performance has been the impact of our substitutes.

Everyone who came in – Seánie, Paul Dullaghan, Noel Brodie and Mikey Cullinan – made a contribution. Joe Considine is planning to come back training with us in the next few weeks when his football commitments ease off, while Ivor Whyte is making really good progress after recovering from a cruciate knee injury, and Seán Flynn's shoulder injury should also be well cleared up by the time our next game comes around. Any team which wins a championship has to have sufficient depth, and we really look to have it now.

We all went into Ennis that evening to celebrate, starting in Mossy's. The place was buzzing. The weather was beautiful, June was coming and the season was pregnant with promise and hope for us.

Some victories are taken for granted, but to win a big championship match with your friends and teammates is a beautiful feeling, and tonight is one of those moments. The feeling of being a band of brothers fighting for the same cause, a feeling forged in good and bad times.

At one stage, I pulled up a stool beside Patsy, who was sipping a pint of Heineken through a smile that was lighting up the whole bar. 'Ah Jeez, there's nothing like this,' he said. 'It's just some feeling to win with your own club. All your own buddies. It's not the same with another club. There's no comparison. This is what it's all about.'

A couple of minutes later, Ken Kennedy passed us on the way to the bar and he just smiled at us. He had been sick heading into the game and at one stage in the second half he turned around and told me to be really alert because he was struggling with the pace of the game. Still, he had given us everything. And so had his brother Damien.

When Patsy got the job, some people doubted whether the Kennedys would give total commitment to a new managerial regime which had effectively removed their father. There was no need to doubt any more.

'They've been brilliant,' said Patsy. 'They've given me absolutely everything. It says a lot about them.'

After a while, we moved up to the Brewery Bar on the square, where most of our young crew were fetched up. The music is louder and the skirts of its female clientele are always shorter up there. Towards the end of the night, I got talking to John Carmody. 'We're going to get stronger when we get everyone back and there will be great competition for places,' he said. 'But we really need to push it on now. Because it takes absolutely everything to win a Clare championship. It's a savage hard championship to win. It always was.'

Most of the lads made their way to Cruise's Bar and the Queen's Hotel nightclub, but before Seánie, Donal Cahill and I headed for home, Seánie had to get his usual post-pints feed: a Hawaiian burger and large chips from Enzo's takeaway. The man has an unbelievable sweet tooth and an appetite like a horse, but playing club hurling allows him summer indulgences which he had to suppress for 13 years when he played for Clare.

We were all still munching on chips when we pulled up outside Donal's house, around 2 a.m. We got talking about the game and I relayed a story to the two lads about a conversation I'd had with Gráinne Hassett – Lorcan and Conor's sister – in Mossy's earlier that evening. She said that she was surprised at how big the crowd was and she was curious to know if players could hear what was being said among the throng while the game was going on.

I said that I never took any notice of the crowd during a match – and then I thought of our championship game against Sixmilebridge last year in Shannon. During one passage of play in the opening ten minutes that evening, when it was helter-skelter in the spilling rain and we were under pressure to clear a ball in the bottom corner, I heard this rasping, distinctive voice from the crowd which immediately registered with me: it was Ger Hoey.

We all just shook our heads at the sadness of the memory. We stayed in the car for another 35 minutes talking about Ger – how much this evening would have meant to him and how happy he'd have been with the performance. And for sure, he'd have been out celebrating with us tonight. Stuck in the middle of it. Loving it. Ecstatic that Doora-Barefield seemed back on the road again.

Seánie lives just half a mile down the road from Donal, and before I dropped him off I just looked at him.

'This is the year to do it,' I said to him. 'We have to do it. We just have to.'

'No doubt about it,' he responded.

We sat talking in the car for another 15 minutes. About Ger. About the club. About our ultimate aim for the year. Without losing the run of ourselves, we started to visualize the county final in October like a couple of kids. When we won county titles in 1998 and 1999, Ger had his eldest daughter Elaine as one of the team mascots. Seánie has three sons now and I have one son and we hoped that they'd be the team mascots this time around, please God. We could almost picture them, togged out in their little maroon-and-white jerseys and their little hurleys, and not knowing what was going on. Hopefully, the next generation of Doora-Barefield players.

'When we won our county medals in the past we were young, and we'd appreciate them an awful lot more now,' Seánie said to me. 'It's eight years since I won anything now, even with Clare. I would just do anything to win it this year. This is definitely my last cut at it. And it would be some way to go out.'

On the way home, I was giddy with the thought of it all because I just want it so badly. Excited too because I really think we have a great chance now. A really great chance.

9. Going Down

Déjà vu. July 7th and, for the second year in a row, we've found our-selves staring into the abyss of relegation from the league. We've gone from being regarded as the Manchester United or Chelsea of Clare club hurling to being viewed as consistent league relegation candidates. Blackburn Rovers. Sunderland. Hull City.

I couldn't tell you exactly how many Clare Cup titles (Division One) that we've won over the last 15 years. Definitely three, maybe four. When we won the title in 1998, the final was played in Novem-ber 1999, a week after that year's county final, and we treated it as a warm-up for the Munster semi-final against Toomevara two weeks later. The weather was so bad that day that Jamesie O'Connor and Donal Cahill – who were injured – left at half-time and went off to a local pub in Tulla to watch South Africa and England in the rugby World Cup quarter-final. They weren't even back by the time we were being presented with the cup.

We could afford to treat the league like a joke back then because we were still good enough to win it if we made a moderate effort. Not any more. It seems like we're only able to get up for champion-ship games any more, which is a huge problem in trying to maintain any consistency. When we went into our last game against Éire Óg last year, the stakes were huge because the loser was going down, but we blitzed them in the second half and that performance was later identified as a turning point in our season. Now? Our final-day oppon-ents, Clarecastle, are safe and have an outside chance of qualifying for a semi-final if other results go their way. And we know that they'd like nothing better than to put us down.

It still shouldn't have come to this. Apart from the game against Cratloe three weeks ago, every game we've lost has been by a score or less. Some of those defeats were games thrown away, while bad luck nailed us in a couple of close matches. In our first match against Clooney-Quin, which we lost by a point, Davy Hoey took a penalty with ten minutes to go; the ball ricocheted off their keeper's hurley, hit the back stanchion of the net and flew back out. Even I could see from the other end of the field that it was a goal but the umpires somehow missed it. The same evening, we missed about eight score-able frees. Our regular free-taker, Conor Hassett, was supposed to play, but the Clare players weren't allowed to line out with their clubs that weekend ahead of a league game against Cork. The club were hoping Hassett would be released because he wasn't even on the panel for the game on Sunday. But he wasn't.

We thought we got a perfectly legitimate goal with the last puck of the game against Inagh-Kilnamona but the referee disallowed it for a square ball and we were beaten by two points. Still, we had enough chances to win two games that day, and our consistency has been so poor that we can't take refuge in bad breaks or poor referee-ing decisions. We're flirting with relegation because we've become conditioned to losing tight league games.

The Clarecastle game was originally fixed for last Friday, the day before our team-bonding weekend trip to the Aran Islands was sched-uled. But Darragh O'Driscoll's sister was getting married on Friday and a number of the lads were attending the afters. The option then was to play the game on Tuesday, two days after lads returned from the Aran Islands like zombies.

That was discussed on the field in a huddle on the day of our last league game, after we beat Sixmilebridge. I was totally against the trip. 'We can't go on that trip if the game is fixed for Tuesday. Jesus, it's hard enough to beat Clarecastle with a fully fit team, never mind a team that's fucked from liquor.'

There was no response to the comment. Conny later told me that some guys were looking at me as if I'd two heads on me. As far as they were concerned, the trip had been planned, guys had arrange-ments made and it was going ahead. Management said that a decision would be made over the next few days, and on Wednesday we got a group text to say that the game against Clarecastle was going ahead the following Tuesday. I wasn't happy, but I wasn't going to go against the wishes of the group.

Only eight players from the senior panel went on the trip, which was a clear statement about either the unity of the group or the point of the exercise. To me, it was pointless with what was coming down the tracks. Some guys were working, more guys couldn't have been bothered, but some lads were clearly planning ahead for the Clarecastle match.

The day before the match, we trained in Gurteen and you just knew some guys were shook up. What's more, a U-21 football championship match had also been fixed for that evening, which wasn't ideal preparation for them, so close to a big hurling game. Anyway, management decided to run the drink out of guys' systems. That training was certainly no benefit to me or my arthritic hips, so I just worked hard in the wall alley for almost half an hour while the boys plodded around the field behind me.

It was a wet evening and the air was sticky with humidity. At one stage, Ken Kennedy came up to me during a water-break, sweat and raindrops dripping off him like he'd just emerged from the shower with his gear on. He hadn't been on the trip and he wasn't impressed. 'That's fair bullshit the night before a game so important. It's all right to run the shit out of guys who were drinking all weekend, but the whole squad shouldn't be doing this running.'

He was right. Already, negative energy was seeping into the collective mood.

It was always going to be a tough struggle against Clarecastle anyway. Greg Lyons has gone to the USA for the summer, while Cathal O'Sullivan has gone travelling to South-east Asia for six weeks. Kevin Dilleen is playing for the Clare footballers against Donegal on Saturday evening and there are no guarantees that he will be released. It's the same story with Conor Hassett, because Clare are playing Galway in the hurling qualifiers as well on Saturday evening.

Jeez, this is going to be some dogfight now.

★

The away dressing rooms in Clarecastle are split into two different rooms, with the showers and toilet area in between. We always set the physio table up in the smaller second room, and I always tog off in there any time we play in Clarecastle, just because the majority of the group use the bigger room and there's more space in here. This evening, though, everybody was gathered in one room – an indication of how the panel had been thinned from when we were last here against Sixmilebridge six weeks ago.

When I was going to the toilet, I heard some of the lads outside discussing how strong the stale stench of Deep Heat was in the room. I just smiled to myself. I've broken my nose three times playing hurling, and the last time I broke it my nose was smashed in three places from a lash of a hurley and it effectively destroyed my sense of smell.

By the time I went back in to put on my gear, it was clear from the staccato nature of conversation that this was a big game. The room was quiet, too quiet. After we togged off and completed the warm-up, John Carmody approached me coming off the pitch on our way back to the dressing rooms.

'There are no excuses tonight because we've got our strongest team available on the pitch,' he said. Dilleen and Hassett had been made available to us, and Clarecastle were only missing Jonathan Clancy. It was also a sign of how the power has shifted in Clare hurling in that there was only one established county player between the two squads. A decade ago, St Joseph's and Clarecastle would have provided around 12 players to the Clare panel.

Clarecastle were making their way out as we went back in to put on our jerseys, and it was obvious that they were up for the game. Aside from our rivalry, they have their own motivations. They had been heavily beaten by Crusheen in their previous game, which had all but killed their chances of a semi-final spot. Now they were looking for a performance and atonement in front of their own crowd.

Fahey alluded to that beforehand. 'They were poor against Crusheen but they're going to come out firing tonight because they have to. They've a strong team out, they're just down Jonathan Clancy, they mean business and they mean to win. They'll be psyched up to their eyeballs, but we need to be controlled and disciplined here. Crusheen didn't concede any frees against them, so it can be done. It can be done, but if there has to be rough stuff dished out, we dish it out. We don't fucking spare them, because they won't spare us.'

Carmody made a similar point before Fahey stepped back in again. 'This is crucial. It's not for Seánie or Christy or Ken that we're playing for our survival. It's for the younger players and the young lads coming down the line. St Joseph's are a Division One side, always have been, and relegation is not going to be a blot on my copybook. They would love to put us down but we're ready for them. Get out and give it everything. Knock sparks out of them.'

Just then Ken interjected. The tension was still palpable inside the room and he was concerned that it had affected some guys' focus and approach. 'Lads, I can sense it already. Unless we get our heads sorted, we're in big trouble. Do ye realize the importance of this game? Do ye realize who we are playing and what they'll do to us? Get fucking tuned in now or we're in serious trouble.' Then Ken started jogging on the spot, before calling for everyone to join. 'Let's give it ten'. Everyone pounded the ground, roaring in unison. 'ONE, TWO, THREE, FOUR, FIVE, SIX, SEVEN, EIGHT, NINE, TEN.' After a few seconds, Conor Hassett called for us to go again. I never join in that ritual because, as a goalkeeper, I just need to concentrate on keeping my head clear.

As I ran down to take my place in goal, I passed the referee, Rory Hickey, in the middle of the pitch. He had refereed the Munster football final between Cork and Limerick the previous Sunday in Cork, and he'd awarded a questionable penalty to Cork in the first half. Cork had won by one point.

'Some scribes are out to get me already,' he said to me.

'Don't be worrying about the scribes,' I said back to him. 'You better keep your head down around the town over the next few days in case Donie Buckley spots you.' (Buckley, a Kerryman who lives in Ennis, is the Limerick football trainer.)

We won the toss and decided to play against the stiff breeze, but we started poorly and let them have the initiative early. They had two points on the board inside the first 90 seconds. A few minutes later their corner-forward, Seánie Moloney, came in along the end-line and was bearing down on goal. I thought he was going to try to drill the ball through me, so I advanced to narrow the angle. He kept going and, as his momentum took him past me, I stuck out my leg and tried to bring him down. I only stalled him and he squared the ball back across the goal to the advancing Clarecastle posse of forwards. I was back in goal by the time Derek Quinn won possession. He got off his shot and it took a deflection off one of our defenders and flew past me. Before I took the puckout, Hickey came in and yellow-carded me for the challenge.

We were behind 1-2 to 0-1 after the first quarter when Ken got into a tussle with a Clarecastle forward, and it soon developed into a belting match. The two of them were wearing hurleys off one another, and in the mayhem the Clarecastle man swung wild and hit him across the head. By the time Ken was on the ground, some of our boys were in, baying for blood. More of us arrived in to break it up and it was sorted out soon enough. It was another indication of how things had cooled between the two clubs. If something like that incident had happened ten years ago, there would have been a jihad on the pitch.

The two boys hadn't a hope of staying on the field. The two umpires had been roaring at them to break it up before it got really heated, and after Hickey consulted with them Ken and the Clarecastle forward were sent off. At that stage, some of our boys rounded on the umpires. Darragh and Marty hammered them for sending off Ken, while Fahey arrived down also to have his say. 'Only one man should have gone. And that was the guy who hit on the head.'

I couldn't agree with that. One of the umpires looked straight at me afterwards. 'What do you think?' he asked me.

'Two red cards, absolutely no question about it.'

It wasn't that I was being disloyal to Ken, but you can't have faction fighting on a hurling pitch.

I knew that Ken was going to be a far bigger loss to us than their forward would be to them and I had to think about reorganizing our defence. Clarecastle cottoned on to the extra space in our full-back line straight away. Their centre-forward, Tyrone Kierse, was playing out near midfield, so they left a huge channel free down the centre of our defence and they ran their next two attacks straight through it. On the second occasion, Eamonn Callinan got in on the end of a break and was coming straight through the centre when corner-back Marty O'Regan dragged him down inside the 14-metre line.

'Too cheap, Marty,' I said to him. 'The boys were coming across and if they didn't get him, I had him.'

Kierse went for a goal from the penalty, but he drove it too high and it flew over the bar. We were five points down and only hanging in just before the break when disaster struck. We were casual out the field when the ball should have been cleared, and it ended up being driven high into our danger zone. It was dropping short to the right of the goal and I was roaring at Marty to get up and spoil the ball and let it drop wide. But Derek Quinn got in under him and both of them tried to catch the ball. The ball broke off Quinn's hand and I had to react sharply to it. I didn't want to pick the ball and leave it exposed so close to goal so I tried to shove it out the side. But Quinn got his hurley to it and scrambled it back across the goal. A couple of our defenders were manically trying to retrieve the ball but Callinan pulled on it first and drove it to the net.

It was a bad goal to concede and I should have done better. We'd really fallen into a huge hole now and it was going to take some effort in the second half to drag ourselves out of it.

We were down 2-8 to 0-6 and the management were in deep conference outside the dressing room as I passed them on the way in. There was complete silence inside before Seánie eventually broke it.

'We were 12 down at half-time last year and we came back to draw the match,' he said. 'We just keep plugging away now and we'll get it back.'

Even though I rarely speak at half-time, I felt I had to. 'Seánie's right, we've got to stay positive. We've all got to hold our hands up for that display, myself included for that last goal, which was bullshit. But we've just got to go back to basics now. Get the blocks and hooks and tackles in to get enough possession of the ball. Keep chasing our performance goals to get our outcome goal. If we do, the scores will come and we'll get back into it and we'll take them. We were absolutely pathetic in the first half against them last year and we came out and blew them away in the second half, and we can do it again now. But let's just keep our heads and work our way through this.'

Conor Hassett added to that by reinforcing the need for us to work harder, but management obviously had a different take on matters. After they arrived in, Carmody let fly.

'Are we just going to drop the heads now and feel sorry for ourselves and get fucked out of this league? That goal before half-time just fucked us up. It has been coming because guys won't get down and do the basics. It should have been cleared twice out the field before it came in.'

By the time Fahey spoke, he was roaring at us. 'We're too fucking nice. For eight years now we've been too fucking nice. I'm sick of Clarecastle and bowing down to them when we should be fucking hammering into them. Instead we're standing back and letting them do what they want. Too fucking nice and I'm fucking sick of it. We're talking the talk but we're not walking the walk and doing it on the pitch.'

This is a problem I've consistently had with management. Our stats work has been too ad hoc and inconsistent and we didn't have any stats feedback for what had just gone on. Maybe they had stats done but they prioritized addressing our attitude instead. I thought there was too much talking and not enough information.

A couple of players spoke up and then Carmody spoke again. 'Let's get out there and get straight back into it. If we're going to go down, let's at least go down with a bit of pride. We've been too tame in a game of this importance and that's just not fucking good enough.'

Carmody was right on that point. St Joseph's stands for far more than what we'd just produced in the last 30 minutes. Our display was almost an insult to our supporters and what they believe we represent. At that moment, one thought came into my head. What would Ger Hoey do now in this situation? If he was playing in a game like this, he'd give everything inside him to help dig out a result. For a brief second, I thought about saying it out loud, but I decided against it. I didn't think it was appropriate, with his brother just five feet away from me – and anyway, I didn't think it was what we needed to hear from an emotional perspective. We needed to suspend emotion and be more calculated and clinical about our display now.

From the throw-in, we went right at them. We got the first two points of the half and then Seánie planted the ball in the net. We had the deficit pared back to a point on the 40th minute after Seánie set up Damo Kennedy for our second goal. We had the momentum behind us, but we lost it midway through the second half by conceding some stupid frees, which allowed them to re-establish their lead.

We chased them down for the remainder of the game but we just couldn't get level. With scores so precious, I tried to bring down a ball going over the bar with about five minutes left. It was looping at an awkward and dangerous height and I didn't get clean control of it first time after stopping it with the stick. As I gathered possession, I got buried by one of their forwards and then the referee blew the whistle. I just put the ball down and got ready to take the free out when I heard the Clarecastle crowd roaring and shouting at me. I looked out at the referee and he just pointed behind me to the umpire who was waving the white flag.

'Jeez, that was hardly gone over,' I said to him.

'It was.'

As I was getting ready to take the puckout, one of the Clarecastle selectors, Barney Lynch, was passing at the back of the goal.

'Christy, when the ball goes over the bar, it's a point, you know. That's what the white flag is for.'

'Are you serious, Barney? I didn't know that's what the white flag was for.'

I tried to pick out Conor Hassett on the wing, but two Clarecastle defenders broke the ball and it came straight back up the pitch again. Within a minute, they'd pushed the lead out to three.

We were desperate for a goal. In injury time, Seánie got in around their defensive cover at an angle. He should have kept going but he tried to pick out Fergal O'Sullivan in front of goal, and the ball was slightly overcooked and it flew beyond him. As soon as Clarecastle cleared it, the game was over. We were beaten by 2-16 to 2-13. It was way too big a score to concede. That's relegation form. Clarecastle had just packed us off to Division Two.

There was a cheer from their supporters at the final whistle, but I honestly couldn't say if it was a boisterous response to our plight. The feeling as we left the field was just hollow, primarily because we'd played so poorly in the first half when the game was effectively decided. This was a big game. And we haven't beaten Clarecastle in a big game now since the 2004 championship semi-final.

I was one of the first into the dressing room and I just patted Mark Hallinan, who was sitting inside the door, on the head. One of the few positives we could take out of the game was that our youngest player had performed. Everyone just togged off and headed for the showers, but as soon as management entered the dressing room, John Carmody called everyone straight back out.

'Lookit, it's done now and ye are good enough to come straight back up next year,' he said. 'I could rant and rave here for the next 30 minutes but I'm not going to. It wasn't tonight that we were relegated. It's been coming. And unless guys are going to get their arses to Gurteen, the same thing is going to happen in the championship. We're not getting the bodies to training and you could see it there tonight. It's all right now, but unless it changes we'll be in the same boat after a quarter-final – here with our heads down. Everybody here has been looking for weekends off to go on stags, weddings, trips away. Well, it has to stop now. Unless it does, we'll meet a Clonlara or a Newmarket on fire in the quarter-finals and we'll be fucking wiped out. That's what's on the cards unless guys start coming to training. And if you're not turning up, I'll tell you myself to fuck off and not come back.'

The frustration was visibly driving Carmody mad and it's hard not to blame him. His commitment to this team is absolutely outstanding and he can't understand how players from this club can't replicate it. He's not from Doora-Barefield, he isn't getting expenses to do the job, and all he's getting is a head full of grief. Sure, that would drive anyone half crazy.

As I was getting into the car afterwards, Marty O'Regan was waiting to get into the car beside me.

'Should I have done better for that second goal?' I asked him.

'You should,' he said back.

'I know, I'm like a dog over it. I just didn't want to pick it and leave it exposed. Fuck it anyway.'

'It didn't matter anyway because we're not fit enough,' he said. 'We just haven't enough work done.'

I rang Seánie the following morning. I expressed my dissatisfaction with management's decision to go on the trip to the Aran Islands, but he didn't think that had been the main issue last night. He raised other valid points: too much talk about Clarecastle beforehand and not enough focus on ourselves; too much talk about breaking hurleys off the opposition and not enough cool-headedness when it mattered.

'That's a fair point,' I said to him. 'You'd just wonder, is that part of the reason we're giving away so many hare-brained frees?'

Then I brought up our lack of statistical analyses at half-time. To be honest, I think management have largely dispensed with that approach since the Cratloe match. We got blitzed in the 15 minutes before half-time that day, conceding 2-6 without reply, and the stats we had collated weren't much good at half-time. We deduced from the previous few games that we were struggling in the second quarter. And maybe management now felt that the time to address this was before the game, by firing us up, and not at half-time, when it was too late.

'I think there is a place for them [stats] but we don't need to go overboard on them either,' said Seánie. 'The bottom line is that guys just need to start working their holes off now for the next few weeks.'

We realized that a draw would have been enough to force a three-way play-off. Still, we're gone down to Division Two now for the first time in 16 years and there's no getting away from it.

And if we're on a slide, we need to arrest it. Fast.

10. Pain

Two nights after losing to Clarecastle, we went back training. It was a beautiful summer's evening and the numbers were really good. So good that we were able to play an internal training match for the first time all season.

Davy Hoey was centre-back on my team and he was trying to mark his man by remote control – you just knew by his body language that he wasn't interested and that it was the last place he wanted to be. At one stage, Patsy came down behind the goal with a water bottle and the look of a man with an itch to scratch.

'Look at Hoey,' he said to me. 'He's just standing up. What the hell is wrong with him?'

I tried to reason with Patsy. 'You have to cut him some slack. Jeez, that man has been through some turmoil this season. You don't know where his head is at.'

Patsy was having none of it. 'No, I don't agree with you. I know he's been through hell, but he should be going through a wall this year for Ger's sake. He should be doing everything in his power this year for Ger.'

'In fairness, Patsy, I don't think it's that simple. It doesn't work like that.'

Davy and Patsy are close friends and the only reason Davy came back this season was because of Patsy. Nobody else would have got him back hurling, especially after Ger passed away. At the beginning of the year, Patsy showed brilliant man-management skills with Davy. He'd regularly meet him for mid-morning coffee in the Brewery Bar or in McDonald's. Nothing heavy, just light-hearted banter.

Lately, though, Patsy has lost patience with him. The breaking point probably came on the weekend we played Inagh-Kilnamona in a crucial Clare Cup league game last month. Davy, who's a top golfer, was playing an inter-club game in the Jim Bruen competition for Ennis Golf Club – where he works as a green-keeper – and Patsy flipped when he announced his unavailability.

Davy was one of our best players against Sixmilebridge in last month's championship and he's a key figure for this team, especially at centre-back position. He has always been one of our best players: Man of the Match in the 1999 All-Ireland club final, Munster club player of the year the following season. He has massive experience as well – he was Clare's best player in the 2002 All-Ireland final against Kilkenny.

It's unreasonable to still expect that same level of consistency from him because he's 33 now and, unlike most of us in the club, Davy hasn't always prioritized hurling ahead of other activities. He's run into trouble with management in the past through his annual trek to the Oxygen music festival in July, but he was always a free spirit, somebody more drawn to surfing in Lahinch than slogging his guts out on a hurling field during the summer. Especially on a beautiful evening like this. He likes his few pints and his cigarettes, which doesn't exactly help to ease the pain on the training ground. Still, Davy absolutely loves hurling, but he's had to compartmentalize it as he's dealt with the grieving process over the past five months.

At times, he knows he hasn't been as committed as he should. The night before we played Ballyea in the championship, he went into Knox's Bar with a friend and had five pints. At one stage, he spotted Patsy in the bar and was convinced that his manager was only there to hunt him out of the place. He immediately ordered his friend to get him a gin and tonic, hoping that Patsy might think it was a 7-Up. But he wasn't fooling anybody.

Patsy was prepared to let it all pass, but Davy has since used up all his credits and his manager isn't prepared to trade in loyalty and friendship any more. Against Clarecastle two days ago, Patsy whipped Davy off, ten minutes into the second half.

After training finished this evening, Davy ambled into the dressing room, unshaven for a few days and with the weight of the world seemingly pressed on his shoulders. Before I began to tog off, I

The St Joseph's Doora-Barefield team before the 1999 All-Ireland club final on
St Patrick's Day at Croke Park . . .

. . . and after it

Bloodied but victorious:
Ger Hoey after the 1999
All-Ireland final

Ger Hoey accepts the
trophy for the Clare
senior hurling title
from Father Michael
McNamara, October 1999.
Both men passed away
suddenly in 2009

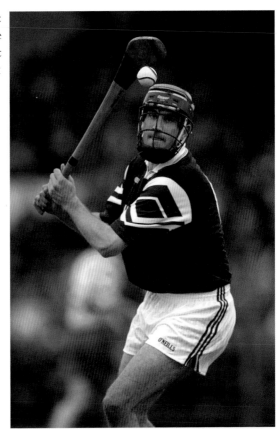

Portrait of an artist:
Seánie McMahon, one
of St Joseph's greatest
ever players, in 2001

Seánie McMahon, Christy
O'Connor and Ger Hoey
march before the 2001 county
final against Sixmilebridge

Ken Kennedy in action in our opening championship game in 2009 against Ballyea

Christy O'Connor surveys his options after fielding a high ball on the line

Coach Patsy Fahey
encourages his players
from the sideline

Through a difficult
season, team captain
Darragh O'Driscoll's
leadership shone through

Jamesie O'Connor, St Joseph's most decorated player, squares up to his Clare teammate Brian Lohan in a 2004 match against Wolfe Tones

Five years later, during a short comeback after a serious knee injury, Jamesie sits among the St Joseph's subs

Eoin 'Conny' Conroy pursues Clarecastle's Conor Plunkett

After the trauma and pain of losing his brother, David Hoey focuses on the sliotar as he tries to win possession against Kilmaley

Team photo before the
county quarter-final
against Newmarket

Christy O'Connor tries
to stop a point against
Newmarket, but the
points keep coming . . .

squeezed my frame on to the bit of bench Davy had claimed for himself.

'How are things, Davy?'

'Fucking pissed off after being taken off the last night. I wasn't great, but the midfielders weren't working hard enough and the space in front of me killed me. I was the scapegoat. Pure bullshit.'

I wanted to shift the focus away from hurling. 'Don't mind Tuesday night, we were all fucking useless. How's the form with you in general?'

He shook his head and his face creased with a grimace. 'To be honest, I just don't have the energy for it at the moment.'

I asked him if he had anything planned for after training. He said he hadn't.

'Do you know what, I'll get a few bananas, a loaf of brown bread, a few bottles of Club Energise and a packet of biscuits and I'll call over for a chat. You on for it?'

'Yeah, good stuff.'

By the time I got to his apartment, Davy had the kettle boiled and was pulling on a cigarette. As he sank into the couch and began to talk, his detachment from hurling and its molten passions became clearly visible.

'I just don't have the energy for it, and getting beaten by Clare-castle just sapped more out of me. At the moment, I just want to give up. I don't really want to hurl. It's so tough at the moment.'

He is bothered by his increasing separation from Patsy – but not bothered enough to do something about the lethargy that is driving Patsy crazy.

'To be honest, if Patsy wasn't the manager, I wouldn't even be hurling,' he says. 'But our meetings for coffee have taken a side-step since I started missing training. I'd say to myself, "I won't ring Patsy because he'll only eat the head off me." It's my fault more than Patsy's.

'I have hated myself at times over the last few weeks because I've felt like a fraud. I just haven't been putting the effort in. I've let Patsy down and I know it. You can see it in him that he is taking it so personal. Everything is so personal to him. Patsy just wants it so much more than I do and there's nothing I can really do about that. And maybe I'm just doing it for the wrong reasons. Maybe I should be doing it for the team as opposed to trying to do it for Ger.'

Ger's name is a constant theme in our dressing room and he is the silent inspiration for our season. But it goes far deeper than that for Davy. He played on the same team as his brother – Davy at number 5, Ger behind him at number 2, always backing him up. The hurling field isn't a refuge from the grief because Davy sees his brother everywhere he turns.

'When I play with the club, I always think about him and the times we had. When we played together, it was just such a successful time for the club. I bonded with a lot of players but, in the brotherly sense, it was just something special. Nothing else can bond you like that. Especially at home after matches with Mam and Dad, to see what it meant to them. And then I see my parents now. It's hard.

'Hurling is just the last thing on my mind now. Pain. There's just pain constantly there. And then at the back of your mind, you're thinking, "He's passed, we got to move on with our lives, and that's what he would want." But it doesn't work that way. The whole funeral, the whole outpouring of emotion, it was very hard. I remember the hospital, the night he died. Seeing [Ciaran] O'Neill, Seánie, Cabs [Donal Cahill], Jamesie. I couldn't go near Seánie because I was so emotional and I'm very close to Seánie.

'There were so many people at the funeral and most of them were hurling people. You nearly felt for the club but it was so heartening to see so many ex-players there. And then with all the hurlers there, I feel a bit of pressure to kinda perform now. I'm trying hard and I want to do it so much. But it's just not there at the moment.

'I'd be having chats with Siobhán and she'd be asking me how training is going. She is so interested in it as well and I think I'm kinda doing it for her sake as well. And I know that she doesn't care what I do. But there's a part of me saying to myself that I have to try and do the right thing.

'I can't handle training. I'm not fit and I can't handle the running. I remember Ger doing runs and I picture how he would run and how much he'd burst himself. He'd come home after training and say, "I beat Jamesie in a sprint tonight." He'd be delighted with himself. And I'd be trying to mirror that in some way. But I'm just fucked, I can't do it. It's a strange place to be, I can't describe it. Every place I turn, he's there.

'At the moment, training is just doing my head in. I finish work normally around 3.30 p.m. and I'd be lying on the couch here, just waiting for training. And my head would be just spinning with stuff. Then I'd go out the odd day to Templemaley [cemetery] and I'd be thinking that I have to keep going for his sake. I have to keep going, I have to keep going. It's hard to describe it. You know the bond you have with your brother, then he retires, you keep playing and then the emotion of the All-Ireland in 1999, ten years on. There are so many things just going through your mind. There are so many things you miss.'

Eight years separated Ger and Davy in age but there always seemed to be a canyon of difference between their personalities and outlooks. Ger was a rock of sense, a settled family man, a high achiever in his job as a bank manager; Davy was more laid back, more inclined to let the road take him wherever it would. Yet Joe Considine put it neatly one time; he said there was a lot of Ger in Davy, and a lot of Davy in Ger. You just had to really know them to see it.

'People always said we were so different, but we weren't that different,' says Davy. 'We used to go drinking together and the last time we went on a session together was Christmas Eve before he died. We came back to his house and we started playing U2 songs. I loved my music and he did too. We were roaring and singing. I fell asleep on the couch and Ger fell asleep on the recliner. I woke up in the middle of the night and I didn't know where I was and Ger was gone. I went back to sleep and then I woke up again at 8.30 in the morning and there he was with his AIB togs, hurling socks and jersey and runners. I looked at him and said, "Where are you going?" And he said, "I'm dying but I'm going for a run." That was just typical of him. I would

never have been able to do that. I suppose that's where the real difference was between us.

'Ger was my big brother. He was a great brother to me and he
couldn't do enough for me. I went through a fair few jobs and I
remember saying to him one time, "When am I ever going to get a
bit of luck?" And he said to me, "Toughen up, you make your own
luck." I always remember that comment because he was so right. The
harder you work, the more luck you get. He instilled a lot of things
in me about hard work and now I work like a dog. He just did everything in the right way. If I hadn't got him, I don't know where I'd be.
I could have gone off the rails. But he never ever once gave out to me.
He never judged you. He was my brother and I could say anything to
him. Just typical brother stuff. I just miss all that. But the thing I miss
the most is playing golf with him. He was mad into his golf. It just
wasn't meant to be.'

Davy's mind is constantly uneasy. The defeat on Tuesday night has
just put his brain spinning into overdrive. Clarecastle are our biggest
rivals and nobody disliked losing to them more than Ger Hoey. Deep
down, Davy knows how disappointed Ger would have been after
Tuesday night. And it's eating him up.

'We were hammered the other evening,' said Davy. 'The thing that
annoyed me most was that we didn't even come to the fight. Myself
included. Ger trained as hard as I've ever seen anyone train, and if he'd
seen what went on Tuesday he would have been disgusted.

'I was heartbroken after the game. I think back and I ask myself,
"What would he have done?" And then I just ask myself, "Why the
fuck am I bothering with this stuff?" Sure it makes no sense at all.
I want it and then I don't want it. There are times when my head is
saying, "Maybe I can do it." But at the moment, my body is saying,
"Definitely not." I'm just emptied.'

He pauses and shakes his head, before looking at his gear-bag
thrown beside the couch. 'But I'm just hoping that this negativity
will only last for a few more days,' he says. 'And that I'll have the
hunger for it then again.'

★

Training has clearly been stepped up. On the morning that Deccie Malone got married, Friday, 17 July, we trained at 6.30 a.m. Some players couldn't make it because of work, but there were 18 present and most guys were accounted for. We had trained hard on Tuesday and Thursday, and training again just nine hours after we'd finished the previous evening was probably counter-productive. But management wanted to gauge commitment and desire, and nobody was holding back.

Seánie McMahon wasn't training because he'd to be at work in Shannon for 7 a.m., but he called in on his way. 'Good turnout,' he said to me, on the edge of the pitch before the session began. 'Perfect conditions for training.'

The sun was up and the ground was rock hard, but the grass was saturated from the early-morning dew and the pitch was like a skating rink – ideal conditions for first-touch hurling training. I know from past early-morning experiences training with Clare. When Clare popularized 6 a.m. sessions under Ger Loughnane in the 1990s, the outside perception was that Clare were running a boot camp and the training was commensurate to that of the US Marines. Yet sliotars would bounce off the turf like golf balls slamming against concrete. Loughnane would break open numerous packs of brand-new sliotars and your first touch had to be so good to survive those sessions – and the lash of Loughnane's tongue – that you'd come away feeling like you'd glue stuck on the bas of your hurley.

Most club teams can't afford a conveyor belt of brand-new sliotars, unfortunately. The average cost of a sliotar is around €7, and you could need around 60 for a proper rapid-fire session with one team. Given how easy it is to lose sliotars and how quickly some of them become unusable, that's a serious financial strain on a club over any season.

We haven't had a batch of new sliotars now in a while and many of the balls in the bag are complete duds which turn into either small rocks or soft potatoes as soon as they get wet. They're not suitable for first-touch hurling, but after our first drill much of the session involved stamina hurling and long striking.

It felt like we were finally beginning to generate some momentum again; but when we trained again on Sunday morning at 12 noon, it was soon evident that we'd gone backwards from the exertions of the weekend. Only ten bodies turned up because a host of the panel had gone to Galway last night for a stag. Still, Patsy couldn't afford to alter the schedule and the session involved more stamina hurling and a blast of shuttle runs at the end.

'It just shows, lads,' he said, as everyone was gasping for air by the end of the session. 'You can't be going out on the tear the whole time and expect to be fit.'

As far as management were concerned, the line in the sand had now been drawn. We had four weeks to our next championship match and there were no more allowances being given. This was the last stag. The last blow-out. The summer was slowly turning into autumn and the business end of the championship was closing in fast. That Sunday evening, a text was sent out to everybody: 'Training this week on Tuesday, Thursday, Saturday and a challenge game against Wolfe Tones on Monday. No more excuses. It's time to get down to serious business.'

Before training on Saturday though, our whole schedule ground to a halt. Another tragedy had struck Doora-Barefield. That morning – 25 July – our parish priest, Fr Michael McNamara, passed away.

Fr Mac was a huge part of St Joseph's. He had been a selector with the senior team for the previous two years and he'd also been a selector with us when we reached the 2004 county final. Most of the players in the panel who were married had been married by Fr Mac. He had just officiated at the wedding of Deccie Malone. He was due to marry Darragh O'Driscoll and his fiancée Bernie in less than two weeks' time. And Conny and Sinéad in September. But less than six months after he'd given a beautiful and moving homily at Ger Hoey's funeral mass, we now had to bury him as well.

The suddenness of it all added to the sense of shock. Three days earlier, Fr Mac was driving out the Tulla road to speak to a young couple soon to be married when he was struck down by a searing pain. He pulled in to the side of the road and an ambulance was called and took him to hospital. The following day, Fr Mac rang Fr Jerry Carey in Ennis to tell him that he needed masses covered in the parish for the next few weeks because he was having an operation to clear an aneurysm. But the following day, Bishop Willie Walsh rang Fr Jerry in tears. Fr Mac didn't survive the operation.

As a mark of respect, our challenge match scheduled for Monday evening was pulled and training was cancelled until Thursday. Although Fr Mac's funeral mass took place in Ennis Cathedral – no church in Doora-Barefield would have taken the crowd – the parish and the club played a huge role in the liturgy of the mass and the subsequent burial. The club formed a guard of honour outside the cathedral as the cortège eventually pulled away to make its way to Barefield church.

Many people expected Fr Mac to be buried in his home parish of Kilmaley. Yet when some landscaping was done around the church last summer, Fr Mac told the landscaper and the church sacristan that he wanted to be buried on Barefield church grounds – with the proviso that his grave should face Kilmaley. He surely didn't expect to be taken so soon, but the sentiment highlighted how much Doora-Barefield meant to Fr Mac. And how that warmth for the parish and its people had rested in his heart.

Over those few sad days, the community spirit within the club and the parish was particularly evident. 'The overriding comment we got after Father Mac's funeral was the tremendous community spirit shown during all the services,' said Jackie Morris, a member of Roslevan pastoral council and the finance committee. 'And much of that spirit was down to Father Mac. Because he felt that the community were the Church.'

When he arrived in Doora-Barefield in 2001, Fr Mac immediately saw the need to involve the community in the parish activities. He set up pastoral councils in Doora, Barefield and Roslevan. There were 40 members in the Roslevan pastoral council, and one of its main functions from the outset was to develop community facilities, which Fr Mac felt were essential to creating a sense of community to the ever-increasing population of Roslevan.

In a parish that is developing at a rapid rate, there are approximately 8,500 people in the Doora-Barefield parish. About 5,000 of those residents are in the Roslevan area, which knits into Ennis and which had effectively been re-zoned as a second town centre in recent years.

When we grew up in Roslevan, it was a largely rural area on the periphery of Ennis; but since 1994, 13 of the 22 major housing estates that have spawned in the parish are in the Roslevan area. Yet the only major focal point in that region is the Roslevan Shopping Centre – which is in front of our old clubhouse and field, which we sold in 2005.

There is no school or church in the area, and mass is said in a small community hall. After the club moved out to Gurteen, there was no green area or community outlet of the kind that St Joseph's had always provided. Winning an All-Ireland club title a decade ago really united a massive parish – the largest rural parish in the diocese of Killaloe – but it also gave a real sense of identity to the Roslevan area, which many new homeowners assumed was in Ennis.

Now that our success has waned and the population has continued to increase, the vast majority of residents don't view Doora-Barefield through the prism of a GAA identity any more. And in the meantime, the increased number of houses within the boundaries of the parish of Doora-Barefield hasn't been matched by the provision of general social amenities necessary to encourage community building and healthy social interaction.

The key focus of efforts to create a new community spirit was the proposed development of a new church and community hall in Roslevan. In the original submission to the local authorities, one of the recommendations was a site for a 16-teacher primary school, childcare and playing pitch in the Roslevan area. That had to be abandoned owing to the recession, but Fr Mac and his pastoral councils were still prepared to keep pushing the boat out, primarily because many of the problems associated with an urban area were beginning to be felt in this formerly rural parish. Growing numbers of young people have limited social and recreational outlets.

So in that submission to the local authorities, the pastoral councils had recommended the inclusion of a number of progressive but fundamental social developments including a multi-purpose community centre, with broadband connectivity, to be provided in Doora, and a youth development centre within the parish.

Fr Mac was a man driven by community spirit and not by Church authority. At a time when the Church is becoming increasingly disconnected from society – particularly young people – Fr Mac appreciated that importance of community spirit and recognized the impact it could have on young people.

He was a man who just got things done. When he ran a parish auction in 2006, the initial purpose was to clear parish debt; but Fr Mac saw it as a means to creating greater parish spirit. It clearly did: the initial fund-raising target was €30,000 but the level of enthusiasm swept that figure to €100,000. That in turn led to the annual parish social, which has been running ever since.

'Father Mac was a great leader,' said Jackie Morris. 'Very strong-willed and focused. He is a massive loss to us. But I suppose we have to ensure now that we keep going forward with what he started. It is what he would have wanted.'

The club feel exactly the same way because Fr Mac was part of our journey over the last number of years. He was a fanatical hurling man and he always wanted us to do well. To be the best we could be. To be true to ourselves. And as we continue our journey, we owe the man that much now.

Darragh O'Driscoll got married on Thursday, 6 August. At 3.12 p.m. that day, just after the ceremony had finished, everyone got a text message: 'Senior training at 12 noon on Sunday. All, and we mean all, togged at 11.55 a.m. There is a meeting 4 players only called by Darragh and Damien immediately afterwards.'

Darragh has been an excellent captain, and this message just highlighted the commitment he has shown to this team. He wasn't going on his honeymoon until Monday, but he still saw the welfare of the squad as a priority before he left.

After a good session on Sunday, John Carmody had the final word from the management on the field before the players' meeting began. He was setting the tone ahead of our third championship match against Ogonnelloe next weekend. 'We want to send out a message to the rest of the county,' said Carmody. 'We're not just going to beat this crowd, we're going to drive them into the ground.'

After everyone had togged off and showered, Darragh kicked off the players' meeting at 1.41 p.m.

'We have 24 weeks done and we've got 11 weeks to go,' he said. 'The county final is fixed for this day 11 weeks. And I've already planned on being in bed early the night before to get ready for it. All we can ask for is that we give it our all. I was thinking last night of the people we have lost, and we have lost two great people. Father Mac was a very proud Doora-Barefield man and a very proud St Joseph's Doora-Barefield man. He gave a lot to us. And I don't need to say how important Ger Hoey was to us all.

'I was just thinking that, no matter what happens, whether we get to a final, semi-final, quarter-final, I hope that we can look back after it's all over and say that we gave it our all. Because that would be a fitting tribute to Father Mac and Ger. It would be what they would want. And what they deserve.'

After Damien Kennedy briefly talked about the importance of treating Ogonnelloe with sufficient respect for next week, Darragh asked if anyone else wanted to speak. If nobody did, he said we'd wrap it up. There was a lull for a few seconds, and then I interjected. 'Lads, I want to hear what the younger lads have to say because it's the same old voices talking the whole time. I just want to know what ye are thinking.'

Then there was another pause. 'No pressure, lads,' said Davy Hoey.

Nobody offered their opinion, so Seánie, a veteran of 19 years, broke the silence. 'Lads, I know I'm not one of the younger lads but there are just a few things I want to say. First things first, I really think we have a great chance of winning the county title. I think it's set up for us. Last year, the reason we didn't beat Newmarket was because we were basically fucked. I was never as tired coming up to a game because we had over-trained. This year, we haven't been killed, guys have had their break and we're fresh. I feel fresh anyway. We can start building it up now and take it from there.

'But some things need to change from now on. What we have done up to now will not win a championship. It will just not be good enough. We need to push ourselves harder in the drills, drive ourselves on that bit more. Really go for it. You can take your break afterwards, but just burst yourselves and then you can rest.'

Seánie then addressed another concern. A couple of weeks ago, he collared Ken Kennedy, Darragh O'Driscoll, Mikey Cullinan and me after training and outlined how all the senior players seemed to be gravitating towards each other during the ball drills. He didn't feel that the senior players were integrating sufficiently with the younger players. It was something that we'd really taken on board in the meantime, but that unconscious segregation was evident from a glance around the room.

'I just think that it's something we need to be aware of,' said Seánie. 'Just look around here now. Senior guys are sitting beside seniors and younger players are with younger players. I'm not saying that there is a divide or any big division. But we're all in it together and we need to push one another. It will just bring us all closer together. But every man here must believe that we can win the championship. If every man here does believe that we can do it, then we will.'

Seánie's words, as always, were soothing. They made it easier for young players to have their say, and Mike McNamara, one of our best forwards, was the first to offer his opinion.

'I am just speaking for the younger players,' he said. 'If you look around, a lot of players are going to go in the next few years. Seánie, Christy, Ken – they're the guys we have always looked to for leadership. We know that they're going to do it, but some of us have always looked to them and not taken on enough responsibility ourselves. Well, when they are gone, what are we going to do then? There's no point looking around then and suddenly realizing that they're not there and we're not used to taking the responsibility they always took. The younger players here just need to start showing more leadership and I think we will drive it on. I'm not talking about shouting or roaring in the dressing room. We will do it on the pitch with our hurling.'

I was sitting beside Mike and I patted him on the arm because I felt it was an important contribution. Conny was sitting the other side of Mike and he briefly stared at me with that furrowed look, which instantly told me he was formulating in his mind what he wanted to say.

'Lads, the point has been made to the younger lads numerous times not to be thinking that you have loads of time to make it happen,' Conny said. 'You fucking haven't. And I know from experience. When I first made the team in 2004, we got to the county final and I expected it to be like that every year. Then I got my jaw smashed the following season and missed the whole championship. And I haven't been able to nail down a permanent place since. That's five years gone in a flash. Bang. Fucking gone.'

Darragh O'Driscoll immediately continued on that theme. 'The younger guys here are really talented players,' he said. A host of them were all sitting together in the corner by the door and Darragh named them as he spoke. 'Whitey [Niall White], Anthony [Halpin], Enda [Lyons], Shane O'Connor, Shane O'Grady, Seán Flynn – ye are more talented than we were when we were yere age. But ye have to drive us on now. We will take inspiration from ye. Don't be afraid to fuck us out of it if we're not putting enough effort in, because that's what we need. Ye need to challenge us and we will challenge ye. And we will all be the better for it.'

All through the meeting, I swore to myself that I wasn't going to talk. But just as Darragh was about to wrap it up, I felt I had to. There was stuff that I needed to unload and I was concerned that I might not get the chance to say it again.

'Lads,' I said, with a smile, 'I swore to myself that I wasn't going to talk because I know ye're probably sick to the teeth of listening to me. But I'm going to say it anyway.

'This is my 20th year in goals for the Doora-Barefield senior team. Some of ye – Enda, you weren't even born when I first started with this team. Half of ye probably think that I should be long gone by this stage, but the end is near for me now. And I just want to tell ye all what winning this county title would mean to me.

'I have three county medals, two Munster club titles and an All-Ireland. But lads, I want this county title as badly as any of those medals. None of those really matter to me now because I need this one. I remember talking to Seánie the night we beat the 'Bridge and we spoke about how special this one would be. We were almost too young to really appreciate those medals, but this one would be so sweet for us all, not just us. Especially this year, after the people we have lost.

'We have to treat this now like a business, because we're in the business of winning it. But we also have to be driven by emotion. We can't be sidetracked by it but we have to be propelled by it. Just think of the people we have lost and, Jesus, we have to just burst ourselves to try and honour them. It's the least we can do for them.

'I have my own emotion to deal with and that is my motivation. The one thing that is driving me is that I can already picture the final whistle at the county final when we have won it. I have so much emotion inside of me and I know that it will burst out of me at that moment. It will be a release for me. Because it's probably the only way I can get it out of me. To win with ye. To win with my best friends and teammates.

'Jesus, lads, I can't tell ye how badly I want this. I have never wanted to win anything as badly in my life. We'll all drive each other, but please, just help me get there. Just get me over that line.'

Conny and Mike Mac each whispered something to me when I was finished but I was mad with myself and I didn't take in what they had said. I thought I'd brought too much personal baggage into it. I was thinking of Róisín while I was talking and there was a quiver in my voice near the end. Some of the younger lads would have known me only as a half-psycho keeper who goes off the rails every now and again. Now they were seeing me as a near emotional wreck.

On my way home, I was shaking my head in the car. Beating myself up. Then Conny rang. 'Well spoken, sham.'

'Ah, Jeez, I think I went over the top,' I responded. 'There was probably no need for half of that stuff.'

'No, it was from the heart,' he said. 'And I think guys really responded to it.'

I hope they do. Still, I don't know why I became so emotional. It just got a hold of me. Maybe I've put extra pressure on myself by saying what I've just said. But I don't care. I just need to get over that line.

11. Return of the Man

Back in May, when, like every club in the country, we held a Lá gClub to mark the GAA's 125th anniversary, the feature event was an exhibition game between the current team and the All-Ireland winning side from ten years ago. The 1999 team wore our blue jerseys – the Munster colours which we'd first donned for the 1999 All-Ireland semi-final because of a clash of colours with Athenry – and we made our way on to the pitch through a huge guard of honour that had gathered outside our dressing room.

Six of the current team were playing with the 1999 side, and most of the remaining players who had retired had kept themselves in good shape, so it didn't take long for the old chemistry of a great team to bubble back to the surface. It was only an exhibition game played at a pedestrian pace but there was still a clear contrast in technical efficiency between the two teams. The current team just didn't have what the 1999 team had: the telepathy, the innate understanding, the fieldcraft and clever use of possession.

Of course there was some exhibitionism, routinely encouraged by the commentator, Michael 'Blackie' O'Connor, who could be heard over the loudspeakers. But the expansive and intelligent style of play from the 1999 side was an embodiment of the class which had made that team one of the best club hurling sides in history.

In the middle of the field, my brother Jamesie was orchestrating the show: spraying ball all over the field, embroidering the play together with little stitch passes, and notching a couple of real quality scores. For some of the younger kids watching, it was probably their first time seeing Clare's joint most-decorated All-Star.

When the match was over and the players were mingling with the crowd on the edge of the pitch, two club stalwarts, Pat Frawley and Micheál McMahon, approached me.

'Can you not try and talk Jamesie into coming back?' Frawley asked me. 'You're his brother, surely he'll listen to you?'

'I know it was only an exhibition game,' said McMahon, 'but he was still head and shoulders above anyone else on the pitch. God, he'd make a massive difference to the senior team.'

I didn't speak to anyone else, but I broached the subject with our physio, Eugene Moynihan, on Tuesday night. I asked him if he thought Jamesie could make a comeback.

'I think he could,' said Eugene. 'He regularly plays soccer on the AstroTurf, doesn't he?'

'He does, yeah, a couple of times a week,' I replied. 'He runs the show there too, runs rings around guys.'

'Well, if he can do that on the AstroTurf, which is an unforgiving surface on knees, I think he could definitely come back.'

Three weeks later, en route to Thurles for the Cork–Tipperary Munster hurling quarter-final, I broached it with Jamesie. It was just two days after we had beaten Sixmilebridge in the championship and I told him what Eugene had said.

'Come on to hell,' I said to him, 'give it a shot. We're going to do everything we can to win it this year for Ger. Give it one lash. See how it goes. If it doesn't work out, walk away from it.'

He didn't dismiss me out of hand. He was very close to Ger Hoey and he could see the value in what we were trying to achieve.

'Ah, I don't know,' he said. 'I just don't think my knee would be up to it.'

'I appreciate that,' I responded. 'But if you don't feel it is after one or two sessions, just walk away from it. No one will say anything to you.'

I didn't mention it to anyone else, but the team captain Darragh O'Driscoll and manager John Carmody had discussed the issue themselves and they called to Jamesie's house that Wednesday night to talk to him about a potential return. Carmody said that they were only looking for him to come back for a ten-week period. We weren't playing championship again until mid-August, so they wouldn't expect him to return to training until that time. He didn't drink or smoke, he always kept himself in good shape, and they didn't see the benefit in flogging him on hard ground in June or July. If his leg held up to the strain, a couple of weeks would get him hurling-sharp again and set him up as an impact substitute.

Jamesie didn't make any promises but he said he'd give it serious consideration. It was always going to be a huge decision because he has been effectively retired now for five seasons – the last serious game he played was the 2004 county final. In a challenge game against Kilmaley before the following season's championship, he tore the cruciate ligament in his right knee. Because of a mis-diagnosis, he didn't become fully aware of the extent of the injury until the following March. The required reconstruction would have meant missing another season and he decided not to have the operation. So he just pulled the plug and retired.

It was a massive blow to the club because without the injury he would have played on for a few more seasons. His presence for the 2005 county semi-final against Wolfe Tones might have been enough to get us to the final, and the loss of his leadership and experience in a developing forward line was one of the main reasons we narrowly failed to emerge from our group in the 2006 and 2007 championships.

The possibility of Jamesie's return has been hovering in the background over the last couple of months, but none of the senior players put him under any pressure to make that decision. They were content to let the idea ferment with him because he was one of the club's greatest players and everybody accepted that he didn't owe anything to St Joseph's.

His leadership on and off the field was among his greatest strengths. A week after we won our first county title in 40 years in 1998, he told us that we were going to win the All-Ireland club title. Nobody believed him, but by the following March we were champions. If nothing else, his presence, experience and leadership would be a huge help to us at the business end of the championship.

On Tuesday, 18 August, Patsy and John Carmody called us into a huddle after training. We were training again on Thursday, but at the unusual time of 8.30 p.m. We couldn't go any earlier because there was a minor football game on, while our junior hurlers were playing Éire Óg in the championship in Gurteen at 7 p.m. 'But the main reason we're training on Thursday night,' said Carmody, 'is because there's a man coming back to train with us. Jamesie O'Connor. What is that man going to bring to this squad? I don't need to say any more, lads.'

Two nights later, I pulled into Gurteen at the same time as Jamesie. I smiled over at him as he got out of the car with his gear and hurley.

'Jeez, I thought I'd never see that sight again,' I said to him.

'Well, take a good look,' he replied, 'because you might never see it again after tonight.'

At that stage the junior game was still ongoing, and as Jamesie made his way into the dressing room with his gear you could clearly see heads turn and the whispering begin. When he walked into the dressing room, a big cheer went up. The Man was back.

Out on the pitch before training began, I approached Patsy, who was clearly buzzing with the latest addition to his squad. 'I don't know if he's going to stay around for long,' I said to him. 'But either way, you need to keep him involved. Whether that's coaching forwards or talking to the team, just make sure he stays on board.'

'Definitely,' responded Patsy. 'If he doesn't play, he'll be our eye in the stand for games.'

After the session ended, I went over and asked Jamesie how he felt. 'My touch is as good as it ever was,' he said. 'It's just like riding a bike, you never lose it. But the knee still feels pretty weak. I don't know, sure we'll see how it goes anyway.'

After I togged off and made my way into the showers, I was met with a wall of steam and a chorus of singing voices in the shower room. 'The nicest shower I've ever had in this place,' said Cathal O'Sullivan. 'They're roasting.'

'The pump is on all evening because of the two other matches,' I said to him.

Cathal immediately dismissed that observation out of hand: 'That's rubbish. They're only boiling hot because of your man [Jamesie]. If the showers were cold, he'd never have come back.'

After we'd towelled down and got dressed, Jamesie and I made our way into the small meeting room just off dressing room number four. It was a big night for the senior team, with the return of one of our greatest players, but it was an equally big night for the club in terms of our future development: the club executive had called a meeting to discuss the hiring of a new coach.

There were 16 people squeezed tightly into the small room: the club executive, trustees, members of the development committee, the minor club executive and some of the best underage coaches in the club. It was a huge plus to see Mike Guilfoyle there, because he has done outstanding work with the underage teams over the last few years.

This was effectively a pitch, from our sub-committee charged with looking for the coach, to the key figures in the club. We had already drawn up a charter, which was read out and then debated. Some people were hard to convince. One senior club member seemed to think that the root of the club's ills lay in the senior team. In his opinion, the senior hurling team was the club's key brand, and it was struggling to capture the imagination of young people in such a competitive market.

I certainly wasn't letting him get away with that. I jumped down his throat: 'That's a complete joke of an assessment. The senior team is doing really well to be as competitive as it is. Do you realize how hard it is for us to be competitive when we're a dual club and that we've had so little underage hurling success and so few young players come through in the last few years? Some of the senior players are trying to wring every last drop of energy out of themselves to win a senior title because the way we're going, we'll be doing well to stay out of intermediate in the next few years when a lot of those players go. We're bursting ourselves at the moment to try and win a senior title, but we can't keep going for much longer. That's why this appointment has to happen. This is for the future.'

Then I machine-gunned everyone with statistics I had prepared: no minor title since 1990; no U-21 title since 1994; no U-16 title since 1995; no U-14 title since 2001. We were giving walkovers to teams in U-16 hurling, while the underage football operation had turned into a machine. 'This is a no-brainer,' I said. 'This has to happen.'

Jamesie backed me up. 'I have been up the north coaching and when I see the standard of Under-10s in Loughgiel Shamrocks and I compare that standard to our Under-10s, it does bother me,' he said. 'I think we are a club in crisis and we need to get a handle on it. I'm not blaming anyone because there's great work being done by the underage coaches. But we just need to do more. There is an appetite to get our act together at underage coaching at county level, and I think there is an appetite to do the same here in the club. But we have to take the bull by the horns and do it ourselves. Because nobody else is going to do it for us.'

The mood within the room was conservative, but the vibes were still good. Of course there were questions asked. The secretary, Dan O'Connor, mentioned the health and safety regulations about hurling in the schools which would have to be explored before we set about appointing a coach. Somebody else mentioned that a coach could only do so much to prevent the huge fall-off rate after U-16 because of the lure of rugby, soccer and other activities. Then the discussion broadened into a debate as to why the U-16 hurling team gave a walkover the previous week. What could a hurling coach do to guard against that happening?

'Look, we could be here for the next hour talking about the difficulties we have,' said Jamesie. 'We're always going to have the problems of urbanization and losing players to other sports – that's just a fact of life. We can make all the excuses we want, but we simply don't have a choice here. The fall-off rate of hurlers is just too great in this club, especially between 16 and 21. I was talking to Colm O'Rourke [former Meath footballer] recently, and he told me that Simonstown Gaels introduced six 19-year-olds on to their championship team this year.' Then he looked over at me. 'Do we even have six 19-year-olds playing hurling in this club?'

I did a quick tally. 'I don't think so. There definitely aren't six 19-year-olds who take hurling very seriously, anyway.' Spotting an opening, I unleashed another torrent of statistics that I'd prepared in drawing up the charter for the proposed new appointment. Ranging from Clare development squads at U-15, U-16, U-17, to the Clare minor, U-21 and senior panels, the club had only three representatives on those six squads this season. Even more of a concern was that only one of those three players saw any real competitive action.

If you were to trawl through most of the big clubs in Munster now – Toomevara, Mount Sion, Ballygunner, Newtownshandrum, Sarsfields (Cork), Adare, Thurles Sarsfields – the average number of representatives those clubs supplied to county panels ranging from U-15 to senior would conservatively be estimated at around 14. When you compare our representative statistics to that average, it's obvious that the reality now is that we're a big club only in name.

'The night before we won our first Under-21 title in 1993, Tony Kelly said that we were going to play a huge part in the future success of Clare hurling,' I said. 'And we did. Our players were nearly the backbone of Clare teams for the next ten years. And it really bothers me now when I see all these Clare hurling teams and there's nobody from Doora-Barefield on them.'

There's no question that the face of Clare hurling has changed. On the Clare U-21 hurling team which won the Munster U-21 title for the first time only three weeks ago, five are from Clonlara, who won the county senior title for the first time in 89 years last October. Three of the back seven are from Crusheen, defeated county finalists two years ago, who have never won a senior title. On the training panel of 36, there are just four players from the big four clubs (Sixmilebridge, Wolfe Tones, Clarecastle and ourselves) which won six successive Munster club titles in the last decade. We're the only ones who don't have a single representative on the squad.

'Being out on the field in Dungarvan [after the Munster U-21 final success against Waterford] was a special feeling,' said Jamesie. 'But there was a slight tinge of regret there too that we didn't have anybody on the panel. I remember going to watch [Ciaran] O'Neill and

Ger Hoey playing for Clare underage teams when I was younger and there was always a great sense of pride to having your own club-mates play for Clare. Christy, Phelim [Collins], Donal [Cahill], Seánie – I remember going to watch them play for Clare and we always had big underage performers for the county. And now we have nobody. That can't continue. We can't allow it to continue.'

I honestly don't think there was ever going to be any disagreement about what we were trying to achieve through appointing an under-age coach. The meeting was never really about trying to justify the appointment; it was merely about confirming its necessity. But if there was going to be a hard sell, some of us weren't leaving the room until the deal was sealed.

At the end of the meeting, Micheál McMahon proposed that we accept the move in principle and it was seconded by Bernie Hallinan, the minor club secretary. Then the senior secretary, Dan O'Connor, just nodded over to me in acknowledgement of what needed to happen next. It was now up to our small sub-committee to go and get our coach.

When we played Ogonnelloe in the championship last week, Patsy delivered one of his most impressive pre-game talks of the season. Before we began our warm-up, he gathered us all in a huddle and then walked us to different parts of the field as he forensically outlined the game plan and explained what was expected of us in those areas. It was cool-headed, calculated, informed and intelligent management.

Less than an hour later, he was involved in a minor brawl and found himself at the bottom of a ruck in the middle of the field.

Just before the interval, the Ogonnelloe goalkeeper and a couple of their defenders were annoyed with a challenge made by Seánie and a melee broke out. Patsy decided to make his way in from the line and get involved, and whether someone clipped him, or he slipped, he was soon picking himself up from the deck. And then, as we were making our way in at half-time, Patsy and John Carmody became embroiled in a slagging match with the referee, which certainly didn't help our cause after the break.

With ten minutes remaining, we were level against a side expected to be relegated. They were only ever going to stick with us if we handed them frees and the referee doled them out like confetti. We definitely got on the wrong side of the ref, but the fact that they got eight of their ten scores from placed balls was a real sign of a lack of sharpness and discipline on our part. Although we won by 0-18 to 0-10, it was the most unimpressive performance we'd produced in years.

Patsy's on edge lately. He's not happy with how the team is performing, and getting relegated in the league has been a major blow to his confidence. He clearly feels under pressure now, a strain that can be alleviated only by winning a county title. And that's not going to happen unless we can find some major form from somewhere.

He flew into a rage when we played Wolfe Tones, Shannon, in a challenge game five days before the Ogonnelloe game. The game was fixed for Shannon to help us acclimatize to the pitch before the weekend, and everyone was told to be there at 6.55 p.m. and togged off and on the field by 7.05 p.m. for a 7.30 start. Some of us were late – myself included – and were still togging off at 7.10 p.m. when Patsy arrived in and lambasted us. He was fully justified.

Then we went out and produced a woeful half of hurling. We were trailing by nine points at the break and Patsy couldn't contain his anger any longer. 'I was down in Kilkenny recently watching their hurlers train and I met Joe Hennessy, the former great Kilkenny hurler,' he said to us, with plumes of smoke billowing from his ears. 'He asked me where I was from and I said, Doora-Barefield. And he said, "Ah yeah, Doora-Barefield, great club, that was a wonderful team which won that All-Ireland club title. God, ye produced some wonderful players for Clare over the years."

'I'm hearing this stuff all over the country about what a great club we are. Well, unless we get our fucking act together, we won't be a great club for much longer because we'll be wiped off the map. We'll soon be forgotten about and nobody will be talking about us then.

'I just can't understand us. We come here tonight, five days before a key championship game, and we aren't even fucking tuned in. Who are we codding? Ogonnelloe will be fighting for their lives on Sunday to stay out of relegation, and we're walking around as if we're in the Queens [nightclub]. You can clearly see who has been training and who hasn't, and there are too many guys missing training. I have missed one training session this year. John Carmody has missed just one session this year. Vinny Sheedy hasn't missed a single training session all year. And why the fuck can't ye give us the commitment that's needed to win a county title?

'We've had nothing but tragedy this year. One tragedy after the next. The club needs a lift. The whole parish needs a lift. And we said that we'd be the ones to give our people a lift. Well, we better start picking it up now or we're going to let everyone down.'

His words did shake us from our torpor and we produced an acceptable second-half performance. But Patsy's words also reminded me of something Davy Hoey said to me a few weeks earlier: that we should be doing it for the right reasons and not making it into a crusade for Ger. And now Fr Mac has been added to that crusade.

That is something the Tyrone football manager Mickey Harte has spoken about very astutely over the years. Harte has had to deal with two huge tragedies during his years with Tyrone: the deaths of Paul McGirr and Cormac McAnallen. Over the years, Harte has often answered requests to speak to clubs who have suffered a tragedy through the loss of one of their treasured members.

People deal with tragedy in different ways and there have always been a number of strands to the philosophy Harte preaches: be there for each other and don't make your sporting lives a crusade to remember the dead; if you really wish to hold those you have lost in high regard, think of what good you can find in them and bring it into your own life; you never really have to go out and win anything for somebody you really respect – you simply have to do your best.

To be honest, we have never addressed the loss of Ger Hoey in that manner. We never really sat down as a team and discussed it, when maybe we should have. Ger's name and presence is constantly in our dressing room and there is enormous emotion in the senior players around his loss. But many of the younger players didn't know Ger.

They didn't play with him. They can't relate to him. They can only guess at what he meant to us.

We probably should have talked about all of this during the year, but it's very hard to talk about Ger with his brother so involved because we're all so aware of his unique feelings and emotions. But maybe it wouldn't do any harm, because Davy seems open to talking about Ger's loss and dealing with it as a team. In any case, all we can do for now is what Harte suggests: be aware of what Ger brought to life and take inspiration from that.

On Sunday, 23 August, five days before our last group game against Broadford, the tension between management and the squad got dramatically worse. A challenge game against Ballybrown from Limerick had been arranged for Gurteen that evening, but torrential rain had fallen over the previous 24 hours and our pitch was unplayable. That morning, a group text was sent out to notify everyone that the game had been switched to Ballybrown's pitch in Clarina, about six miles outside Limerick city.

As soon as we arrived everyone togged off, but there was no sign of management. They had all travelled together in the one car and nearly everyone was ready to go by the time the car pulled into the car park. As they made their way towards the door, a couple of lads asked for the sliotar bag so they could begin warming up. They were immediately told to go straight back inside and sit down. There was an edge to their tone and something was clearly about to go down. Patsy and John Carmody stood in the middle of the floor.

'Right, lads,' said Patsy, 'anyone who was drinking last night, step into the middle of the circle.'

The senior footballers had played their last group game yesterday, but with a senior championship match on in five days' time the hurling management had already issued a strict no-drinking order to prevent any dual players from going out last night. A group text sent yesterday at 11.55 a.m. finished with the line: 'No alcohol for anyone over the next six days, serious competition for places so tomorrow is a chance for everyone.'

Patsy knew that ban had been breached. He took a spin into town at 10.30 p.m. and browsed through Mossy's pub. Some guys knew they had been spotted.

So, Cathal O'Sullivan, Ivor Whyte, Gary Hassett and Brian Collins stepped into the circle. Ivor is a brother of one of the selectors, Steve Whyte, while Gary Hassett and Brian Collins are two peripheral players on the panel but two very honest and good young lads. Most of the ire from management focused on Cathal O'Sullivan. He wasn't long back from six weeks travelling in South-east Asia, but he'd been our captain last year and was one of our most experienced players.

'For fuck's sake, Cathal, what were ye at?' Patsy asked him.

'It was only three drinks after the game,' Cathal responded. 'That was all we had.'

'I don't care, ye were told no drink,' snapped Patsy. 'There's been too much fucking around going on here and this is just a symptom of the disease that's creeping into the panel. It's only going to take a few guys to bring the whole thing down.'

Then Carmody stepped in. 'Lads, ye were told no drink. Cathal, is it because you were sulking after you didn't start the last day? You were captain of this team last year and we expect more from you. There's a saying that winners do what losers don't, and what ye did last night was the stuff of losers. Do any of ye really believe that we're going to win the senior championship? Because what ye did last night says to me that ye don't. This club is messing around now for eight years without a senior championship and will ye just get yere act together and get it right. Colm Mullen is off the panel for Friday night and Kevin Dilleen is close to being off the panel because he hasn't been training with us. Certain guys just need to get their act together and we all need to start pulling in the one direction from now on. Because if we don't, we're fucked.'

Carmody then asked the four lads if they were going to apologize to the group. They all did.

It was Jamesie's first match back since he made a brief reappearance against Portumna in a challenge game in 2006, and I was walking out beside him as we made our way on to the pitch for our warm-up.

'Welcome back again,' I said to him. 'A bit different from the old days.'

He just looked at me and raised his eyes to heaven.

As we gathered at the top corner of the field to go through our stretching routine, Damien Kennedy tried to dilute any negativity that was still floating in the air. 'What happened, happened; but it's done and dusted now. The lads have apologized, so let's just move on. No more about it.'

We were well in control during the first half and I had a good chat with Terrence 'Spider' Kenny, the former Limerick hurler who was doing umpire.

'How are ye going?' he asked me.

'Not great, to be honest,' I replied. 'We're finding it very hard at the moment to combine football and hurling. We were playing football championship yesterday and you can clearly see out there that guys are tired. And we've a big championship match on Friday night.'

Then he told me a story about the year Ballybrown won the Munster club hurling title in 1989. They were also involved in an intermediate football semi-final that season and they hit the crossbar with a late shot that would have given them victory against New-castlewest. 'If that goal had gone in, there's no way we would have won the Munster club title,' he told me. 'It would have taken too much out of us. You just can't do hurling and football together. It's impossible.'

We created about five clear-cut goalscoring chances in that first half, but we failed to take any of them. Then they hit a purple patch just before the break, which left us ahead by just three points at half-time, despite having played with a very stiff breeze. In the team huddle at the break, Ken Kennedy addressed our lack of composure in front of goal and our lack of a killer instinct. 'If we're only up by three points at half-time on Friday night, we're going to be in serious trouble because Broadford will smell blood and they'll go for us. The game has to be put away from them by that stage so they don't get any belief that they can beat us. So when ye get the chances, just score them. Especially goal chances.'

After Ken had spoken, John Carmody adopted a different tone.

At least we were creating goal chances, and a goal would eventually come. 'There have been a lot of positives to our play,' he said. 'So just keep going, keep going. It will happen for us.'

Ken didn't seem to think so. As we were making our way down the field to take up our positions for the second half, he sidled up to me.

'Did you hear that bullshit? Going well? For God's sake, this crowd are only intermediate. We should be blowing them away.'

'I know, I know, but we have to stay positive,' I responded.

Then as we both looked back up the field it was like staring into a wall of light. A watery sun was dipping low in the autumn evening and visibility was almost nil with the glare from the wet grass.

'Chris, be calling and covering behind me the whole time now because I can't see a thing,' Ken said to me, just before the ball was thrown in.

I just looked at the umpire. 'He can't see a thing but he expects me to see everything. He must think I have X-ray eyes that can see straight through a blinding sun.'

Five minutes into the half, a long cross-field ball from their midfielder went straight into the net. When you're a goalkeeper there are never any excuses, but did I see the ball? If a jumbo jet was coming at me, I wouldn't have seen it.

I knew then that it was going to be a difficult last 25 minutes. We were facing into a stiff breeze, a lethal sun and a soggy pitch with a team half flaked from having had so many dual players playing their second game in 24 hours. Although we started throwing in substitutes all over the place – including Jamesie – we were still looking for a performance. Ballybrown were really up for it now, having got a lead and with a sizeable home crowd roaring on their every score. They had an army of bodies on the sideline, which was being marshalled by Tom Ryan, the former Limerick manager. We were a senior team and a scalp which would provide an injection of good vibes for them before their next championship game.

They ended up beating us by ten points.

Holy Jesus.

★

The following night, I was at a meeting in Gurteen to help draw up a newspaper advertisement for applicants for our new underage coach. Halfway through the discussion, I got a call from Conny, but I didn't take it. As soon as I was about to dial his number after landing in home at 10.45 p.m., he rang me. He had some news for me that was eating him up.

'Come here,' he said, 'Patsy just rang me there earlier on to tell me that I'm not on the panel for Friday night.'

'What are you talking about?'

'You heard me. I'm not on the panel. He said that there were 34 togging out at the moment and that I wasn't going to be togging on Friday. He asked me to be a hurley carrier, but I don't know about that. I've only said it to Seánie, Ken and yourself and I just want to get your opinion.'

'I'll ring you back,' I said to him. 'I'm ringing Patsy straight away.'

'No, no, no, don't ring him, I don't want that. Please don't. Just leave it and we'll sort it out.'

Patsy is a very good friend of mine and, while I have made a conscious decision this year to keep that friendship divorced from his management, I can't agree with him on this one. Conny brings so much to our set-up. When he trains, his intensity is a huge influence on the temperature of training, especially in games of backs-and-forwards, because he normally flattens whoever comes near him. He was a critical influence in altering the mood at half-time against Bally-ea, while he also had a really positive input before the Sixmilebridge match. He is a leader and a character, the sort of person you always need in a dressing room.

He paid the price for not being around for the challenge match against Ballybrown at the weekend, but the guy is getting married in 12 days' time and he was sorting out wedding plans with his fiancée, Sinéad. Anyway, the man trains harder than a US Navy Seal. Recently he recruited a private trainer, someone who used to work with the boxer Ricky Hatton. Management don't see that work he does on his own in Dublin, but it's not as if they have a reason to doubt his commitment. Conny was one of our best players with the juniors against

Éire Óg last week and when the majority of the juniors on the senior panel went home afterwards, he stayed on and trained with the seniors for a session that didn't finish until close to 10 p.m. And then drove back to Dublin.

Conny's obviously not in management's plans, but I think he's been treated harshly recently. The man co-runs his own company in Dublin, Titan Marketing, and when we played the Galway intermediates in a challenge in Tubber three weeks ago, he had driven from Dublin to Cork that day on business, and then from Cork to Tubber on the Galway border in north Clare for the game. We were down a huge number of bodies, against a squad that had 37 players togged out, and I felt we really needed his physicality on the night. Seánie wasn't togged out but was in the stand, and he told me afterwards that he caught Patsy's eye at one stage and pointed to Conny in an attempt to encourage Patsy to get him on the field to start winning dirty ball. He only got the last eight minutes.

Then the poor old devil paid a huge price for it afterwards. He told Sinéad that he was working and he never mentioned the match because he knew it would entail him getting back to Dublin after 1 a.m. He came back to my house afterwards for some food and to charge up his phone. As he was eating a sandwich in the corner of the kitchen, just after 10 p.m., he put his index finger up to his mouth to tell me to keep it quiet as he rang Sinéad.

'Hi, babe, I'm just after finishing up now and I'll be heading up the road in a few minutes.'

I just shook my head at him as he got off the phone. 'You're an idiot. I'm telling you, you'll get caught. Women have a knack of finding out these things. I learned my lesson the hard way with Olivia. She caught me telling lies about matches and training a few times and it caused holy war. You're better off to come clean.'

This is another conundrum of the club player. Whereas the inter-county player can justify the manic commitment to his wife or partner because of the profile and rewards, the ordinary club player doesn't always have that bargaining power. As a result, he often has to engage in clandestine operations. My work colleague, Michael Foley, told me one time that I was going to the same effort to hide my involvement with a bunch of minor hurlers as someone who was engaging in an extra-marital affair. But a couple of loose words on the phone one evening to one of the selectors, and I was rumbled.

It's inevitable. The morning after our game against the Galway intermediates, Conny was under pressure to get out to work, and he asked Sinéad to get his jacket out of his jeep. As soon as she opened the door, she got the stink from the wet gear wafting through the air inside. She checked his gear-bag and noticed his wet gear and the fresh grass stuck to his boots. She stormed back into the house.

'Where were you yesterday evening? You told me you were working.'

Conny had no choice. He had to come clean.

Sinéad, who had spent the previous evening writing out their wedding invitations on her own, just picked up the batch of invitations and fired them at him.

Conny just loves the club and he would do anything for this team. But there is a deeper meaning to his passion over the last year. Twelve months ago, his father Gerry suffered a brain haemorrhage. Along with Conny's brother Seán, Gerry Conroy was this team's best supporter. He never missed a game, even if it was a challenge match against some team up in Galway, and he was our rallying cry in the huddle before we played Sixmilebridge in last year's championship because he'd been struck down two weeks earlier. Gerry can't go to matches any more, and deep down I know Conny's motivation is for us to get to a county final and for his father to witness it.

Now that he's been dropped, all his efforts feel like a slap in the face. 'I think I'm being made a convenient scapegoat for some of the ghouling that's going on around the place at the moment,' he said to me over the phone. 'But I held my counsel. I could have taken Fahey apart for some of the shit that's been going on, but I didn't. He needn't talk to me about commitment; I'm trying to commute from Dublin for hurling and keep people employed up here. I don't know what I'm going to do. I'll probably just take it on the chin and turn up on Friday. Sure I can't watch the match from the stand, I'll go stone mad. No man is bigger than the team and maybe I'm not training as hard as I can either. But a man has to have his pride as well and I could tell them to go and fuck themselves.'

Seánie and I weren't happy with how he'd been treated and we spoke on the phone about it early the following morning. We couldn't see where it was coming from and we both agreed that Patsy had slightly lost the run of himself. I thought that he had been very clinical and decisive earlier in the year but that he had let emotion take hold of him recently, and this had affected his decision making. I brought up the incident against Ogonnelloe when he became involved in the fracas on the pitch.

'In fairness to him,' said Seánie, 'somebody caught him and pulled him down on the ground.'

'That's bullshit, he shouldn't have been anywhere near the place,' I responded. 'That's the last place he should have been. He needs to step away from all that and retain a cool head on the line.'

Then Seánie made a point. 'What's going to happen now if Conny says that he's not going to do the hurleys on Friday? Will Patsy tell him to shag off?'

'One of us should ring Patsy,' I said. 'We need to get a hold of this now because we can't afford to lose him from our dressing room.'

Seánie said that he would ring him and then he'd call back. An hour later he was back on to me. Patsy told Seánie that it was more or less John Carmody's call and that they'd wanted to trim the panel for Friday's game. Seánie then rang Carmody, who said that nothing had been finalized yet. After Seánie reasoned with him, Carmody agreed to include Conny on the panel for Friday.

Conny had already accepted that he wasn't going to be part of the panel on Friday, but he left a message on Patsy's phone to say that he was still '100 per cent committed for Friday'. Now that he was back on the panel, Conny wasn't convinced that the management's decision to return him to the squad would be wholly beneficial in the long term.

'It's no harm for management to be unpopular,' he said to me later that afternoon. 'I was reading there recently about Tom Brady [New England Patriots' quarterback] saying that he doesn't want to be friends with his coach; he just wants to be coached. When he goes to the training ground he doesn't want to be told how great he is by his coach; he wants to be coached to become a better player. And that's the bottom line, with any of us.

'I had no problem taking the hit and letting everyone else know that I wasn't happy about taking the hit. Because it would have sent out a message to everyone. I'm not annoyed with yourself and Seánie for battling my case, but this is a back-down from management now. The boys have backed down and they're probably not going to drop anyone. I bet you no one will be dropped now, including Mully. I think they missed a glorious opportunity to be ruthless and drop three or four of us. To really shake things up.

'Now, if we win on Friday we'll have a four- or five-week lay-off and there's going to be more disruption because lads will get side-tracked again with football or some other thing. I was at the wrong end of a bad call, but I was willing to take my medicine and use it wisely to get us going again. And I feel that there needs to be a clear-the-air meeting because the way we're going, we're just going to fuck away the chance of winning a county title.'

The following morning, I was greeted at the door by the postman, John Williams, who is also the Corofin hurling goalkeeper. 'Ye're a cute crowd, bringing an All-Star out of retirement to try and win the Canon Hamilton,' he said to me. 'The whole place is talking about it.'

It was the *Clare People*'s back-page story this morning. Jamesie is definitely back now anyway.

12. Let the Healing Begin

Here we go again. Despite everything that has happened over the last few days, you can still almost sense complacency infecting us like a virus in the lead-up to our last group game, against Broadford. Even though Newmarket and ourselves are the only two teams to have won our opening three games, six points probably won't be enough to put us straight through to the quarter-finals. A defeat to Broadford and we're more than likely back into the pit for a play-off.

Three days ago, a blind man could have seen that the attitude wasn't right: some lads were just slobbering through the drills, almost as if waiting for closing time of the game on Friday. I was doing my own goalkeeping training on the other pitch with Paul Madden and Mikey Rosingrave and I didn't feel involved enough with the group to suddenly arrive with the sirens flashing and start lecturing them. At one stage I went into the dressing room for my puckout hurley and Ken Kennedy followed me in. He wasn't training because he was nursing a hamstring strain from the weekend's game.

'You need to say something to them,' he said. 'They're all over the place.'

'Jesus, Ken, guys are sick to the teeth of listening to me,' I said. 'Maybe someone else will sense it and knock it on the head.' Nobody did.

We have three wins, but it's mind-blowing how we seem to think that the job is done in the group, especially after such an insipid performance against Ogonnelloe two weeks ago. On Wednesday morning, Seánie McMahon rang me – he'd been to the cryotherapy clinic the previous evening because he's been struggling to shake off a strain in his back.

'Lookit, we're blue in the face from talking about this stuff, but it has to come from you now tomorrow night,' I said to him. 'Just lay it on the fucking line to them. If they don't listen to you, we can forget about it.'

Before training on Thursday evening, Seánie spelled it out as clearly as he could. 'It's the same fucking story with us again. We're gone casual and we've absolutely no reason to. We think the job is done, and it's not. We went into a group game against Corofin two years ago with the same bullshit attitude and we were beaten. Our Under-21s went into a quarter-final last year against Meelick-Parteen in a game that we should have won by ten points and we were turned over because we weren't mentally ready for it. From now until tomorrow evening, we get ourselves steeled for an unmerciful battle. And we come to the battle ready to fight for our lives.'

Those comments are nothing the lads haven't heard from Seánie before, but his authority and immense standing as a player always lend huge weight to his words. He rarely raises his voice when he speaks but you can almost read the passion and emotion in the creases of his face.

It's always impossible to speak after Seánie, but I just wanted to re-emphasize one point. Our senior footballers are out in the championship next Tuesday, and if they win that game they're out then again the following Friday.

'Look,' I said, 'if we get dragged into a play-off, we're absolutely fucked. We'll be playing hurling and football games on the same weekend, and guys won't be able to walk. Our season will be as good as over.'

I travelled into Cusack Park on Friday evening with Jamesie and Mikey Rosingrave. It was the first time that Jamesie was togging out for a game in the Park since the 2004 county final. As we entered the gate, the groundsman Martin Flanagan spotted him.

'Hey, I've put ye in the dressing room closest to the gate. So you won't have to walk as far.'

The team wasn't named until we arrived in the dressing room, and it was a strange selection. Management were obviously trying to shake things up, but it reminded me of what our physio, Eugene

Moynihan, had said to me a couple of weeks earlier: that guys didn't really know where they stood and that the uncertainty was affecting players' form and confidence. Competition is the lifeblood of any squad, but we're not Kilkenny, and Eugene had a point. I got the impression that management felt we'd have enough to beat Broadford even with a risky selection. And if things did start going against us, we'd just empty the bench to finish off the job.

Traditionally, Broadford would have been renowned as a tough east Clare outfit. But this was a young and skilful team who had just come up from intermediate and who should have beaten Sixmilebridge in their previous game. Our approach was simple: we wanted to physically bully them off the field.

'Warm up the shoulders, lads, because we're going to be using them,' Ken said in the huddle just before we left the dressing room. 'Let's frighten these guys.'

'Loads of people around the county are saying all week that there's going to be one big upset at the weekend,' roared Patsy. 'Well, there's going to be no upset here.'

We started well and were four points up after 20 minutes until we gave away a ridiculous 20-metre free. Niall White fouled his man 30 metres from goal and then protested by throwing his hurley on the ground and the referee moved the ball in ten metres. Craig Chaplin buried it.

We got a goal back almost immediately and were in a good position at the break. Three points up and with the breeze at our backs to come. Then we went out in the second half and capitulated.

It was one of the most disheartening half-hours of hurling we've produced in living memory. They got a run on us and we just basically lay down and let them walk all over us. They hit four successive points before we had our first score of the half from a free to level it up. Then Conor Hassett was red-carded for an off-the-ball offence.

Management had sprung Jamesie from the bench to try and rescue a perilous situation. The first chance I got, I hit him with a short puckout to midfield and the shot he took went barely twenty yards.

They pushed on and went ahead again with a couple of minutes remaining. They would have been out of sight if they'd converted half their chances, and we couldn't buy a score. The last five minutes were like a slow march to madness.

Two minutes into injury time, Chaplin had a free near the sideline from about 70 metres to close out the game. The ball appeared to have the distance but it was hanging in the breeze and was dropping close to the crossbar at an awkward height. Ken was roaring at me to let it go wide but I couldn't be sure that it wasn't going to dip – and anyway, I knew if the ball went dead that the game was over. So I batted the ball out to the side to keep the game alive and give us one last chance to go down the field and get the equalizer to put us through.

We had a couple of chances to clear it but their corner-forward muscled his way into the tackle and eventually won the ball. He squared it to their wing-forward and he put the ball over the bar to put them two ahead. I could hear Ken roaring at me as I quickly gathered the ball, but the second I pucked it out, the referee blew the final whistle. Then Ken cut loose. 'You cost us the game. For fuck's sake, that ball was going wide, what the hell were you at? You just cost us the game.'

I shook hands with a couple of Broadford players but there was only one thing on my mind as I left the field: 'I'm not accepting that shit.'

Ken was just about to enter the showers when I got into the dressing room and I went straight in after him.

'Get away from me,' he said.

'No, you hold on a minute here, you're out of order,' I responded.

'Shut up to fuck, will you, you're back-answering lads all day and I'm not listening to it any more.'

'What are you raving about? Is giving lads advice and telling them to follow their men now back-answering? No, you shut the fuck up and listen to me.'

He tried to push past me but I put my hand on his chest and stopped him. All the while, players were awkwardly passing us by as they entered or left the shower area and I was aware that this was a show

that the team didn't need at this point. Still, I wasn't letting Ken away
with it because he'd have just brushed it aside if I left it until the next
training session to address it.

'I was trying to do the right thing for the team. I couldn't be sure
if that ball was going wide and I have a split second to decide. I can't
let anyone else make up my mind, only myself. And anyway, I was
trying to do the right thing for the team by keeping the ball in play.'

'But they scored a point from it.'

'It doesn't matter a fuck if they scored five goals from it, it's the
same thing to be beaten by twenty points as it is by one point. As
soon as that ball went dead, the game was over.'

Ken just walked into the showers, but I was glad I'd had my say. A
couple of minutes later, after I had towelled down I was entering the
dressing room when I saw Danny Chaplin, the Broadford manager,
standing in the middle of the room. He's a genuine hurling man, but
then I caught wind of his words. 'This is a massive win for us. Not
just because it keeps our season alive but because it's against the
standard-bearers of Clare hurling.'

Holy Christ, I just turned around and went straight back into the
showers. No offence to Danny Chaplin, but we're no longer the
standard-bearers of Clare hurling and that's the last thing we need to
be listening to. There was a time when we'd have beaten the pick of
east Clare, when Broadford might have been lucky to have three
players on the team. But not any more. At the moment, we wouldn't
beat 15 Katy Barrys.

The mood was desperate inside in the dressing room. Raw, edgy,
internal tension – the worst kind. You could nearly peel it off the
walls. Anger with management, anger with the performance. Basically, a bunch of guys just seriously pissed off. And in a mean mood.
If somebody had said the wrong thing out loud, God only knows
what could have happened.

Personally, I was disgusted with the performance. It's bad enough
to be beaten, but the manner of the defeat was soul-destroying.
They'd blown us off the pitch in the second half with their pace and
the speed of their hurling, but the bottom line was that a crowd of

young lads had just rolled over us. And that's a sickening feeling for a team regarded as one of the most physically powerful in the county.

Jamesie and I didn't speak a word as we made our way back to the car. Just as we were sitting in, I smiled to him. 'Welcome back. I'd say you're glad you signed back up for this shit.' Then I changed tone. 'I know what you're going to say about that incident in the showers. I know you're not impressed, but he was out of order and I wasn't letting him away with it.'

I informed Jamesie of the context and just left it at that. I drove him out to Gurteen, because he had to collect his car, and we just sat talking for half an hour. The more we chatted, the heavier the mood got. He had come down to me from the stand just before he came on as a substitute to instruct me to go shorter with the puckouts. I was just telling him now that part of the reason I was going long was because guys weren't tuned in and that their first touch was so poor that the ball was more than likely to go back over my head if I went short.

'Yeah, you're probably right. You're not dealing with the likes of [Ger] Hoey and [Ciaran] O'Neill now, who you know are always going to be tuned in.'

Jamesie was only back training three weeks but he had seen enough to convince him of how far off the pace we really were.

'How many guys are really hurting tonight? How badly do guys really want it?' There was no need for an answer.

Then he talked about the training. 'I'm only back a few weeks and I'm well able for it. There's not half enough intensity. We were doing a drill the other night and lads were nearly standing around getting cold. There's not enough pace to the sessions.'

'You need to say it to Fahey now,' I said to him. 'It has more authority if it comes from you. You need to say it to him about taking more of a coaching role if you're not going to be considered as a starter.'

'Well, a lot of what we need now can't be coached,' he responded. 'Lads either want it or they don't, and I don't know if they really want it.'

About ten minutes later, Patsy pulled in to Gurteen. He dropped

Steve Whyte off near the AstroTurf and then he spun back down in our direction. 'Now's your chance,' I said to Jamesie. 'Say it to him.'

Patsy rolled down the window and just lifted his eyes to heaven. He's four years younger than Jamesie and three years younger than me. He's a close friend of ours and we didn't want to seem like we were talking down to him. But he's the coach now and he has to take a large share of responsibility for the performance.

I cleaned the chamber while Jamesie loaded the bullet. I mentioned the gamble of the selection and Patsy defended it. A minute later, Jamesie pulled the trigger. 'There's not enough intensity to the training, Patsy. We need to be doing more. We need to be working harder.'

In fairness to Patsy, he took it on board. Numbers had been a problem, but that shouldn't be an issue from now on. Just before he left, he asked Jamesie to do a bit more coaching. He said he would.

As I was driving home, I was thinking of Jamesie's inglorious return. The main reason he had come back was to try and help the club win a championship and to honour Ger Hoey's memory. And now this. When he did come on in the game, there was barely a murmur. Our supporters were so concerned with our form that they barely even noticed him. Or else they felt that we hadn't given them the entitlement to cheer and welcome back one of our greatest ever players. To be honest, I almost felt embarrassed for him. His leg still isn't right and, from talking to him in the car, I know his heart isn't in it. And I'm sure he's just disgusted that the standards that the likes of he and Ger Hoey set for this club have slipped so drastically.

By the time I got home, I was still in dire form. The manner of the defeat was one thing, but we're not playing well enough to win a championship.

For a couple of years, playing senior championship matches had almost become torturous. We hadn't enough quality forwards to put up big scores, so every match was a dogfight to the wire. You always relish a battle, but it was becoming tedious, almost like a dour football struggle in winter. Then last year we were liberated. We were fitter than we are now and were playing much sharper hurling. We were posting big scores, and four of our seven championship matches were effectively over with 15 minutes remaining. Now it's back to the same old stuff again. Dour, low-scoring dogfights. Of course there's a real element of honour in winning those games, but they make you weary as well. And now we're more than likely going to have two more battles in a play-off to make the quarter-finals.

The lads were going into town that night but I couldn't be bothered to join them. I was like a lunatic for the rest of the evening and Olivia eventually let me have it. 'If it's going to have this much of an effect on you, just pack it in,' she said. 'It can't be worth it.'

The incident with Ken was still bothering me, but deep in my heart I was beginning to admit that the wheels were coming off the track and that the dream was over. We weren't playing well enough. We didn't deserve anything with our commitment. You always try and stay positive, but it's still difficult to avoid the unavoidable: that we're just not good enough any more; that we just don't have enough in the tank; that we just don't want it enough any more. And that's a real bitch of a feeling.

Around 4 p.m. the following day, Conny rang me. A meeting had been arranged between players and management for tomorrow evening. 'It's going to be a fucking bloodletting,' he said. 'Some of the boys are going to cut loose.'

Then an hour later, he rang me back. 'Did you hear the result in the 'Bridge–Ballyea game?'

'No.'

'A draw.'

We're through.

The meeting was still going ahead, though. It was just as well, because red flags had been popping up all over the place. Emmett Whelan had reportedly left the panel because he'd been substituted 11 minutes after he'd been brought on. Yet he was only just back from eight months in Australia and had got game time ahead of guys who'd been training all year. The word on the ground was that Cathal O'Sullivan was also jumping ship. He wasn't long back from six weeks travelling in South-east Asia, but he felt he was still being pun-ished for breaking the drinking curfew last weekend. Moreover, management told him he was only being considered for a midfield place when he'd been a career defender.

The previous evening, Damien Kennedy and Davy Hoey had nearly come to blows. Damo made some remark about management, Hoey countered by criticizing his performance, and somebody had to step in between them. Poison was seeping into the camp from every angle. The father of one of the players on the bench had con-fronted Patsy immediately after the game, just as he was coming into the tunnel. He told him that the performance reflected how he ran his team. Patsy just kept walking.

Conny rang me back again on Sunday to tell me that some of the boys were bitching like a flock of gossiping women. One of them had told him that he should open fire on management over how he was treated in the lead-up to the game. He said that he'd call to collect me for the meeting at 8 p.m.

'I'm not going to be a fool for anyone,' he said on the way out to Gurteen in his jeep. 'The boys want me to do their dirty work for them but I'll cut that off at the Khyber Pass. I'll be one of the first to speak and I'm going to be pro-management here tonight.'

Almost everyone on the panel was present. Whelan and Colm Mullen were absent, and John Carmody opened the meeting on that point. He outlined how Whelan had dropped three balls and had mistimed two passes and he said he was sorry that Whelan wasn't around to discuss those reasons why he'd been taken off.

Then he broadened the point. 'Some of the stuff that I've heard since Friday night has disgusted me. I've heard numerous times that the best team we had out was above in the stand. All this kind of shit. The reason we're here is to get it out in the open. If anyone has a grievance, we're all big enough to deal with it and address it.'

He wasn't holding back. Although the player whose father had lectured Patsy was no more than a few feet away from him, Carmody said that he'd bitten his lip at the time. But that if he did it again, he'd 'do time for him'.

Carmody said that he could justify the team selection and he went through every player individually and outlined the reason he'd started. As for the guys on the bench, he said that some of them hadn't been considered because of injury, while more hadn't taken their chance to nail down a place over the last few weeks. With regard to Greg Lyons more or less hopping off a plane after three months in the USA and being brought on, Carmody was unequivocal. 'Greg is one of our best players. We were thinking of a quarter-final and that's the reason we needed to get him on the field.' In his opinion, Paul Dullaghan was the only player in the room who had a reason to feel hard done by. And he'd been concussed in a football game the previous week.

In his eyes, this was coming down the tracks a mile off. He was right when he said that the only time we had full numbers on the pitch was the Thursday evening session before the Ogonnelloe and Broadford games. Not getting enough bodies on the pitch had largely contributed to our recent performances.

'I have a wife, three kids and a business,' said Carmody. 'My kids are involved in hurling, football, athletics and loads of other stuff. I'm involved with a camogie team and another underage team, but I can still make time for this team because I have given ye a commitment. Guys are making excuses not to come to training when they should be making excuses *to* come to training. And some of ye have fuck-all on when you consider what other lads have on. Ye have absolutely no excuse in the world not to be here.

'Look around ye! Look at the players that are here! Jeez, this championship is here for ye. There are only about three or four decent teams left. Newmarket are the team to beat, but they still have to prove that if they hit the wall again, they can get over it. Clonlara have a very good side but they don't have much beyond their first 15. But to win a championship, you need to be fucking savage, and ye're gone soft. There's no meanness there. We didn't break a hurley against Broadford. Eoin, did we even break a hurley?'

'No, I didn't throw in one stick,' said Conny, who'd been handling the replacement hurleys on the far sideline.

'We're going nowhere until we get bodies on the field again. This is yere club, lads. Let's just come together and let's fucking do it.'

Before Patsy spoke you could read from his body language how much he was hurting. 'I've been with other clubs, lads, but it does hurt a lot more when it's your own club. I've taken some stuff on board since Friday. The intensity and fitness has to come up in training, but it's been difficult to draw up sessions with the footballers playing as well. Our forward play has been a real problem but Jamesie is going to do some work on that, and we just have to keep our heads now and start working hard again.'

As team captain, Darragh O'Driscoll had clearly come prepared. He had a sheet of paper on his lap and his notes were written under four headings: Attitude, Workrate, Attendance, Bitching. He addressed each point intelligently and constructively and he reaffirmed Jamesie's concern about training not being intense enough. There needed to be more games of backs-and-forwards or conditioned games in training.

When it came to discussing management's performance, there was one dominant theme which Darragh had gathered from the group. Discipline.

'The feedback I'm getting is that some players were getting disciplined and others weren't and that discipline needs to be more equitable.'

Darragh encouraged everyone to speak, and after a brief silence of about 30 seconds, Conny stepped up.

'Last Friday was the first time since 2000 that I didn't get a senior jersey and I was really pissed off when I was told. But then I looked at it and said that management were probably right because I hadn't been doing enough. There are plenty of guys here not doing enough, but all I'm listening to is bitching. Sure that isn't worth a fuck to anyone. Where is that going to get you? Where would it get me? If you have a problem, store it in your locker and then bring it to training with you tomorrow night and the night after and the night after. The guy that has your jersey, rip his fucking head off in training to get it back. Let him have it. Rough him up. Walk down on top of him if you have to. And if you get your chance in a challenge game, make sure you don't waste it.'

Seánie was sitting right beside Conny and he felt Carmody had been too soft in some of his assessments. 'From one to seven we were excellent the other night but from there up, it just wasn't good enough. I'm up that end of the field and what I have done is just not good enough. What we're doing will not be enough to win us a championship.'

Ken's grievances had a longer history than Friday's game. 'No disrespect to Ballybrown but it was a disgrace that an intermediate team should be beating us by ten points in a challenge game the week before a championship match. They're a decent side but that was ridiculous. I said at half-time that we need to start burying goals and you [Carmody] said that we were doing fine, and there was no way that we were. We need to turn into Kilkenny. Start burying teams. We're too nice. Anyone who comes in around me, I'll fucking nail them, but that's my job and that's the bitterness we have inside in the full-back line. But don't be telling us as backs that we're great either because we haven't met a set of forwards that can open us up. When we meet a Newmarket or a Clonlara, then we'll see how good we are. But we won't even get that far unless we really harden up and just get mean in training. We're not at the pace required. We should have beaten the shit out of Broadford but I don't think we're learning much from the challenge games we're playing. We can only learn from playing challenge games against the top teams like Portumna.'

There was a time when we didn't have to look for a challenge game against the top club sides in Munster and Galway because they were the ones looking for a game off us. But we don't have the currency to trade in that market any more. Portumna wouldn't waste their time playing us now because they'd wipe us out. We played them up in Portumna three years ago, six weeks after they won their first All-Ireland, and they were just toying with us two weeks before we played our opening championship match. Patsy said that he'd been on to their manager Johnny Kelly trying to arrange a challenge game, but having a big name as a club isn't enough to get their attention any more.

The discussion began to focus on the weakness of our forward play, but the same voices were dominating the discussion. Seánie had reiterated the importance of young players having their say and he mentioned an article which had appeared in the *Sunday Times* that morning. It was an extract from Alan English's new book on Ireland's rugby Grand Slam, which detailed how Rob Kearney had spoken up at a meeting about how the Munster players seemed to show more passion with their province than they did with Ireland. 'A young fella of 22 put it up to the likes of O'Connell and O'Gara and these boys and it was a major turning point,' said Seánie. 'We need that input here. We need to hear what ye're thinking.'

I suspected that wasn't going to happen, so I increased the pressure. 'OK, *everyone* here has to talk. We'll put a two-minute limit on it, but just say what's on your mind.'

I knew the two-minute limit was too ambitious, and that we'd probably be here for another two hours, but there was no other way around it. I knew guys that were there who hadn't spoken, and who weren't going to speak, but who had festering issues.

It was obvious from the outset that there wouldn't be any holding back. Marty O'Regan lectured Conor Hassett on getting sent off and it opened up another debate. 'A Broadford guy hit you the other night and you took the bait, Hass. You need to be cuter. That was pure headless stuff. You're our one inter-county player. You need to be leading us.'

Then Darragh weighed in on that subject. He reckoned that we'd turned a load of referees in Clare against us with our on-field bitching. There are definitely a couple of referees out there that have it in for us. We experienced that first hand last year in one championship match when two umpires told me before half-time to warn our backs and our management about the amount of bitching to the referee. When umpires are thinking along those lines, you know you're in trouble, and in the second half the referee made some decisions against us that were a disgrace.

When Jamesie spoke, that was the first point he touched on. He addressed Niall White for the manner in which he conceded the free, and the extra yards, which resulted in Broadford's goal on Friday. 'Whitey, that's just not good enough. That kind of petulance has crept into this club and it is visible in some of our underage teams. It needs to be cut out.' Then he turned on Carmody and told him that his assessment was too meek and that we needed to grasp reality.

Ivor Whyte was next to get a sideswipe from Jamesie. 'You wasted too much ball. Something always good happens with your man [Seánie] inside and you were just hitting it over his head. Five points from play in a challenge against Ballybrown doesn't give you a licence to shoot for points with every ball.'

He was clearly in a mood to keep going.

'Is Mully here?' He wasn't. Jamesie looked over to the corner to Davy Hoey. 'What you and Mully did at half-time was a disgrace.'

Mullen and Hoey had gone down to the tunnel at half-time for a cigarette. Jamesie paused for about five seconds. 'Jesus, we need you. This team needs you.'

He was clearly on a roll so he just kept going. 'Lookit, I didn't think I should have been brought on the other evening. I have a 50 per cent tear on my cruciate ligament and the surgeon told me that it's not a matter of *if* I might tear it but *when* I might do so. I'm not going to win anything for ye. When I was asked back, I thought about Ger dying and this being such an important year for the club, but I don't get that sense. Like how badly do guys really want this? We can go on about forward play and that – and I will do what I can – but the bottom line was that we were outfought by Broadford. And that is unforgivable. They wanted it more than us. If we do nothing else this year, we have to make sure that that doesn't happen again. There is something noble and honourable about going out if you're beaten by a better team, but there is something sickening about just bowing out. And that's the real sickening thing about the past for some of us: that there were years there when we just didn't do things right and we weren't mentally right and that was the reason we didn't win things. Not because we weren't good enough. I was involved with a Flannan's team with Shane [O'Connor] last year and we got beaten in a Harty Cup quarter-final but I never enjoyed being involved with a team as much because they were so honest and we got the most out of them. That is what it's all about.'

There was a real hush when he spoke. Not just because of his standing within the club but because of why he'd come back. Jamesie didn't need to come back after four years away. He had done it all. What was in it for him? He was only risking his knee and his reputation. Some of the younger guys should have been grateful that they were getting the chance to play and train with him instead of bitching about not getting game-time.

Seán Flynn, who along with Conor Redmond is the best young leader we have in the club, had no problem elaborating on the need for the younger players to assume more responsibility in the squad. Enda Lyons had spoken earlier about some of the dual players being young guys who 'needed breaks' from training. That was Flynn's starting point.

'The five lads who were taken off the other night were not taken off because they're young lads or because the older lads or management don't rate them. We just need to harden the fuck up.' Then he looked over to Enda in the corner. 'We need to harden the fuck up.'

By the time it came to my turn to speak, I looked over at Ken. He had his head down, but I just wanted to explain to the group the reason for our blow-up in the dressing rooms.

'You know how much time I have for you. And if you have any problem with what I'm going to say, you can have your response after I've finished talking. Everybody here knows that you'd probably kill me if you hit me a belt, but I wouldn't have been happy with myself if I had let it pass. The bottom line here is that we all back one another up. The last thing I always say to you before every game is that you back me up 100 per cent and that I'll back you up 100 per cent.'

Ken nodded back to me and I kept going.

'That unity has to be there with all of us. When Munster won the Heineken Cup in 2006, they conceded a try to Biarritz in the first two minutes because John Kelly missed a basic tackle that led to a try. When they were all under the post, he said that he had got it wrong and that it wouldn't happen again. They all rallied behind him and drove him on, and that was the way it had to be.

'There's just one other thing I need to get out in the open here. Do lads have a problem with some of my talking during games? I need to know. There was one incident in the 'Bridge match when a ball came off the upright and I was roaring at Marty that his man was right on him and he went to pick it. Marty and Hoey fucked me out of it and Ken told me that I was frightening lads on the ball. I never fuck lads out of it if they make a mistake but maybe I am a bit over the top, and if lads feel that I am, let me know.

'I'm just trying to get the organization right at the back and ye all know I can see what ye can't. There was one incident the last day when I was roaring at Mark [Hallinan] to come back into the hole and Hoey was telling me to leave him on the wing, but Mark caught a great ball and I'm just trying to make sure that space is covered. It's basic zonal defensive stuff. That's the reason I'm always calling somebody back into the line beside me for long-range frees or sidelines. Because if one of the full-back line gets dragged out, the guy on the line can cover the space so I don't have to leave my line. That's just basic teamwork. And if that guy clears the ball, I'll encourage him to the last. I'll drive him on. And if he misses it, I'll still drive him on because that's the unity that's required.

'Look, ye all know how much this means to me and I'm not going to go back into it again. I want this so badly that at times it nearly frightens me. I get more nervous now than I ever did because I know the end is coming for me. But that is what it's all about. That is the juice, playing with your best friends. Seánie and James and Darragh and Ken. The buzz is still winning with your best friends. I don't know what the hell I'll do when I pack it up; I'll probably go stone fucking crazy. What we have to do now is just give it our all. Let's just give everything for eight weeks of our lives now because we'll never forgive ourselves if we don't put it in and that's the reason we don't win a county title. If we're not good enough, fair enough. But let's not have any regrets. I said it to ye at our last meeting that what's driving me on is the vision of the final whistle in the county final when we're county champions and all the emotion inside me will come out then like a geyser. Just get me there. Let's all get there together.'

When Noel Brodie had spoken, halfway through the meeting, he touched on one specific topic. He mentioned the famous speech given by the Al Pacino character, Tony LaMotta, in the film *Any Given Sunday*. Brodie didn't refer to the popular line about fighting for the inches that make the difference between winning and losing, between living and dying. He focused instead on the line where LaMotta says, '. . . either we heal as a team or we are going to crumble', that 'we are in hell right now and we can stay here and get the shit kicked out of us or we can fight our way back into the light'. Brodie's words are probably just what we need to hear right now. 'We have hit the bottom of the barrel now and we can't go any lower,' he said. 'And we need to heal as a team now before we can go forward.'

The process is to begin with training tomorrow, and Brian O'Reilly will be back on Wednesday night to work on our fitness. The next month is going to be hard work, but we need to get back fighting for those inches, and tearing ourselves and everyone else around us to pieces for that inch. And there's a lot of healing to be done along the way.

13. Top Dogs

Life has a way of coming back to bite you in the ass. The win rate on our puckout statistics has been dire in our last couple of games and some of the senior players have been locked into a disagreement with management about changing policy. Our strategy of going long the majority of the time just hasn't been working and, in an attempt to convince management of an alternative, Jamesie walked us through a forward-play and puckout-strategy session on the underage pitch last week. Given that it takes roughly three to four seconds for a ball to drop when it's struck long, giving defenders and midfielders sufficient time to get coverage, our preferred puckout strategy now is to go short or else create a two-on-one scenario on the break through clearly defined signals.

We played Kinvara in a challenge game last night, and as soon as Jamesie came on as a substitute in the second half I drilled him with a short puckout inside our own half. In the process of catching it, he chipped a bone and dislocated his thumb. In any case, he's gone for the rest of the season.

I know there's an element of relief for him, because he wasn't enjoying it. His knee is still giving him trouble and he hasn't the same fireproof confidence in himself any more because he just doesn't have the fitness and hurling work done. In his mind, playing competitive hurling is no longer something that motivates him, and he doesn't deserve the indignity of being possibly cleaned out by some ravenous young gun, voraciously intent on taking Jamesie O'Connor's scalp. He was risking more serious long-term damage to his knee by coming back, but he was willing to take that chance to help us try and win a county title to honour Ger Hoey's memory. Jamesie doesn't have to prove anything to anyone as a hurler, but at least he tried. And everyone respects him more for it.

'When I think of it now,' he said a few days later, 'I wonder, was it me coming back because I really wanted to, or was it me coming back because people wanted me to come back? And to be honest, it was probably the latter. There's no way I wanted it as much as I used to. I've three kids, my knee still isn't right. And it's a young man's game now.

'I wasn't ready for the Broadford game but, to be honest, I think my vision of what I could do and management's vision didn't seem to concur. I maybe saw myself playing corner-forward off Seánie. Get the ball into him and I'd work off him. Maybe manufacture a free close to goal, or make an intelligent run, and if I got the ball in my hand I'd have had a good chance of popping it over. But suddenly I'm on wing-forward against Ballybrown and I'm a target for puckouts. It was the same against Broadford. I came on at centre-forward against Kinvara. I just wasn't able for that any more.

'Even the meeting we had after the Broadford game, I was kinda asking myself what am I doing here because I've been at so many of those clear-the-air meetings over the years. I'm nearly sick of them at this stage and I was saying to myself that I'm not back long enough to start giving out to fellas. I wasn't going to speak at all, but then you said that everyone had to speak. So after I started, I decided to get some stuff off my chest about a couple of players' commitment and attitude. You hope that you get the right response afterwards and that fellas take it in the right way, but I'm not really sure if that's the case. Ten or twelve years ago, there was a real hunger there and the players we had left no stone unturned to win for Doora-Barefield. Unfortunately, I'm not sure if that's the case any more.

'When you said it to me going down in the car to the Cork–Tipp game that ye were going to do everything ye could to win it for Ger, I suppose I just wanted to try and help ye out. I should have finished it there and then in the car – told you no way, that it wasn't going to happen. But I suppose the competitor was still there in me, Ger was a great friend and I was curious as well as to whether I could still maybe do it. And I just couldn't.'

We've all accepted now that Jamesie is gone, but he's still going to be a loss to us because we've been haemorrhaging players in the last few weeks. Conor Hassett received a one-match suspension from his straight red card in the Broadford game, so he's definitely out for the quarter-final. Davy Hoey and Kevin Dilleen are both doubtful with injury, while the possibility of getting Joe Considine back disappeared after he broke his jaw in a football match. Greg Lyons is in college in Edinburgh, Niall White always seems to be working nights, while Shane O'Connor was laid low with an infection and has been concentrating his time with the minor footballers.

In fairness to Emmet Whelan, he returned to the panel a few days after the Broadford game. He is another serious option for us now but there isn't the overflow of training players provided by the juniors any more because they recently exited the championship. The dual players have to play Liscannor in a senior football relegation semi-final the week before the hurling quarter-final and, all of a sudden, our training numbers are way too low for this stage of the season.

The Kinvara game also proved that we're still off the pace. We began well but shipped 2-2 in five minutes before the break and completely lost our way in the second half, eventually losing 2-17 to 0-14. Management had the match recorded – some guy was perched on top of a white van with his camera and tripod – and it was agreed afterwards that different groups would meet up to watch the game. 'Watch the second half first and get the bad stuff out of the way, because we did a lot of good things in the first half,' said John Carmody afterwards.

Although we've had the whole year to prepare, the quarter-final is closing in quickly now. We were supposed to play on 26 September, but the fantastic All-Ireland success of the Clare U-21 hurlers shoved that date back until 4 October. Of the six teams we could meet – Clonlara, Clooney-Quin, Cratloe, Inagh-Kilnamona, Kilmaley and Newmarket – the bookies would probably give us a realistic chance of beating three of those sides.

Yet, with the exception of Newmarket – and they haven't won a county title since 1981 – none of those sides would be seen in Clare as traditional powerhouses. Four of the six clubs we could meet were all intermediate clubs within the last decade, while the remaining quarter-finalists, Broadford, were last year's intermediate champions.

We're probably the biggest name left in the competition now, but we're viewed as a legitimate target by anyone.

When I spoke to Patsy a couple of days after the Kinvara game, we both agreed that the one team we'd like to avoid was Cratloe. We had physically bullied them around Clareabbey last year, but our concern was that a team of young speedsters would just run us off the pitch in Cusack Park. 'You know, a part of me wants Clonlara in the quarter-final,' said Patsy. 'Just to help us focus guys' minds.' Clonlara are the reigning champions.

He just shook his head and sighed in exasperation. At the moment, the man is nearly broken. Disillusioned almost beyond belief. 'One year of this and I'm out,' he said. 'I just can't take it any more. This job would wreck your head.'

The job that he had craved is now cracking his morale and splintering his spirit. Managing Doora-Barefield means everything to Patsy but, as the year has progressed, he has struggled to separate the reality of management from kinship and friendship. He feels increasingly let down by the lack of loyalty and respect shown to him by some players who he regards as close friends. He's been burned from chasing players and deflated from a basic lack of courtesy that any manager deserves. The expected protocol from any player who can't attend training or a challenge match is to text or call a member of management. But some guys have consistently ignored that consideration.

'There's always someone missing, somebody always has an excuse,' said Patsy. 'Lads have said that they'll do whatever it takes, but they won't. They're all fucking talk. I'm just sick of it. Guys just don't want it. With the tragedy that's gone on in the club this year, guys should be busting themselves. But they're just not willing to do it. I'm telling you, when some of the senior players go, this club is in real trouble. Serious trouble.

'We haven't dropped the hammer on guys but there's been no comeback. Some guys are still boozing, they just can't stay in at weekends. We got hammered for going to the Aran Islands on our pre-planned bonding weekend and people were blaming it for us getting relegated. Only two of the team which started that game against Clarecastle were on that trip; but some serious drinking went on at home that weekend, which nobody knew about. Well, we found out about it. There was a wedding and a party on and some guys didn't spare themselves. If drink was the cause of us getting relegated – and I don't think it was the reason – it was the drinking that went on in Ennis. Not the Aran Islands.'

He's so frustrated at the moment that he spoke to Liam Griffin – the former Wexford manager – yesterday in an attempt to find some ideas on how to manage the current situation. 'I just can't get my head around it at the moment,' said Patsy. 'And neither can John Carmody. He just can't understand why some guys don't want to make more of an effort. They're putting it in but they're not really prepared to go the extra mile that is required to win at this level. We probably should have let some guys go, got rid of them. But what do you do then? Where are we going to get them? I'm sure it's the same in most clubs.'

Some of us have challenged a few of the serial offenders who have been skipping sessions, but what can be really achieved if you have to go chasing guys? If they don't want to come training, how badly do they really want to play or win? Can you totally rely on them when the real heat arrives during a game? Coaxing players to train is soul-destroying.

Despite the size of Doora-Barefield, our lack of underage hurling success and our booming underage football culture have made it more difficult for young players to make that transition to adult hurling. As a result, we don't have enough numbers coming through to foster competition and put sufficient pressure on established players. In that context, we can't really discard prominent or young players for their lack of commitment because it could threaten our existence as a senior hurling club. Rewarding commitment and giving opportunities to more peripheral and honest players would be the noble way to go, but very few managers see the valour or merit in taking that chance with a team capable of winning a county title.

You'd often wonder, is it just us? Are we unique in that we have struggled in recent years to get fellas to train over the summer? I don't think we are, because you hear clubs all around the country talking about the same problems, especially when their season is at the mercy of the county team. After the great Limerick hurler Steve McDonagh retired from inter-county hurling, he said that he learned more in his first two years back with Bruree than he had in 12 years with Limerick. The experience and struggles he discovered at club level really opened his eyes, and his observation could act as a metaphor for many clubs around the country.

'Young lads now are affluent and it's not reasonable to expect them to do what lads did ten years ago,' said McDonagh after Bruree won their first county title under their own name in 2006. 'They go off to concerts or stags during the summer and it would drive you wild at times. But what can you do? You have to let them go. In the ideal world, you wouldn't want to bend the rules but we don't have any choice in rural Ireland when you depend on everybody. It would be very easy to fall out with fellas. You can't really crack the whip any more.'

We're not a rural club and may have a vastly bigger population than Bruree, but that doesn't necessarily mean that we have more playing numbers. The progression we have made from a largely rural parish to an increasingly urban one has diluted our identity. Our U-16 keeper, Aaron Landy, a great lad who sometimes trains with the senior keepers, told me recently that some young hurlers his age in the club are just more interested in football, soccer and rugby and hanging out with their friends in town.

After our U-21s were beaten in March, Patsy asked them to stay involved in the club, because the U-21 campaign was only a stepping stone to hurling with the junior and senior teams in Doora-Barefield. But more than half of that squad hasn't picked up a hurley since then. A couple of weeks ago, I had a chat about that issue with John Carmody, who was able to assess those difficulties from the perspective of being from another club. 'It's a huge problem here, and the club really needs to look at its structures,' he said. 'Because, from what I can see, a lot of the young lads from 21 down don't have any sense of what being part of a club really means.'

You look on other clubs with real envy at times. Clubs where hurling and football is almost what defines their existence. At times, you'd feel that such a level of commitment could lead to a degree of insularity and deprive a parish of a more open-minded outlook. But it guarantees a phenomenal community spirit and a booming culture of player participation.

Our problem may arise in part from our relocation from our traditional base in Roslevan, which is now at the heart of an urban centre. Estates mushroomed and no ancillary facilities were provided. The only real green area was the pitch in Roslevan, but that's gone now, so there is no focal point where young kids can meet. Gurteen is the only option, but the facility sits on the periphery of the parish.

Construction on our new clubhouse will begin next year and, at a recent meeting with the minor club executive about hiring the new coach, the minor treasurer, Seánie Lyons, made an excellent point. He spoke about setting aside an area – with a couple of pool tables, a dartboard, and a coffee dock – for young players to hang out and spend time around the club before and after training. It's an excellent idea – it would provide the kids with a focal point and strengthen their identification with the club.

When we were growing up, and were sometimes engaged in a battle against certain clubs from east and south Clare, they might refer to us as a townie club because our base in Roslevan was perched right on the edge of Ennis. We used to resent that term and we often took delight in ramming it down their throats on the scoreboard. But we effectively are a town club now in many ways, because nearly two-thirds of the parish's population live in a predominantly urban area. And we have to change our mentality to cater for that reality. From the bottom up.

Only last week, I was speaking to Paudie Butler, National Hurling Co-ordinator, about some details surrounding hiring our new coach. The talk soon drifted to our difficulties with urbanization. 'I know ye have problems there, but at least ye're going the right way about it,' he said. 'Because if the hurling people in the club don't do something about it, it will all fall apart on ye. Ye've had an awful lot of new people come into the parish in the last few years. They are looking for an identity and whichever creates the most appealing prospect, they will join that. And in an urban club, that can be swimming, cycling, rugby, soccer or hurling. It's up to the club to see that the kids are there for anybody. There may be 50 kids in sixth class in the schools in yere parish and they are there for anybody. It's like a supermarket now and if the club can provide attractive games and attractive coaching, ye will get them. It's easy to say that urbanization is the problem why young lads are not interested in hurling. That's not true. They *are* interested. But are ye giving them a structure to play games? That is important because a lot of underage games are cancelled. So the club has to take responsibility for giving young lads that option.'

We all know what's ahead of us now. Before the 1999 All-Ireland club final, our manager, Michael Clohessy, took to the floor in Croke Park. 'A journalist rang me last week and asked me, where is Doora-Barefield,' he said. 'Well, after today, everyone will know where Doora-Barefield is.'

That victory put us on the map, but Doora-Barefield is such a vastly different place now from what it was ten years ago that there are people living in Doora-Barefield now who don't even realize that they're living in the parish.

After training on Thursday evening, 17 September, management informed us of our training schedule for the weekend. We were playing Kilmoyley from Kerry in a challenge game at the LIT grounds in Limerick on Saturday at 12 noon and we were all going to the Greenhills Hotel afterwards for a meal – a rare treat. Then on Sunday, we were training on the beach in Quilty at 8 a.m. Ken Kennedy was on the treatment table in the dressing room by that stage, so I made a point of telling him about the challenge game as soon as I spotted him.

'Look, these boys might not be Portumna but just because they're from Kerry, that doesn't mean that they won't be a serious challenge for us,' I said to him. 'They're a hardened crowd. Plus, they've got Dalo [Anthony Daly] training them and he'll have them well pumped up for us.'

'Yeah, I know, they'll give us a decent game,' he responded.

Before the game on Saturday, Patsy called us all into the goal-mouth, where we crowded into a huddle. After going through the team and what he expected from each individual, he addressed us in a tone mixed with frustration and anxiety.

'We need a result today, lads, we badly need to win a game. At the moment, I'm not enjoying it and ye're not enjoying it. And we'll drive ourselves demented if we don't get a performance. Two weeks before a quarter-final, we desperately need to start performing.'

We lost by 1-14 to 0-14, a goal from a Shane Brick 20-metre free the difference at the end. From our last two challenge games, a couple of trends are already becoming clear. We've hit 14 scores but we've failed to score a goal and we're fading out of games. If fitness is an issue – and it appears it is – we're in serious trouble because we don't have enough time now to top up the tank with gas. Given that we're not averaging as many points as last year, we're going to need goals to win games – but we're not even creating the chances. We need to ana-lyse everything very closely now, but if you were to think too much about it, you'd wreck your head.

Unfortunately, the horror chamber was opened again the follow-ing morning when only 13 turned up for training. A couple of guys were working, some lads were going to the All-Ireland football final in Dublin, but five lads just didn't bother. In terms of proper hydra-tion and fuel intake beforehand, going back to west Clare would have required a 6.30 a.m. wake-up call, but management wanted to gauge commitment and attitude so close to the quarter-final. Once again, they got their answer from some guys, and it is eating away at the morale of the squad like a virus.

Our final challenge game had been arranged for Wednesday night against Adare, the Limerick champions, but I rang Seánie first thing Monday morning. 'Things are way too negative at the moment and we'll suffocate ourselves with it,' I said to him. 'It's hard to be positive but we've got to try and blow this negativity out of the water, because it's killing us.'

'Yeah, it's a concern,' he replied. 'And we've got to do something about it.'

We have got to choose our attitude now, especially Patsy. More importantly than him being a coach now and enlightening us with new drills and tactics, he has to lead us. To create a more positive mindset. Before training on Tuesday evening, I rang Patsy. It may have been beyond the limits of accepted player–manager dialogue, but I felt the issue had to be addressed.

'Patsy, I'm not telling you your business now, but I think you're being a bit too negative at the moment,' I said. 'There's a really negative vibe around the squad. I know it's not coming from you, but I think your frustration is adding to it. I know you're pissed off with guys, but we need to turn this around now and it has to come from you, starting with tonight.'

He wasn't interested. 'I take your points, but my negativity is coming from the negativity of guys not making it to the training field. We're just not getting the bodies on the field. There has never been a day where I've turned around to John [Carmody] or the selectors and said, "Yeah, everyone is here." There is always someone missing. Either they're injured, have excuses, or they just couldn't be bothered their ass to turn up. I just can't understand it. Look at Sunday for Christ's sake – 13 guys at training. Two weeks before a county quarter-final. A complete fucking joke.'

I was a bit concerned with where this was going. 'I accept all that, but we're less than two weeks away now from a quarter-final and this negativity needs to be knocked on the head tonight. If you want, I can do up some positive stats about our season and give them to you for you to deliver.'

'No, I'm not talking tonight,' he responded. 'It's time for action now, and guys need to start showing me they're serious through hard work on the pitch. Whatever I have to say, I'll say it next week before the quarter-final.'

'Jeez, Patsy, it will be too late by then. You need to do something tonight.'

'No, I said I'm not talking tonight.'

'Well, somebody better say something,' I said.

'If you feel it's important,' he responded, 'you can take the stretching beforehand and I'll give you five or ten minutes before training starts to talk to the lads.'

'OK, either Seánie or I will talk to the lads then.'

The second I got off the phone, I rang Seánie. 'Patsy's not interested in trying to address this, so will you do it? It might seem better coming from you.'

'No. It's in your head, so you need to deliver it.'

As soon as I put down the phone, I started jotting down a few notes. Two days earlier, Kerry had won the All-Ireland football title after the greatest resurrection in their storied history. After stumbling through the qualifiers, they went into an All-Ireland quarter-final where they were expected to be blown to smithereens by Dublin. After they turned the gun on Dublin, it set them up for the All-Ireland.

You couldn't dream of comparing us to Kerry, but I thought the analogy between where both teams were at before their respective big-game quarter-finals was a decent place to start. I also spoke to Kieran Shannon, the writer and sports psychologist, who is also a good friend of mine. He had some good pointers as well.

Jamesie was taking the session in Gurteen that evening. After the stretching was completed at the corner of the top field, in front of the AstroTurf, I called the lads into a huddle. Seánie and Jamesie knew what was coming, but I never got a chance to run it by Darragh O'Driscoll beforehand. Numbers were pretty high and there were only three lads missing from the squad.

'Look, I'm only going to speak for three minutes because it needs to be said. I just feel that we're swimming in a sea of negativity at the moment and we're going to drown ourselves in it. You have to feel good to play good, you don't have to play good to feel good. If we're all waiting to play good, we might never feel good about ourselves and we might as well write off the season here now. We're putting ourselves under too much pressure at the moment and there's this feeling going around that we're going nowhere because we haven't been able to win a game recently. This needs to be addressed now because if we're seven points down with 20 minutes to go tomorrow night against Adare, we'll waste those last 20 minutes because lads will be thinking, "Jeez, another game lost," and we'll get nothing out of it. We need to empty the tank tomorrow night and get the maximum out of ourselves. Fuck the result, just burst yourself for 60 minutes and stay positive throughout the game.

'Everybody here has to be positive from now on because this is where the road to the quarter-final begins. You've got to come to that game positive tomorrow night, you just have to. Each guy here, say to yourself before the game that you're going to give yourself three targets: whether that's a personal hook-block-tackle target that you have to meet, how many scores you're going to try and set up, how many puckouts you're going to win, that you're not going to concede any stupid frees. Whatever it is, give yourself a target and chase it. And if it's not working out for you, just keep going after it and stay positive.

'People often ask me, "What's Seánie like in a dressing room?" And I always tell them that the two phrases I always associate with Seánie are "Next ball" and "Hard work". Do ye ever hear the man saying much different in a dressing room? It's not rocket science; if we keep working hard, it will turn for us.

'Look, I'm not comparing us to Kerry, but Kerry are the perfect example for us. I was at their game against Sligo and they got out of there with their lives. They fell into an All-Ireland quarter-final against Dublin and what did they do then? They reaffirmed their positives; their big-game experience, their record in Croke Park, their record against the Dubs. It doesn't matter how they got there, they got there. It's the same with us. We're in the quarter-final now and it doesn't matter a damn how we got there. Broadford might have needed to top that group but we didn't. We're a championship team that gets motivated by the big days. Same as Kerry. That's what we do.

'Now, let's reaffirm our positives. The three games we've played against Ballyea, the 'Bridge and Ogonnelloe, our backs were to the wall in all three but we came out on the right side of them. We played poorly in two of them but we still got the result. We've conceded just three goals from play in our last ten championship games over the last two seasons. We just don't concede goals – against anyone. No team in this championship has a better goal-concession ratio than us this season. That's not down to me; it's down to our defence. We've a serious defence. People say we don't have pace at the back, but what team has ever opened us up? Newmarket did last year when we were half asleep and we were destroyed from over-training.'

I took a breath and continued: 'Four of the six teams we could meet in the quarter-final have never beaten us in senior championship. And the two that have – Newmarket and Kilmaley – what would we give for a crack at those two?'

At that moment, I caught Darragh O'Driscoll's eye. 'What would you give, Darragh, for a crack at Newmarket with ten minutes to go when it's a right battle?'

He looked at me with glazed eyes. 'I'd fucking love it.'

I kept going: 'They won't fucking roll over us again if we meet them because we'll be ready for them this time. And if it's Kilmaley, we'll be gunning for them too because we'll always owe them one after 2004 [when we lost the county final to them by a point]. Somebody said to me the other day that Inagh-Kilnamona were flying. I was impressed with how they took Tulla apart, but I don't care how well they're going; they do not want to meet us. They can go on about wanting revenge for last year but, deep down, they don't want to see us coming near them because we put doubts in their heads last year. I knew that game was over ten minutes into the second half because they couldn't get the ball past our half-back line. We bullied them around the place, fucked them out of our way. No matter how well they're going, if they meet us, those doubts will be still there.

'Anyway, what have they done? What the fuck have Newmarket done? Fair play to Clonlara, they're a serious crowd. But let's see how they respond when they're in a war with us! Stick your chest out now. All the big guns – Clarecastle, Wolfe Tones, the 'Bridge – they're all gone. We're the fucking top dogs now left in this championship. We're Doora-Barefield and we don't forget that. Just think of what this club stands for. Think of what we have done. We spin it whatever way we have to now. We mightn't be going as well as we'd like, but we use whatever positives we have for our benefit. What are we being so negative about? Look around ye! Look at the positives in this group. Look at the fucking power!'

I was scanning the eyes in the group around me. I fixed a stare on Cathal O'Sullivan and hit him a shot into the chest with my fist. He didn't flinch, just gritted his teeth.

'Look at the power Cathal has. You might as well be hitting the wall. Look at the experience around here! What other team has that? For Christ's sake, we've one of the greatest players who ever played the game standing over there [Seánie]. What would any other club left in the championship give to have him in their corner?'

By that stage I was wired. One point I had wanted to make was the contribution of Ken Kennedy and Marty O'Regan. They had been our two best players all year because they'd been playing with an arrogant, almost belligerent attitude towards their opponents, physically dominating them, railroading anyone who got in their way of the ball. They were putting in savage body hits, opening guys up whenever they got the chance, but it was mostly disciplined and intelligent play. For God's sake, Marty made 35 plays against Broadford – mind-blowing statistics for a corner-back in 60 minutes. If we followed the lead of Marty and Ken, we'd physically dominate any team left in the competition. Using that example just went out of my head but I felt I'd done enough talking by then so I just nodded over to Seánie.

'We have everything going for us, but what's bringing us down is that we're not working hard enough,' he said. 'We start now the second the session begins and when we come to play Adare tomorrow night, we work like fucking dogs.'

Given that we were playing 24 hours later, Jamesie's session was mostly tailored around forward play and creating goal chances. We finished the session with a conditioned game of backs and forwards, but in the final minutes Ivor Whyte turned sharply for a ball and collapsed in a heap. His cries were piercing the cold night air and Patsy just blew the whistle and concluded the session. We gathered around Ivor and a couple of lads carried him into the dressing room.

It looks like his knee has gone. Again. Three days before we played

Inagh-Kilnamona in last year's quarter-final, he tore his cruciate ligament. After the operation, he took up residency in a gym to build his knee back up, and his return to full fitness during the summer was a major boost to our championship aspirations. Now, it looks like another season is gone for him.

I texted him the following morning to see how he felt, and the prognosis didn't seem good. 'It's still badly swollen and it feels like what happened last year,' he texted back.

I met him at lunchtime and he was a little bit more upbeat. 'Eugene [the physio] thinks it might only be the medial ligament,' he said.

A couple of hours later though, his worst fears were confirmed. His cruciate ligament was gone again.

It was another huge hammerblow. Another good player gone. Yet when I arrived into the dressing room in Gurteen before the Adare game that evening, the tone of the mood felt different. Almost giddy. I had completely forgotten that the draw for the quarter-finals had been made at 6 p.m.

'Who did we get?' I asked Mikey Cullinan.

'Newmarket.'

A kind of excited energy shot through me. Interesting. Difficult, but interesting. Just at that point, I caught Davy Hoey's eye. 'Great draw,' he said. 'Just what we needed.'

Ken Kennedy, who was togging off beside Davy, was equally happy. 'I'm delighted we got them. It's time to set the record straight now from last year.'

Although they were the only unbeaten team in the competition and they'd emphatically dominated the group of death, it was still a decent draw for us. Even though our form has been poor, if we'd been drawn against one of the lesser teams, we might not be as tuned in as we'd need to be. And if there is any resistance or pride left in us now, a joust with Newmarket will surely draw it out of us.

Maybe it's just meant to be. We initially drew Kilmaley, but when the last two names were drawn – Clonlara against Inagh-Kilnamona – they realized that those teams had already met in their group and couldn't possibly meet again. The whole draw had to be done again.

And the second time, we got Newmarket, with the winners to play either Clonlara or Clooney-Quin in the semi-final.

We couldn't have got a harder draw, but there was only one thing on our mind and John Carmody focused on it as soon as he entered the dressing room. 'Ye've all heard the draw and ye know what's ahead of ye. And if ye have any doubts, just remember the sick feeling ye had in yere stomachs coming out of Cusack Park last year after they'd walked all over ye. Do not forget that feeling.'

Before we went out, I went through our puckout signals, to make sure everyone was on the same wavelength. Then Seánie reaffirmed the importance of our new puckout strategy, especially in the context of having drawn Newmarket. 'Against Clarecastle, they brought their half-forward line out to midfield, and they're going to do the exact same to us on our puckout. So we've got to get used to our strategy here now and be ready for what's coming in ten days. Half-backs and midfielders, make the space and Christy will find you.'

There was just one more thing I needed to say on that before we left the dressing room: 'If I'm going short, stick up your hand and catch the fucking ball. I don't want to see any of this craic of guys taking it on your stick. You won't have time against Newmarket. Get it into your hand and then move it.' Patsy just nodded at me.

Our performance was a sign that we finally seem to be getting it right. We didn't win. But we didn't lose. We drew a very competitive game: 1-14 each. Adare are going for three-in-a-row, they are the best team in Limerick by a distance and they weren't holding back. They'd all their big guns out – Mark Foley, Timmy Houlihan, Conor Fitzgerald, Donncha Sheehan – and we should have beaten them because we had more possession. We only scored 14 points again, but we're pretty confident that we can beat Newmarket with 14 or 15 scores because we feel our defence can limit them to less than that total.

Two nights later, we only did a light session because the footballers were playing a relegation semi-final the following day. They were beaten less than 24 hours later and management arranged our Sunday session for 7.30 a.m. Everyone was there and, while the club was naturally disappointed after the football result, the mood among the group was positive and energetic.

'We're sharp and we're fresh and I think we're coming good at the right time,' Patsy said to us as we were completing our warm-down. 'I'm a lot happier now than I was a week ago. I feel really positive for next weekend.'

Then John Carmody raised the tone a couple of notches. 'We think about nothing else now all week, only Newmarket. If we suck them into a battle, we'll see then how good they are.'

Patsy then clearly became more animated as he raised another issue. 'One final thing. How many more times is Ciaran O'Neill going to beat us? How many more fucking times? I might have beaten ye in 2007 with Corofin, but by Jesus Patsy Fahey wasn't going to beat ye in 2008. Because there was no way ye were going to let it happen. I have great respect for O'Neill, but he's our enemy now for the next week. And we're not going to let him get one over on us again.'

The situation with O'Neill just emphasizes how intertwined the whole club championship is. Apart from being a former teammate and a close friend to some guys on the panel, he also trains our minor hurlers, two of whom are on the senior panel. Before we played Adare last Wednesday evening, O'Neill's son Alan was pucking around the goalmouth, just after the draw had been made. 'Has your father put you here to spy on us?' I said to him in jest. 'And I hope it's us that you'll be shouting for next weekend.'

'Of course I'll be shouting for us,' he responded.

O'Neill knows everything about us, but he got an updated version after the Adare game because word came back to us afterwards that one of our clubmen – someone intensely loyal to O'Neill – was there taking notes for him. It was disappointing for us to hear, but that's the nature of club life: there are always schisms and fallouts and collateral damage. And there's nothing anyone can do to avoid it.

One thing we are sure of, though, is that O'Neill doesn't really rate us as a team. He still harbours that feeling after his time with us as manager in 2006, when we lost our opening game by a point and he ran us into the ground over the summer. Guys were just burned out, but he interpreted it as softness and weakness. Our capitulation to Newmarket last year may have been a confirmation of that theory for O'Neill, but we're aiming to blow it out of the water now.

We're ready for O'Neill and his crew, and we got the perfect confidence boost at 9.30 the following evening when Conny rang me: 'Just to let you know that the Red Lad will be there to talk to ye Wednesday evening.'

By the Red Lad, he means Paul O'Connell.

14. The Red Lad

I sometimes refer to Conny as Jerry Maguire – after the sports agent played by Tom Cruise in the 1996 film. Through his business, Conny acts as a sports agent to some of the top sports people in the country, but he's actually more like a Rod Tidwell – the Cuba Gooding Jr trash-talking, love-bombing, extrovert character – than a Jerry Maguire.

He's the main character on our team and he has a nickname – that only he uses – for nearly every one of us: 'Blue', 'Joey the lip', 'Rigsby', 'Mac the knife', 'Jorge Santos', 'Le Blanc', 'Hokey', 'Daz', 'Madser'. When we were in Dublin, he used to call Hass 'Reno Raines' – after the character on the old TV series *The Renegade*.

Like Tidwell, the man has his own language. 'I hear you barking, big dog.' 'He's more demons than Lord of the Rings.' 'You're so wise, brother, you're like a mini Buddha.' 'That lad wouldn't work off a battery.' 'Heartbreak city – population one.'

Sometimes he borrows his inspired words off films, especially Will Ferrell characters. 'I'm in a glass cage of emotion.' 'That will give you a deep burn in your triceps.' 'By the beard of Zeus.'

Conny has a unique personality and an amazing ability to connect with people. In 2003, he was voted 'Escort of the Year' on the Rose of Tralee. When he was being presented with his award, he was high-fiving the host, Ryan Tubridy, and comparing an Escort and a Rose to Batman and Robin. There he was, live on TV in front of one million viewers, looking like butter wouldn't melt in his mouth. And all of us laughing at the irony that only a gangster like him could pull that one off.

When he went back to the Rose of Tralee festival a year later as a guest escort, he struck up a friendship with Tyrone manager Mickey Harte, whose daughter Michaela was a Rose. Conny told Harte that he'd take care of Michaela, but the man was hardly able to take care of himself once the partying started. At the end of the week, Mickey told Conny what he really thought of his offer: 'I wouldn't let you look after my dog, never mind my daughter.'

Yet Conny and Harte maintained their friendship ever since, partly through their business dealings. He was at Conny's wedding four weeks ago. And so was Paul O'Connell.

Conny has been friends with Paul O'Connell for four years now, after first getting to know him when he worked on a contract with Powerade, for whom O'Connell is a brand ambassador. On one of their first meetings, Conny drove O'Connell from Limerick to Dublin for a photo-shoot. When he picked him up outside his house, O'Connell arrived out the door with a copy of the *Sunday Times*.

As soon as he got into the jeep, he opened it up.

'Listen here now, boss,' Conny said to one of the most powerful athletes in world rugby. 'If you think you're going to read that paper between here and Dublin, you've another think coming to you. You've got two choices: you either talk to me, or else you read every article out loud to me.'

O'Connell chose the first option and they hit it off straight away. At the time Conny was, as he'd say himself, 'in the darkness' over some domestic row he'd had with Sinéad, and he spilled his heart out to O'Connell. The Munster captain just saw it as bait; he spent half the journey home twisting the dial on the radio, searching for love songs, trying to torture Conny.

Like all of us, though, O'Connell connected so well with Conny because of his immense personality and character. During Conny's speech at his wedding last month, O'Connell spent most of it bent over laughing at its content.

Through that friendship, O'Connell has developed a real understanding of our club, especially what this season means to us. He knows all about our hurt and our recent history; about Ger Hoey, Fr Mac, our desire to win a county title, our quest to beat Newmarket. When Conny asked him if he'd come to talk to us four days before we played Newmarket, O'Connell didn't even have to think twice about it.

Only a few of us knew about his impending arrival on Wednesday night. We kept it quiet because we didn't want word leaking out and it creating a circus around the club. We certainly didn't want it getting back to Newmarket; but that was almost taken out of our hands because there was a U-13 match between the two clubs on in Gurteen before O'Connell was supposed to arrive. On the way into the dressing room, one of the Newmarket midfielders, Paudie Collins, was standing in front of our dressing rooms. Another one of their players, Anthony 'Scony' Kilmartin, was watching the game from behind the goals.

When I went into the dressing room, I broached the subject with Ken Kennedy. 'You haven't a big bag in the jeep, so we could somehow smuggle the Lions captain in here?'

'The boys should tell him to go down to the Shibeen for half an hour and have a few hot whiskeys,' Ken responded.

Seánie McMahon, who I always sit beside, overheard us. 'To hell with them. Who cares if they see him.'

We went outside for about ten minutes to puck around before we were all called back in to sit down. A minute later, O'Connell walked in behind Patsy and John Carmody. Dressed in his Munster tracksuit, he almost had to stoop down as he came in the door.

Some guys who hadn't been told were staring at him with their mouths open.

'Lads, Paul is here to talk to us,' said Patsy. 'And if training isn't going that well afterwards, we'll put him on the tackle-bags.'

So Paul O'Connell, British and Irish Lions captain, Munster captain, probably future Irish captain, and one of the best rugby players in the world, was suddenly addressing us.

O'Connell said that he didn't have anything specific in his head to say to us. He had planned on formulating something on his way from Limerick but he had come through a cobweb of back roads in east Clare and ended up in Kilkishen, where he was forced to ring Conny, who became his sat-nav between there and Gurteen. He said that he didn't know much about hurling but that he'd talk to us about some of his rugby experiences and then he'd get us to ask questions. And we'd take it from there.

From the very outset, it was clearly obvious that he wasn't brash or arrogant. His humble demeanour belied his status as a world-class player, and he was able to relate to us from his own experience as a young player with Young Munster. The broader context of this game didn't matter; he immediately knew that it was the most important game in our lives at this particular time.

He impressed on us how the same basic principles of honesty and hard work applied to all sports, no matter what level you play at. It was clear from his tone how important friendship was to him as a player – how much it should mean to play for the guy beside you. Not all professional sports teams had that unique spirit and motivation, but he was sure that our bond was unbreakable. He said that it was incredible how the 30-year-olds on this team have been watching the 20-year-olds since they were ten and now we were all teammates. In his opinion, there was no other sporting environment which could foster relationships that deep.

He marvelled at how unique and personal that relationship was and how motivating it was for guys to be in the same dressing room as Jamesie. O'Connell looked over at him and said that Jamesie was always an immensely skilful player, but he also struck him as an unbelievably passionate player who gave everything for the team. He said that that type of player in rugby really inspired him. And that having somebody like Jamesie in our dressing room had to be inspiring for us. He told us to draw on that because he felt that being on a team beside someone who had gone way beyond the call of duty always gave him great confidence.

For the next 40 minutes, we peppered him with questions. What was the spirit like in the Munster dressing room? How do they keep that spirit so strong? Do Munster prepare any differently for home games than they do for away games in the Heineken Cup? How does he keep motivating himself? What's the best advice to help address our tendency to start slowly in games? What's the best plan of action for dealing with a game plan coming apart during a match?

He was honest and thorough in his every response. In the middle of the discussion, he was just about to answer a query from Darragh

O'Driscoll when a knock came to the door and one of the lads opened it behind O'Connell. It was Mikey Rosingrave, our third-choice keeper, a fantastic young lad who is only 17 but who is probably the most passionate and committed young player in the club. He had texted me earlier that day about training and I'd texted him back to 'make sure you're there because we have something special planned'. He probably thought it was to work our way through a new batch of goalkeeping drills. He'd clearly mixed up the time that training was supposed to start or else he couldn't get a lift any earlier. Now here he was, standing in front of one of the world's best rugby players with his mouth wide open. The blood drained from his face and he almost fell on to the nearest part of a bench he could find. A few of us smirked at poor Mikey's state of shock, but O'Connell just kept going.

Two of his replies to our questions instantly struck a chord with us. Patsy had told him the team we were playing on Saturday had convincingly beaten us in last year's semi-final. He wanted to know what advice he could give us on facing the same team again now.

Conny had already filled O'Connell in on the nature of last year's defeat. O'Connell said that Newmarket had to see a different animal from the very outset on Saturday. We had to let them know that they knew they were facing a completely different atmosphere. To let them appreciate how much last year hurt us. O'Connell said that the reality of hurling is that you're out there with a weapon in your hand. He wasn't advocating dirty play or belting someone off the ball but he said that if we could intimidate someone, well then, we should be doing it.

About ten minutes later, Jamesie asked O'Connell about belief. He said that we believed we were going to win on Saturday but he still got the impression that, deep down, there are doubts there about our ability to beat Newmarket. How do you get rid of all those doubts?

O'Connell said that of course there would be doubts there. The key was chasing them out of your head by drawing on the positives. Then he turned the question back on Jamesie. He asked him, when he was playing with Clare, if they always believed that they were a better hurling team than the opposition? He asked Jamesie if he thought that they were more talented. He said that that Clare team had some unbelievable leaders and warriors. Great men.

'Yeah,' said Jamesie, 'we just felt that we had the work done. We had worked harder than anybody else. We were fitter than anybody else and we would outfight anybody else.'

O'Connell said that attitude echoed what he had said earlier about hard work and honesty. In his opinion, doubts are the same as your confidence – they can be controlled. If you have the work done, those doubts will serve you well because they will make sure you don't walk out on to the pitch complacent. Most doubts are good things: they make you wary, make you conscious of pitfalls in a game, and make you cover off those pitfalls. He told us that if there weren't doubts in sport, nobody would ever hear of these great stories of guys digging out unbelievable results from nowhere. Doubts are what make sport. If everything was a certainty, there would be no fun. And that's where the joy comes from winning. Getting rid of the hurt and pain after years of trying.

Just before the session was about to be wrapped up, John Carmody thanked O'Connell for his immense input. And then he asked if there was one final piece of advice that he'd like to impart. He just implored us not to walk off the pitch with any regrets. To leave everything we had out there.

And with that, he thanked us for our time.

After a huge round of applause, a lot of guys went up to shake O'Connell's hand. We'd entered the dressing room less than an hour earlier in daylight, and by the time we left it the floodlights had been switched on. It was almost the perfect metaphor for how we felt – energized and hopping off the ground. During the stretch in the top corner, the positive impact O'Connell had made was clearly visible.

He hung around for a while afterwards to watch us train. As we took a quick water-break after about half an hour, I looked over and O'Connell was chatting on the edge of the pitch to Jamesie, Tommy Duggan (the club chairman) and a few more people. He was obviously interested in our club, who we were and what we stood for.

At times it's easy to perceive elite sports people as a million miles detached from ordinary club players like us, but O'Connell was nothing but humble and genuine. Real world-class.

As we were stretching afterwards in the middle of the pitch, Darragh O'Driscoll spoke. He reiterated three points that O'Connell had spoken about: the edge; the personal ambition to be as good as you could be; the motivation. Then he looked over at Davy Hoey.

'Dave, I'm thinking of you when I say this – our motivation is for Ger. We all remember how horrible February was.'

Any comment that was made or aired had a direct thread to what O'Connell had already spoken about.

'We start building the atmosphere from now,' said Ken Kennedy. 'There's no point starting to tune in for this game on Friday. I'm thinking about it all week and I'm getting shag-all work done.'

'We come with a different mentality on Saturday,' said Cathal O'Sullivan. 'Remember what they were saying about us after last year's game – "men against boys". Well, we'll fucking show them on Saturday. So stand up and be a man.'

By the time Patsy got around to having the last word in the huddle, the man was charged like he had a kinetic undercurrent running through his veins. He was pumped, his eyes flashing, mouth working fast, wired to the centre of his squad.

'We start the process of intimidation the second we get off that bus on Saturday. I saw some of ye here tonight saluting "Scony" Kilmartin down behind the goal. Well, that kind of shit is out from now on – if we see any of them around town or at work, we don't even look at them. On Saturday, you shake your man's hand, and then the first chance you get – on the ball – you fucking bury him.'

After we'd showered and changed, management had a meeting with six senior players in the dressing room. We were conscious of the need to keep it brief because we were meeting again on Friday night. We went through our game plan and our puckout strategy. We decided to choreograph the first five puckouts – so everyone knew what was happening – and then it was my call after we'd seen how they set up on us.

The last five minutes of the discussion focused on what O'Connell had said about Newmarket having to see a different animal from what they faced last year. At one stage, Patsy had asked his advice on how we might need to break up Newmarket's momentum if they got a run on us. In any case, it was something that we had often spoken about. That if a row did start, we needed to make sure that there were more of us in there than them. Just to let them know that if they wanted to start anything, we had more physical presence in there than them. But we obviously had to be cute about how we executed it, to avoid getting a card or sparking off something ridiculous or rattling ourselves.

'What Conor [Hassett] did the last day was lunacy,' said Seánie. 'I've great time for him, but he's no good to us now on Saturday because he's suspended. There's no point in us going down to 14 over something stupid. We're finished if we do. So if you get hit, you either discreetly hit back or else you put the ball over the bar. Be hard and mean, but no retaliation.'

Seánie has been in every battle known to man, but I still felt that – along with our discipline and focus – we needed to bring something more to the table. As much as they believe we have a soft underbelly, we believe the same about them. 'The bottom line is that O'Neill thinks we're a bit soft,' I said to the small group which had assembled in dressing room three. 'That's going back as far as 2006, when he managed us. I'm sure that's what he has them thinking, and they'll just believe that they're way better than us. Sure Marty [O'Regan] was cleaned out by Colin Ryan last year because Marty was concussed. And Colin Ryan has another think coming to him if he reckons he's going to clean Marty out again.

'I really think they'll crack if we put the heat on them. From every angle. As O'Connell said, be that different animal. Give off that different vibe. Have them thinking, "Where did these guys come out of?" [Ger] Loughnane often made reference to that: "Be roaring and shouting encouragement at each other throughout the game. And roar even louder if we get a score or someone clears a great ball. And have them thinking, 'Jeez, it's true what they say about these guys – they really are half mad.'" We have to be totally clear-headed in what we're doing, but that's what these boys have to see on Saturday; that we're focused – but half demented at the same time.'

On the way home from training, I got a phone call from my younger brother John.

'Well, are ye ready for them?'

'We are,' I replied. 'We're going to hit them with everything we have.'

About half an hour later, Conny rang me.

'Well, how was he?'

'Brilliant,' I replied. 'Excellent. Just what we needed. Jeez, I've a good feeling about Saturday. I really think we can do it.'

In classic Conny tongue, he immediately borrowed a line from the Ridley Scott film, *Gladiator*.

'As Caesar said to Maximus, "Whisper it."'

15. White Fluffy Clouds

Before our final team meeting on Friday night – less than 24 hours before the quarter-final – everything seemed right. The meeting had been scheduled for Fahy Hall in Roslevan at 8.30 p.m. but we had to wait outside until 8.40 because a prayer service was still running inside. Still, that time gave us the opportunity to chat among ourselves and to gauge the mood. And the mood felt perfect.

I had a good talk with Davy Hoey. He hasn't played a full league or championship game since June, but he's regained his fitness and his appetite over the last few weeks and has neatly slotted into the centre-back spot. We had met up in Gurteen on Tuesday evening to practise short puckouts and he really seemed to have come back to himself. Much of that credit has to go to Seánie McMahon, who has been constantly ringing Davy over the last few weeks. Nothing heavy; just saying the right things.

The only real danger for Davy coming into a game like this, in which we've invested so much, is that he could become submerged by all that emotion. Separating emotion from hard-headed business can't be easy. But he feels that he's got his head around that transaction.

'I'm flying it,' he said. 'I'm going to play the best game I've ever played. I can feel it. I've never felt emotion on this level before a game. I've been out in Templemaley talking to Ger over the last few days. And I'm going out there again tomorrow. I've cried, but it's actually been a good release for me as well. I'm gunning myself beforehand to say something really passionate about Ger, but I'm not sure if I will. We'll see, because I want to keep my emotions in check. I don't want this overriding feeling to take over either – that we have to win for Ger. We win because we're Doora-Barefield. That's what he would want.'

Just before the meeting began, I handed Patsy and John Carmody copies of a document I had typed out earlier in the week. It was titled 'Reaffirming our positives'. It read as follows:

1. St Joseph's have played eight senior championship quarter-finals in the last 12 years and have won all eight – a 100 per cent record. No other club in the county has a better strike rate in county quarter-finals than us.
2. St Joseph's have only conceded one goal from play in four championship games to date – no other club in the county has managed this.
3. Against Ballyea, Sixmilebridge and Ogonnelloe, our backs were to the wall each time and we came out on top. Along with Newmarket, we were the only club to win our first three championship matches.
4. This is just like the Kerry–Dublin All-Ireland football quarter-final.
5. Kerry went into that game written off – just like we are now. Newmarket are going into the county quarter-final as raging favourites – just like Dublin.
6. We're like Kerry – we have all the experience and know-how. Newmarket are like Dublin – coming into this match in a blaze of hype, with huge expectation, supposedly flying it, but without being really tested.
7. We adopt Kerry's attitude now by reaffirming our positives:
   We have huge experience
   We know how to win big games
   We have one of the best players to ever play the game.
   We are physically powerful, probably the most physical team in Clare.
   We are Doora-Barefield, the top dogs left in this championship.
   And we are going to beat Newmarket.

When Patsy began to talk, he focused heavily on the first point. 'Jeez, lads, I wasn't aware that our record in quarter-finals was so good. A 100 per cent record over the last 12 years – that's a serious strike rate at this stage of the competition. And it proves one thing: we know how to win these big games.'

Patsy had about four pages of his own notes, which he went through forensically. He gave a detailed breakdown of Newmarket's players and how he thought they'd set up. Then he went through each one of us and what he expected of us. He focused on Seánie more than any other player.

'I'm expecting a massive game out of Seánie tomorrow and he is going to win the game for us,' said Patsy. 'Our game plan is primarily focused around Seánie. Unless the measured pass or the score is on out the field, we get the ball into him every time. He has the beating of his man, but we can't afford to have Seánie going out to the corner and battling for his own possession out there. Get it into him and then get in close to him for the pass or layoff. There are goals to be got, so let's start sniffing around that goal with every opportunity.'

Our job tomorrow was to perform, and Patsy was just reaffirming our job in the meantime: hydrate; visualize; stay loose; keep to the routine.

The rest of the management had their say, but the meeting probably lasted too long – close to 50 minutes – because guys were anxious and it was getting close to 10 p.m. Just before we finished up, Patsy had the last word: 'I've goosebumps on the back of my neck already. I've never been as up for a game in all my life. I'm expecting a huge performance from us. I know it's in us. I really believe it's in us. The mood and the atmosphere is spot-on. This is our 80th time meeting and we've already played 20 matches. The work has been done. The experience is in the team and the squad. We are ready. Believe we are ready. And let's get ready now to hit these boys with everything we have tomorrow.'

After our stretch and puckaround in Gurteen before the game on Saturday, we had new travel arrangements for heading to Cusack Park. Gurteen is just two miles from the county grounds and we'd normally travel in cars and park near the Glór theatre, across from the pitch. However, management decided that we'd travel by bus for the first time since the county final in 2004.

One reason we always travel in convoy is to save money and, while it may have been a change of routine – which is not always advisable – management wanted to ensure total focus and that guys wouldn't have to worry about finding car spaces before an expected big attendance.

On the short journey in the Quin road, the bus was silent and the atmosphere thick with adrenalin and nerves. For many of us, youthful naivety is no longer an asset. You can dwell too much on fears, but we've all tried to take the positives from what we've heard over the last week. You isolate some of that advice and then refer back to it as a safety mechanism. As Paul O'Connell said, most doubts are assets; they make you wary and conscious of pitfalls in a game, and make you cover off those pitfalls.

You sift through the clutter in your head, ignoring the sights around you which invade your thought process. You picture the game you want to play, but you paint the picture with very basic brush strokes.

Clear head.

Always positive.

Doubt your doubts.

First ball.

Next ball.

And the next ball.

That's all you think about. Again. And again. And again.

After taking a right at the roundabout beside the train station, the bus travelled 200 metres along Clon road before taking a left and then a sharp right along the Causeway road. A decent-sized crowd seemed to be making their way towards the ground as the bus turned right again and eased its way up outside Cusack Park.

'Heads down now, boys,' roared Patsy from the top of the bus. 'Don't look or talk to anyone.'

The first thing I always do when I enter the ground is look at the three flags above the scoreboard to see how hard the wind is blowing. As usual, it was gusting straight down the pitch. If we won the toss, we had already decided to play against the breeze in the first half. We'd planned on lacing that opening half with hard hitting and explosive hurling, and we felt we'd need the elements with us in the second half to try and sustain it.

As soon as we entered the dressing room, the mood felt right. Tense but focused. Just right. This may not be a county final, an All-Ireland final or a Heineken Cup final live on Sky Sports. But at this exact moment, this is the most important game in our lives. Our whole season, our quest to bring some happiness back to our parish after a year of tragedy, is all on the line over the next hour. You can't think like that, but you know by the mood and the atmosphere of the room that this is big. That this is a defining moment for this group of players.

After we got togged off, Jamesie and Seánie addressed the forwards in the showers. After they had finished, Ken and I led the backs and the two midfielders in there to go over some basic but fundamental points.

'Be disciplined but hit hard,' I said. 'And no stupid frees. If you're going to give away a free, make sure it's a good one. Put him on his hole and make sure he knows you're not messing around with him.'

There were two other points I wanted to get across.

'We have got to hold the line at all costs in the half-back line. We can't afford to have ye dragged out the field and have acres of space inside in front of our full-back line. Sit back and let the midfielders and half-forward come down the field and scrap like hell in the middle third. Kevin [Dilleen], you gotta control that middle third for us now. You've got to be our organizer out there. And if the half-forward line aren't coming out the field and doing their job, let them fucking know about it.

'Secondly, we all know where the first five puckouts are going. Well, the third one is going short to either Davy [Hoey] or Darragh [O'Driscoll]. So be ready for it and don't look surprised. It doesn't matter what happens, that puckout is going short. Their full-forward line is going to try and split the space between our full-back line and half-back line because their half-forward line are going to be playing way out the field. So you've got to get into space to give me an outlet.

'And finally, lads, as O'Connell said, empty the tank and have no regrets. Because we're going out to win.'

One of the other four quarter-finals taking place over the weekend – Cratloe versus Broadford – was the curtain-raiser to our game. It was running a little bit behind schedule, which meant that we had to remain in the dressing room longer than we had originally planned.

The worst time before a big championship game is often that wait before you hit the pitch, when the time crawls and seconds can seem like minutes. For me, I always use that time to think of my favourite sports quote. It's from an interview given by Offaly's Johnny Pilkington to Tom Humphries before the 1998 All-Ireland final.

It's 3.15 on Sunday and everything else is forgotten about. I like that. All that matters is the 20 lads togging out, plus the management. The lads who have put in the effort. You don't want to let them down. Everything is forgotten about, all the troubles, all the worry. You have a job to do. It starts then and you tune off the other things. Everybody is focused in on the one thing. You know the sounds, fellas chatting, balls banging, lads getting rubs, all the talk, fellas a bit nervous. It's a nice place to be actually. Gets you away from everywhere, no trouble, no bitterness, no anything else. Just some lads out to do a job.

At the end of the day, this is what it's really all about. Getting ready to go into battle with your best friends, your neighbours, your own people. For me, that is always the ultimate comfort blanket. You may be racked by nerves, but where else in the world at this exact moment in time would you rather be? Nowhere.

In that regard, this dressing room is the only place you want to be. You look around at the faces and you see the focus, the intensity, the honesty, the desire to win for this club. For me, it's always written on Seánie's face more clearly than anyone else's. There's no manic look or gritted expression behind the visor on his helmet; just a serene look of calm and focus. Jeez, the man looks lean and primed. We're really ready.

I go to the toilet as usual and lock myself in for a minute. I bend down on my knees, as I always do, and ask Jesus to bless me and to look after us. To try and guide us over the line.

When I open the door, Ken passes by me and I just wink at him. 'Best of luck,' I say to him. 'Backing one another up 100 per cent.'

'Yeah,' he says. 'Plenty of calling now. And best of luck.'

When I make my way back into the dressing room, I approach Cathal O'Sullivan. 'I'm delighted you're back on this team because we need you. Fucking ruthless now, first to the ball and if it goes past you, I'm right behind you. Backing one another up now the whole time – no matter what.'

We're getting ready to go now. Lads are stretching, hopping balls off the wall. Everyone is finished getting rubs from Eugene in the shower area and we're all in the centre of the dressing room now. I go over to Seánie and shake his hand. No words are exchanged. We just look into each other's eyes. Let's get this done.

We're just some lads out to do a job. But this job is more personal than it's ever been for us before. Everybody – the whole group – is wrapped in a huge huddle. I don't know whose left shoulder I have a grab of but there is serious power there. You scan the eyes for the truth. It's clear. We are ready to go.

The decibel levels are increasing now. The hurley carriers are sorted and there's nothing left to organize. There is calm, but there's also controlled passion and emotion. Patsy has the last word in the huddle.

'This is personal for a couple of reasons. These boys laughed at us after they beat us last year – don't forget that out there. It's been a tough year for us, but we're going to dedicate this performance to two men: Ger Hoey and Father Mac. We owe it to ourselves and to everyone in the parish to do whatever it takes to win this game. SO WHATEVER IT TAKES TO WIN TODAY – NO MATTER WHAT – YOU FUCKING DO IT.'

★

We were on the pitch about three minutes before Newmarket arrived out. As soon as I heard the cheer from their supporters, I glanced over to the tunnel to try and gauge their body language. Christ, I thought they looked a bit all over the place. Certainly cocky. If they're not ready for us, they won't know what hit them.

After we'd gone through our pre-match puckaround, we gathered in a huddle, 30 metres from the town goal. Conny was floating around with a water bottle and he'd already picked up the similar vibe that I had. 'Did ye see the way they came out?' he said. 'Arrogant and casual as fuck. So be ready now to unleash hell on them.'

Newmarket had already won the toss and had elected to play against the breeze in the first half, so we reaffirmed the importance of getting on top early in the game. We squeezed tightly together again and inhaled deeply. This was it. Let's go.

Both teams went at it hard from the throw-in. They had the first couple of attacks but we repelled them. I broke my good hurley during one of those passages of play – which is always a minor setback – but I felt comfortable with how we'd settled into the game. We were getting the hits in hard and early and they'd already set up with a defensive-minded formation by playing a sweeper against the breeze. They were clearly trying to create early space in our defence, but I couldn't see them burning us with how we'd reorganized ourselves.

The opening period was just a slugging match and when the first score arrived on five minutes, it was us who got it. It was a really good score too, well engineered across the field, before Damien Kennedy finished it.

Newmarket quickly replied with two Colin Ryan points, one from a 65, but we were back level soon afterwards with another good score from Greg Lyons. By this stage, Newmarket knew they were in a game. We just had to maintain that pressure.

We were still struggling slightly on our own puckouts. The first five puckouts had gone pretty OK – we won three of them – but their sweeper was limiting our options in trying to create two-on-one scenarios on the break around the middle third. They were playing just two men in the full-forward line but they were splitting the space intelligently in the zones between the full- and half-forward line. After I banged one short puckout to Davy Hoey – which I slightly under-hit – he had to take it on the hurley, which cost him a split second, and it invited the Newmarket cavalry on to him. We got the ball away, but you could clearly hear the groans of our supporters in the stands, along with the audible requests to drive the ball long.

After the ball was cleared, I shouted out to Davy. When he turned around, I put my hand up in the air.

'My fault, I half-topped it. But stay alert. Keep finding that space because there's no point me banging it long for the sake of it.'

The only negative aspect of our game as the half progressed was that we were conceding more scoreable frees than they were. We were getting bodies in quickly to the tackle but we weren't always disciplined enough, and they began to punish us. Colin Ryan converted two frees in quick succession but we put the heads down and kept going. By the first quarter, we'd the game levelled up again, this time from two frees from Seánie, who'd taken over the dead-ball striking duties in the absence of Conor Hassett.

At 0-4 each we were right in the game, but as the half wore on they got a run on us. Wing-back Mikey Cullinan had clearly been injured early in the game and appeared to be struggling with a hand injury. His marker, David Barrett, thundered into the match and rifled three unanswered points from play between the 17th and 24th minutes. After a break in play after that third score, I roared out to Mikey to see if he was OK but he didn't hear me. Before I got a chance to ask him a second time, Newmarket were on the attack again.

They had us on the back foot. We were struggling to get any decent ball into our full-forward line and Seánie had to chase out to the corners – the one thing we didn't want – to try and get his hands on any clean possession. At the other end of the field, Newmarket had slightly altered the make-up of their attack by moving their big centre-forward, Jim McInerney, in to full-forward.

After Colin Ryan nailed another free, McInerney won a good ball over Ken and made it 0-9 to 0-4 in the 25th minute. Ryan then pushed them six points ahead three minutes later, before Mike McNamara landed an excellent score in the 30th minute to bring it back to 0-10 0-5. As the half entered injury time, we had a chance to reduce the deficit to four, but the attack broke down at the critical moment and one of their defenders launched the ball deep into our half.

We needed to defend strongly now – no more scores before half-time. We were six points down against Newmarket at exactly the same stage of the game last year when they got a goal just before the break to end the contest. 'Whatever happens now,' I said to myself, 'they can't get a goal. No goal. Stay strong.'

The ball was worked up the right wing along the sideline when one of their players made the space and shot for a point. The second he struck the ball, it was clear that it wasn't going to have the distance and it was dropping in a zone about ten metres from the goal. Cathal O'Sullivan and Colin Ryan were chasing in after it, but I felt it was my ball. It was a similar situation to how they had scored their goal last year and, for a split second, that went through my mind. But this time I knew exactly what I was going to do. I was coming to bat the ball clear and clean out whoever got in my way in the process.

I crashed into the two players but I got a good connection on the ball first and I knocked it about 15 metres away to two of our defenders. We had a chance to get it clear, but two Newmarket players were suddenly on top of them and they turned over possession. One of them let fly on the ball and pinged it across the goalmouth. Cathal went at pace to control the ball, but it ricocheted off his stick and flew up into the air.

In a flash, Seánie Arthur let fly on it. Bang. It flew like a rocket into the top corner. I never even moved.

A huge cheer went up from the Newmarket crowd. Again. 'Ah, Jesus, no,' I said to myself. 'Not this shit again. Who the hell is writing this script?'

As soon as I pucked out the ball, the referee Rory Hickey blew the half-time whistle again. The scoreboard was down at the other end of the field, but I didn't need to look at it to realize that this was *déjà vu* from last year.

Newmarket-on-Fergus 1-10

St Joseph's Doora-Barefield 0-5

It was another heavy journey to the dressing room. Another occasion when chasing the doubts from your mind can seem like a futile exercise against avoiding the inevitable. No matter how hard you try and sweep them away, the demons are still there, hammering against your consciousness. An eight-point deficit isn't irretrievable, but they are better than us. They're faster than us. They're slicker than us. And they've got the breeze to assist them in the second half.

In the dressing room, there's no shouting or roaring. Everyone is sitting on the bench, getting water and energy drinks on board, trying to sort out the clutter from his own head, individually trying to examine the contribution they have made in the game.

Management are outside the door, assessing the damage. Greg Lyons, who has his jersey off, is towelling himself down in the corner. His mop of hair is wet from sweat after being concealed in a helmet. He is the first to speak.

'We're not doing what we said we would do. We're not getting the right ball into Seánie. We're not even getting ball into him. We're not getting enough tackles in out the field; we're not putting them under enough pressure when they're striking. We're just not doing what we were supposed to do.'

Different players made different contributions on what we needed to do: cut down on conceding frees; don't panic; be more aggressive; get early scores on the board.

As ever, Seánie was completely positive in his outlook: 'Look, we just keep going, keep fighting for that next ball. The next ball is all that matters. We got three goals against them in the second half last year, and we can get them again. If we get it back down to three or four points, they'll panic and we'll take them in the last few minutes. But we've got to believe that we can do it. We have to believe that we can win this.'

There was a different vibe from last year. In that game, we'd been completely outplayed in the first half and we'd been on the back foot from the first ball. At least we'd competed with them this time around.

'Lads, we've got three scores from play,' I said. 'How many scores have they got from play? What is it, four or five? Max. It's the frees that has them ahead. Nothing else. If we're more disciplined in the tackle, this game is still there for us.'

I said it because I wanted us to stay positive. But deep down, I didn't have much conviction in my words. I couldn't get the doubts out of my head – the feeling that that goal had just buried us.

Looking around, I can't see how we can retrieve this. I can't see it because I don't believe it myself. Jesus Christ, I've never felt like this before. What is wrong with me? I just can't get those demons out of my head.

Our nerves are still raw, and painful intimations of another defeat are seeping into our bones. Management have tried to lift us but we're still flat. We're not playing well enough to turn this around against a superior team and we just know it. We can't avoid it.

Mikey Cullinan has broken his thumb so Seán Flynn is summoned from the substitutes' bench to take his place. We try and reorganize our formation, but we seem to be just stumbling towards the inevitable when Jamesie suddenly stands in the middle of the floor.

'Right, everyone get in here now. Get in.'

We all get to our feet and hurry in. A couple of lads nearly knocked over the table in their haste – Jamesie just has that aura and effect on us. We gather tightly around the club's most decorated player.

'Look, there are more important things in hurling than medals and trophies and glory,' he said in a loud and distinct voice. 'There are more noble things in hurling than just those things. You have got to have respect, and we've lost our respect now. We have lost our respect and we have got to get it back. We've got to show what this club is all about.

'Lookit, I was over a Harty team in Flannan's last January. Christy was just after burying his daughter and before we played a match a couple of days later, I said to them, "Ye will be the guys who will carry one another's coffins." That's what hurling and friendship and brotherhood is all about. That's how much it means. Well, a week after that, I was carrying Ger Hoey's coffin. It was one of the hardest things I ever had to do. Most of ye here carried Ger's coffin with me and I don't have to tell ye how hard it was. And in time, we will all carry each other's coffin because of the respect and the friendship we have for one another. So this half is all about one thing now: respect. Get out there and hurl with respect and honour. Make it mean something. Because it means a lot to us.'

Newmarket were already on the pitch by the time we made our way back out the tunnel and as I ran down to take up my position I passed Ciaran O'Neill, who was after giving advice to their full-forward. O'Neill was one of the last six St Joseph's players who carried Ger Hoey's coffin to his final resting place in Templemaley last February. As we passed, he looked at me and I just looked straight through him. We all needed to be clear-headed and efficient now from the very first ball.

As I dropped my hurleys and bag in the corner of the goal, I turned and faced the pitch and the gust of wind immediately pressed against my face. The breeze was strong, stronger than I thought.

Shane O'Brien had their first score inside two minutes, but we regrouped and landed the next three points, two from Seánie and one from Greg Lyons, to leave six points between the sides.

From the puckout, Newmarket came raiding again. A ball came through a ruck of players on the 20-metre line and was rolling dangerously in no-man's-land. Their big full-forward, Jim McInerney, had been running towards the goal when the ball broke, so he kept going at pace and I had to get there before him. It was a 50–50 ball, but I couldn't afford to try and pick it because he'd be on me straight away. With nobody behind me, I had to protect the ball at all costs. So I scrambled to my feet, spreading my body behind the ball and knocking it away to the side where Cathal O'Sullivan got it clear. Just as I'd got it away, though, McInerney caught me on my left shin – completely accidentally – with the blades of his boot.

There was a burning sensation on my leg from the impact but I just passed it off. I was just focused on the next ball. A minute later, I looked down at my maroon sock, which was pulled up just below my knee, and I could see the blood bubbling and soaking through the sock. I wasn't really interested in examining the injury because I was still only thinking about the next ball.

Two minutes later, I went out to hit a free, 30 metres from goal. As I was running back, my leg didn't feel right. It was sore and the blood seemed to be pouring through the sock. So I pulled it down.

Jesus Christ.

All I could see was my shin bone. It was totally exposed, with the flesh having been ripped away in a huge wound.

One of the umpires spotted me straight away. 'Jesus, go down. I'll get him to stop the game.'

And then it hit me. This game is over for me. I'm out of here. My season is over. Jeez, I don't know if I'll ever be back here after this. Ah, no. My dream of winning this county title is over.

As I sat on the goal-line while our physio Eugene attended to me, the tears came to my eyes. I was thinking of Róisín. I had so much emotion inside, I wanted it to burst out of me. I wanted that to happen on this field, but not in this way. Not like this. Please God, no.

A few of the Newmarket players had gathered around to examine the commotion. Seánie Arthur began rubbing my hair, patting me on the head, trying to comfort me. Then suddenly, Mikey Rosingrave, our third-choice keeper, a 17-year-old cub, was kneeling beside me, with his arm around my left shoulder. And in that moment, the tears left me. All I could think about was what a smashing young fella Mikey was.

As they were waiting for the stretcher to come on to the pitch, Paul Madden, our sub keeper, was now standing beside me on the line. As he got ready to take my place, I switched back on to auto-pilot. 'Total focus now, Paul, you've been here before and you're well capable of doing it. Best of luck now.'

As I was being carried off on the stretcher, all I could see above me was white fluffy clouds, puffing out against the backdrop of a canvas of grey sky. In one sense, part of me was slightly relieved because there was no way we could win this game. If they got a late run on us, they could destroy us again. And I just didn't have the heart for that.

But then I started thinking again and emotion got the better of me again. 'Jeez, this is not the way it's supposed to end,' I said to the lads who were carrying the stretcher, even though I didn't even know who they were. 'This was not how this year was supposed to end.'

As I was loaded into the back of a blue van which had been converted into a makeshift ambulance, Jamesie had decided to come with me to the hospital.

'This has gone all wrong for us,' I said to him.

'Forget about it, just forget about it now,' he responded. 'Getting yourself right now is all that matters.'

When we got to the A&E at Ennis General Hospital, the first thing I asked the nurses was if there was a radio around the place, where they could tune in to Clare FM for some updated reports. I'm sure there was but they said there wasn't.

'Send someone a text there, find out what the story is,' I asked Jamesie.

A couple of minutes later, his phone beeped in his pocket. The message read: 'Newmarket ahead by nine, ten minutes left.'

It's definitely gone now.

After getting pumped up on intravenous painkillers, I was just waiting for an ambulance to take me to University College Hospital Galway to undergo plastic surgery. About 20 minutes later, Conny and Joe Considine arrived over to the hospital. They had the final result.

Newmarket-on-Fergus 2-18

St Joseph's 0-10

Colin Ryan got Newmarket's second goal in the last minute, but it was still a hammering. Fourteen points. I traced the history of our recent championship results in my mind and quickly concluded that it was our biggest ever defeat in the championship over the last two decades. Heartbreak.

It was even harder to take, given how confident we felt, going into the game. Given how much we had invested in this game, in this season. We genuinely felt that we could win a county title, but where do we go from here? Can we legitimately have those aims any more?

Given the age profile of the team, will we even be a senior team in four or five years' time?

After getting an X-ray, I then had to sign a form with my VHI number before the ambulance could be sanctioned to pick me up. My case wasn't an emergency, so I had to wait until the ambulance – whose company were contracted to VHI – came from Castlebar. I was wheeled into an empty ward, where a nurse turned on the TV and I tuned into Premiership Soccer Saturday.

Soon afterwards, the club chairman, Tommy Duggan, arrived with my gear-bag. I took off my jersey and changed into a T-shirt. I folded the jersey and handed it back to Tommy.

'You've had it a long time now,' Tommy said to me.

'Twenty years,' I responded. 'I hope I'll see it again.'

'No doubt you will, no doubt you will.'

One of the few positives from the day was the performance of Paul Madden, my replacement. Tommy said that he'd made a couple of very good saves and that his handling was excellent. I was genuinely delighted for him.

'Fair play to him, he's a great lad. Maybe it's just time for me to hand it over to him now. He's the future, not me.'

After Tommy left, Jamesie stayed chatting until the ambulance arrived.

'When you see the cutbacks around this place, today was only a minor setback,' I told him. 'But it's still a sad day for us. Since we came up senior in 1994, we've always set out at the start of any year with the intention of winning a county title. Jeez, I don't know, can we have those ambitions any more? We've got to be more realistic with our targets from now on and just make sure we don't slip any further.'

We had tried our best but we just had to accept where our place now was in the world. What I saw today in Newmarket – a young, coltish team, loaded with skill and class and pace and ambition – was almost a mirror image of ourselves in the late 1990s. The current Newmarket team still has to win a county title, but they have what we haven't: youth. We had only two players under 25 starting today, while most of their squad was in that age bracket. Too many of us are trying to wind back the clock, still desperately clinging to that hope of an autumn windfall. And most of the guys on this team who really want it – desperately want it – just don't have the legs any more.

On the ambulance trip to Galway, I knew it was the last time I'd ever play with some of those guys again. Seánie definitely won't be back. Neither will Davy Hoey. Those boys of summer will slip into retirement now. They have no more to give on the field. Their focus will just switch to the training ground from now on.

I'll miss playing with them. One of the most well-worn dressing-room clichés is that you could trust guys with your life; but there is a genuine feeling of brotherhood with club teams. When you're in a bear-pit and the odds are stacked against you and you look into your teammates' eyes – the guys you have been friends with since childhood – then you see that trust. And it always provides a massive security blanket.

Lying on a trolley in the A&E department in UCHG that night, the texts of support starting flowing in from all the lads and from management. The Newmarket manager, Diarmuid O'Leary, texted me. And so did his chief lieutenant, Ciaran O'Neill. 'Best of luck with the recovery,' the text read. 'Hard luck today, you played well. But just want to let you know that it broke my heart to see that happening to Joseph's. I got no satisfaction out of today.'

Say what you want about O'Neill, but the man is Doora-Barefield to the core. And I genuinely know that he's hurting just as much as the rest of us tonight.

At 11.59 p.m., I got a text from Seánie. 'Keep the head up and look after yourself. Call you tomorrow.'

I responded at once. 'Sound. But just wanted to let you know that no matter what happens from now on, I wanted to tell you that it was an honour and a pleasure to play with you.'

He texted back immediately: 'Appreciate that boss and it was my pleasure to hurl with you too. We'd the time of our lives. Today was cat but we won't forget the great days. You just can't beat playing with your best friends.'

16. Passion

In the days after the defeat to Newmarket, introspection hit most of us like Novocaine: it helped numb the pain but it didn't take away that low feeling. When I spoke to Darragh O'Driscoll three days afterwards, we siphoned the disappointment into separate rooms of discussion: the nature of the collapse; the hurt from being beaten so heavily; our lack of youth on the pitch; the future.

A few of the lads had already told me that Darragh had been very emotional in the dressing room afterwards but that he had spoken really well. In my mind's eye, I was trying to picture that dressing room because I knew it would be the last time that I'd ever share one with some of those guys as players. Paul Madden told me that Davy Hoey had cried. I could picture how devastated Patsy would have been and how low the rest of us would have felt after suffering our biggest championship defeat in two decades.

I was trying to imagine more than the mood because it's nearly always easier to recall the scene of a losing dressing room than a winning one at the end of a season. Maybe that's because your head is bowed and your eye level is focused on the detail of the detritus: empty bottles, discarded sticky tape, broken hurleys, jerseys strewn across the table, fresh grass stuck to a wet floor. Faces are concealed behind the mask of disappointment, conversation stymied from the lack of interaction.

When I asked Darragh to try and describe the dressing room, he said that he'd write me an email on it. The following day, it landed in my inbox.

Christy
   There are a few things I remember from the dressing room but not everything. I was the last one to speak after Patsy had spoken.

The dressing room was silent, heads down everywhere – you can imagine it yourself. Dave Hoey was in tears. I actually hadn't prepared to say anything – you don't prepare to give losing speeches, I guess. As I started to speak, I remember my voice started to break and I paused for about ten seconds to gather my thoughts and to try and stop myself from crying . . . pure silence, everyone waiting for me to start again. A few tears but I managed to stay composed for the rest of it.

I started again by saying, 'What a year', in reference to the turmoil and emotion of the season. I looked around the room and thanked each of the management team by name for their commitment. I saw Tommy [Duggan] and Dan [O'Connor] by the dressing-room door and I thanked them for their contribution in what was a very trying year for them. I remember seeing Paul Hallinan [young hurley carrier] and thanking him for hardly missing a training session all year. Then I thanked the players. I didn't mention Ger or Father Mac by name but I remember coming out with the line, 'We wanted to honour people this year but I'm not fully sure if we did.'

I mentioned the great tradition in the club and the fact that we were a junior club for much of the 60s, 70s and 80s and came through many years of disappointment to the pinnacle of an All-Ireland club title. I said that we always tried to play the game the way it should be played and that we can be proud of that fact. I said we needed younger players to come through to add pace to the team and to drive the club forward. I'm pretty sure I finished up with the line: 'We're Doora-Barefield and we will be back.'

Talk soon

Darragh

Darragh was a great captain, one of the best I've ever played under – totally committed, genuine, brave, a good leader. More than anything, though, his passion for the club and his grasp of what St Joseph's stood for framed a huge part of his make-up. I remember him at half-time in a county semi-final against Clarecastle in 2002 after having dislocated his shoulder earlier in the game. The guy was in absolute agony but he addressed us with tears in his eyes and a tone of heartbreak in his voice. You could always tell how much it meant to him.

He was a guy who commanded respect and someone who played with pride and honour – the three words that many of us in the club liked to think represented everything St Joseph's stood for. And the feeling that we weren't always true to those principles this season has made the disappointment even more acute. It feels like an offence against our core values.

The Newmarket defeat was not the fitting denouement we had in mind, and we're all hurting. But deep down inside, we have real regrets as a team, which has only shovelled more salt into an open wound. We let ourselves down because we know there is more in us. We know that we could have been more committed, more determined, more relentless in our pursuit of our goals, which might have led to glory. Winning the county title was always going to be a stretch, but that's why we needed to push ourselves to even greater extremes to have a real chance. And we didn't.

Then again, maybe emotion got the better of us. And so did fatigue with having so many dual players. They're not excuses, just reality. There were only two dual clubs in the senior hurling and football championships this season – ourselves and Wolfe Tones – and it's becoming more difficult to compete in both codes because most senior clubs in Clare specialize in either hurling or football. That is a huge challenge for us going forward.

Whatever about success though, this season was ultimately about honouring people and that's why Darragh rightly questioned the legitimacy and substance behind that promise in the dressing room afterwards. If there was any season to show what St Joseph's was all about – pride, respect and honour – this was it. And that's the most devastating aspect of the whole lot.

Darragh was an exemplar of that club loyalty and code. Apart from the captaincy, part of the reason why he put so much into this year was because nobody embodied the values he spoke about more than Ger Hoey. In fact, Ger probably inculcated Darragh with those values more than anyone else. It wasn't surprising that emotion engulfed him in the dressing room afterwards.

Darragh came into the team as a young player; but Ger had that ability to connect with people on every level, and their relationship was fostered from playing in the same defence for four seasons. 'When I first joined the panel, I really remember how encouraging Ger was to the younger players like me and Ken,' says Darragh. 'But the one thing I probably remember most about the glory days was the dressing room before big games when the backs would go into the showers for a chat. We'd usually find Ciaran O'Neill in there before us, getting ready for the game by running at the walls. After O'Neill had nearly demolished the place, then Ger would start talking and the rest of us would start listening. He would implore each man to "look at the size of us". To not come off the pitch "without having worked our socks off and if that meant being carried off, so be it".'

Although he was 11 years younger than Ger, Darragh probably developed a greater understanding than most of what the club meant to Ger, primarily because they got to travel extensively together when they both played with the AIB hurling team. Among Darragh's many memories of Ger are two incidents from the 2005 AIB tour to Australia and New Zealand. Firstly, the annual match against the Defence Forces was held in Melbourne as the Army were also touring at the same time. He was selected at wing-back, with Ger due to start in the corner behind him. However, Ger got injured in training and was devastated to be missing out on the big match of the tour.

'Before that game,' says Darragh, 'players and mentors from each side were psyching each other up with the usual calls of "Come on AIB" or "Come on the Army". I looked over at the sideline just before throw-in and Ger was staring at me with a clinched fist. He roared at me, "Come on the Parish." That was the last thing I expected to hear in Melbourne but I was rarely as proud to hear it. The parish gave us both a great sense of identity and it was a great bond when we represented the Bank.'

Two weeks afterwards, their last tour match brought them to

Sydney to play a New South Wales selection. It was Ger's last competitive hurling match and he made sure he was right for it. He was one of the best players on the pitch. 'At the final whistle, I walked over to Ger to shake his hand,' says Darragh. 'To wish him a happy hurling retirement and, I must admit, to slag him that it was no longer a game for old men. Instead of shaking my hand, Ger hugged me and, after a few moments, he said he was delighted to have played his last game with a Doora-Barefield man beside him. I still believe I was more delighted to have been playing alongside Ger. That tour and that memory is something I will always cherish.'

When we began to finalize the arrangements for our ten-year reunion trip to Kilkenny last March, we also began to loosely plan some small way for our squad to commemorate Ger. We weren't really sure how to go about it until Donal Cahill – who had been co-opted on to the committee – came up with the idea of commissioning an artist to do a pencil sketch of Ger from an old photograph. He knew a Dutch artist living in Ireland – Stan van Rensberg – and had been impressed with his work. When Cahill brought some of his drawings along to a meeting one night, we decided to press ahead with that option.

In the process of gathering numerous photographs and trying to decide on the best one which would allow van Rensberg to capture Ger's passion and character for his portrait, we came up with another idea. We decided to get John Kelly, a photographer from the *Clare Champion* newspaper, to assemble a collage of photos on a large framed poster. We would present the portrait to Siobhán and the girls, while the collage would be given to Ger's mother and father.

The collage was made up of ten photographs of Ger in action, which wrapped around the centrefold picture of him raising the Canon Hamilton trophy in the middle of the field after our first county title in 1998. The portrait was sketched from a pose for a pen picture before the 1999 All-Ireland club final. At the bottom of the frame the inscription read: 'Ger Hoey – leader, team-mate and friend. A true inspiration.'

On the night it was presented to Siobhán, we were a little concerned that she might become emotional, but her face lit up when she saw the portrait of Ger. She was delighted with it.

The photographs which we assembled for the framed collage were selected because we felt they offered the neatest collective snapshot of Ger's career: walking with his eldest daughter Elaine in the parade before the 1998 county final; celebrating with his brothers, John and David, and Jim Felle on the field after the same game; about to receive the Munster club trophy along with Ciaran O'Neill after the 1999 Munster final against Ballygunner; bursting out past Athenry's Donal Moran with the ball in his hand during the 2000 All-Ireland club final; being interviewed on the field after the 1999 All-Ireland club final, in which a plaster has failed to staunch the bleeding from a nasty cut across his nose.

The man was always in the wars. Some of us used to call him de la Hoey, after the renowned boxer, Oscar de la Hoya. In four of the ten photographs in the collage, Ger is wearing his yellow helmet, which rarely lasted 60 minutes. A couple of weeks before we played Clarecastle in the 2000 championship, Ger received 16 stitches in a head wound while playing a game with the AIB. Twenty minutes into the Clarecastle game, the helmet was gone, fired to the sideline.

Ger played for the club for only one more season before he and his family moved to the USA. His last game with Doora-Barefield was the 2001 Munster club quarter-final against Ballygunner in Walsh Park. As we made our way off the pitch that day, he extended his hand to me in the bottom corner of the field, just in front of the tunnel. 'The end of an era,' he said. 'A great era.'

Moving on, though, never meant that he was leaving anything behind. Ger's ties with the club were never severed. If anything, they only grew stronger while he was away.

'Even though he might not have been around, he was always there,' says Ger's brother, John. 'That love for the club never left him. The club was his second family. It was most of his life. I suppose he experienced the ultimate journey, from Under-10 parish league up to the All-Ireland club final. Then it was the work journey: Portlaoise, Limerick, the States, Carrigaline and then back home to Doora-Barefield.

Basically, everything was linked. Doora-Barefield couldn't be separated from the big picture. It was always there.'

Ger's death has had a devastating effect on his family, but St Joseph's have also felt a deep sense of loss. What the club has really lost is decades of presence and leadership, years of getting back what Ger Hoey was prepared to give. The chance to regenerate what is important.

'I suppose what the club have lost is huge in terms of administration and leadership,' says John Hoey. 'Ger would have given so much back and it would have been so effortless for him. It would have just been another natural progression. He would have been coaching underage teams and he would have taken the senior team eventually. There's the huge loss that the Hoeys have, but there is a huge loss to the hurling club as well. You're only guessing but you could have no problem imagining Ger as chairman of the club in ten years' time. And staying there for ten years. He was there so long, he had the respect of everyone, even the auld boys.

'The two people I remember most coming in to the funeral were Mikey Mac [McNamara] and Lott [O'Halloran]. I remember them bringing the entire Under-12 team to Corofin once for a match in two cars. Health and Safety out the window. Lads would be stacked on top of each other in the back and then three in the front seat. Mikey Mac's yellow Beetle and Lott had this auld brown Ford, an enormous yoke. I can remember it like yesterday. Ger was the captain of that team.'

John played alongside Ger on that side, both of them in the half-back line. John was one of the most promising hurlers in the club at that time, but he suffered a neck injury when he was 16 and a swollen disc forced him to stop all contact sports.

Ger was responsible for partially resurrecting his career five years later. In March 1991, we were on the way to play Blackrock from Limerick in a challenge game in Kilfinane and we only had 14 players heading through Limerick city. John was in college in UL at the time and Ger corralled him into lining out. John survived and he committed to training again, but his career definitively ended that August when he broke his leg in a junior game against Feakle in Tulla.

As he lay on the field in agony, the Feakle goalkeeper tied his legs together with a sock. There was no stretcher at the ground, so they took the ladder from the scoreboard, padded it with some coats from a few of the Doora-Barefield supporters, and then carried John off the pitch while he lay across the makeshift stretcher. As he waited outside the dressing room for the ambulance to arrive, it started raining. And the Doora-Barefield supporters reclaimed their jackets from underneath John's back. They wanted to watch the rest of the match in comfort.

'To be honest, I really missed the hurling because I was injured,' says John. 'The bond you get in a dressing room can't be replicated anywhere else. It just can't, especially a club dressing room. It's absolutely unique and it's very rare that it's broken. You'd have such pride in your club, especially when your brothers are playing. Then Ger playing behind David on the one line on such a brilliant team. You could clearly see Ger choking with pride. And the pride watching your brother do that is unbelievably special.'

'It's been very hard but, when Ger was buried, I'd say for most of the lads on that wall [from the framed photograph of the 1999 All-Ireland winning team], I can literally imagine it was close enough to losing a brother for them. I've talked to a good few of them about it, and those lads were family to him. They were as good as brothers and I can say that with me being his brother. And there would be no jealousy saying that Ger had another ten to fifteen brothers from that photograph. It was just natural.'

The Hoeys' link to Doora-Barefield still remains as strong as ever. Ger's sister Sarah still plays camogie, while John coaches the U-6s and David has already been recruited for the U-12 management next season. Ger's father Bernie is the unofficial groundsman in Gurteen, along with Jimmy McNamara. And two of Ger's daughters, Caoimhe and Orla, play camogie and ladies football with the club. 'Although Ger is gone, our family link with the club is still as strong as ever,' says John Hoey. 'It will never be broken. Ever.'

The St Joseph's senior team retired the number 2 jersey this year in honour of Ger.

★

In the last few weeks, we've appointed our underage hurling coach. Interviews took place in the Auburn Lodge Hotel in early October, where the interview panel comprised Ronan Keane, one of Clare's Games Promotion Officers, along with Joey Carton and Jamesie O'Connor. Candidates were called for interview and Alan Small – a highly qualified and hugely respected figure within Clare coaching circles at grass-roots level – was eventually appointed to the position.

We feel good to go now. Our sub-committee held a meeting with the three school principals in September and they were fully supportive of the new initiative. It's a hugely progressive step forward for St Joseph's, but it is equally important for everyone within the club – particularly underage mentors – to realize that the appointment is not a panacea for all our ills.

Ten years ago, St Joseph's were All-Ireland club champions and a huge number of people within the club took that success for granted. We didn't build on it with enough hard work at underage level and now we're all paying the price. St Joseph's still have huge respect as a club around the country, but the test now is to ensure that such hard-earned respect is not lost. Success is no accident or twist of romance. It is the result of planning and perpetual effort, and that's the challenge for all of us now.

Already, everyone seems really up for it, including the senior players. We all appreciate how important the next few years are, and the perils that lie ahead. Seven of the team that started against Newmarket were over 30 and those players will retire from senior hurling in the near future. With that issue in mind, a large group of players – from U-21 to senior – came together on 22 November for a 'Players Hurling Forum', where a ten-page framework document was drawn up for next season.

Conny chaired the forum and we were broken up into four groups in which one young player wrote the points raised by the group on a flipchart, before outlining those points to everyone else. The goals for adult hurling in the club over the coming season were discussed against the background of 'what success would look like in 2010'. Our goals were far more realistic than the ones we would normally have set.

Win promotion from Division Two of the Clare Cup.
Beat one of the top 4 clubs in the Championship.
Qualify for the Quarter-Finals.
Get our pride and respect back by playing with spirit.

I suppose, for many of us, we crave getting our respect back more than anything else. Newmarket may have taken our name in the quarter-final but the hurt has just made us all more determined to reclaim it as soon as we can.

We've been fighting that battle for a while now. Two years ago, a small group of us were at a match in Cusack Park when a couple of lads standing behind us began discussing the prospects of the teams left in the championship. When our name came up, they didn't even entertain us as realistic contenders: 'Sure those boys are finished. They've no young players coming through. Football has taken them over. Their good days are long gone.'

We casually smiled at each other, silently vowing to use those words like a flame-thrower on every other team left in the championship. Yet, we didn't. We couldn't even get out of our group that year.

Coming back the following season and reaching a semi-final was about more than just defying the odds; it was a diligent and hard-working response from a proud group of players. This year was more than just aiming to go one step further; it was about the impact and the perspective that death and loss had on our club. Overcoming grief. Healing pain. Siphoning hurt. Renewing hope. Rekindling joy.

On the face of it, ultimately we failed to do what we'd hoped to achieve. Yet did we really? We tried. We dreamed. We hoped. We fought. We healed. We tried again. We failed again. But at least we expressed ourselves through the forum which best defines us as people. Surely that isn't failure?

Sometimes we beat ourselves up too much. We see the final destination as all that matters, when the beauty is always in the journey – the camaraderie, the spirit, the togetherness, the hard training sessions, the battles, the joy in victory, the devastation in defeat, the purity of feeling part of your own unique little tribe.

For now, the good days have gone. The bad ones may only be around the corner but that doesn't mean we turn our backs and walk away. No matter what happens – good days or bad days – the club will always be part of us. It is who we are. It is in our blood. There is no separation.

Two days before we played Clarecastle in the 2002 county semi-final, Seán Mangan, our former trainer and one of Doora-Barefield's greatest clubmen, said to us that St Joseph's were normally the gauge for the mood and temperature of the parish. At the time, we were just after hitting a sticky patch for the first time in five years. 'When we're winning and playing well, the whole place is in a good mood,' said Mangan. 'When we're playing poorly and losing, everyone is in bad form.'

The communal loyalty to St Joseph's is still deep and persistent, but it no longer pervades the parish to the same degree it once did. When people talk about Doora-Barefield, hurling is often the prism through which they view us. It is how many of us want them to view us. That stems from the pride we have in our club, our history, our heritage. The strong principles and beliefs which determined the sense of worth and place that Ger Hoey always carried with him, no matter where he went.

Yet in our very own parish, the majority of our people certainly no longer view themselves through that prism of its flag-bearing hurling team. There are a myriad reasons why we have lost part of our identity as a club and that's why we almost have to start again. To redefine our goals, reset our objectives. Appointing an underage coach is a long-term plan, the fruits of which we may not see for over ten years. Yet that is the investment we are willing to make.

In the meantime, the journey will just continue. Patsy is moving on and so is John Carmody. The word on the ground is that Carmody and Ciaran O'Neill are renewing their partnership with Kilmaley again. Seánie McMahon and Davy Hoey have already announced their retirements, while Conor Hassett is going to Australia for a year, maybe longer. They are serious losses.

We just have to have faith now in our younger players. I have already been appointed U-21 manager for next season and I assembled a backroom team only last week: Conny and Darragh O'Driscoll. There is a good crop of young players there, even if roughly half of them are still minors. They are our next generation.

For now, a long, emotional and trying year has ended for us all. Along with trying to honour Ger, much of my own personal motivation this year came from Róisín. Before every match, I'd bless myself on the pitch, look to the sky and ask Róisín to look out for me. The beautiful little girl that I never got the chance to raise or cherish. The hardest thing I ever had to do in my life was place her in that little white coffin and whisper to her through my tears how sorry I was that I wasn't able to protect her or take care of her. A father would do anything for his child. The huge regret is that I never got the opportunity.

Grief is always there, at every turn. Your son doesn't have the sister he should. You see your wife depressed, and it tears you apart. The grief is just more private because people didn't know your child. They don't know what to say to you. In the early days, they often just avoid you.

The well of emotion that was bubbling inside me all year, I just kept it in check for the welfare of my family. They were my priority. If I was to finally let it all out, there was only one place I felt I could. All along, I could picture myself at the final whistle in the county final, after we'd won and I'd collapsed to my knees and the raw emotion just burst out of me like a geyser.

Maybe it's just the big-boy syndrome where men don't show their emotions, but hurling is where I express myself most. Two of my favourite places on this earth are Gurteen and the handball alleys in St Flannan's College when there is nobody else around. On those evenings, that's where I connect with Róisín more than anywhere else. Maybe it doesn't have to be this huge outpouring of emotion to grieve for my daughter. Maybe this is my way of coming to terms with her death.

In the weeks after Róisín's passing, Olivia trawled every website and booklet imaginable to try and find the words to put some kind of meaning on our grief. She couldn't find them, and then they came from the most unlikely source: Conny. It was from a text message he sent me in February after he got engaged to Sinéad. 'The year will yet offer sprays of sunshine, with Róisín all over it.'

That's what keeps you going: the loyalty, the friendship, the camaraderie, the honesty, the togetherness, the support. Most of which comes from your club-mates, all of us bound up together in this communal brotherhood that almost defines us as people.

No matter what happens, we are Doora-Barefield and we will always stick together. As Darragh O'Driscoll said, 'We will be back.' We will get stronger. We will win county titles again. We will aim to win Munster and All-Ireland titles again. And no matter how long that may take, we will certainly enjoy the journey along the way.

As for my own career, I can think of numerous reasons not to go back playing next year: my age, the injury to my leg and the risks of a recurrence, having to wear a helmet for the first time. But I can't think of one good reason why I shouldn't go back. St Joseph's Doora-Barefield is my extended family. My passion. My future.

And anyway, what else am I going to do?

Acknowledgements

Some of my closest friends advised me against writing this book. They told me that I would be bringing unnecessary hassle on myself and attracting attention to our club for more wrong reasons than right ones. Some people felt that this book would have no relevance around the country. But this is a snapshot of club life and all that goes with it. Every club in the country can relate to this story in its own way. What drives us in Doora-Barefield drives club people everywhere.

There are a number of people I would like to thank, in no particular order: Mike McInerney (St Flannan's), Fergal Cahill, Jackie Morris and Damian Lawlor. I would like to extend special thanks to Kieran Shannon, Michael Foley, Richie Fitzpatrick, Denis Walsh and Tom Humphries for all their friendship, help and advice on this project.

To Anne McManus at Sportsfile, Flann Howard, Joe Ó Muircheartaigh and John Kelly for the photographs. To John Redmond for his photographs and for his continued loyalty.

To Michael McLoughlin and Brendan Barrington at Penguin Ireland for all their help and assistance in getting this project over the line.

To Paul O'Connell for his advice and insight on that great day in Cork. To Eoin Conroy, the Jerry Maguire of the sports world and a huge figure in this book. He was always there. When I got injured in our last game, he sent me a text that evening: 'It's tough but it gives you a great ending for the book.' Thanks for everything, Eoin.

To Seánie McMahon, Donal Cahill, Derek Ryan and Fran O'Connor, super friends and great confidants.

I would especially like to thank my family – my parents Tom and Joan, my brothers James and John and my sisters Sheila and Claire. I've always regarded myself blessed to have such a wonderful family. I would also like to thank Olivia's family, especially her brother Niall, Róisín's godfather and a true GAA clubman.

Mostly though, I want to say thank you to my wife Olivia. The last two years have been the most difficult of our lives, but we remain as strong as ever. To my son Thomas, I wanted him to know about the beautiful sister, Róisín, he never knew, and to see in later life, please God, what our lives were like at that period in his young life. Thomas, you light up our lives so much and I hope that you will value and appreciate this book in time.

Unfortunately, a lot of the text in this book is fuelled by tragedy. Fr Michael McNamara was a proud Doora-Barefield man, whom we will never forget. Our physical trainer in 2009, Brian O'Reilly, also recently passed away. I never got the chance to thank him for all his efforts with us, but I would like Brian's family to know how highly I and the rest of the players in Doora-Barefield thought of him.

One of the primary reasons I wrote this book was to honour and pay tribute to Ger Hoey, one of the most remarkable people I ever knew. I was fortunate to play with some great players but I always regarded Ger as one of the greatest. I would really like to thank Siobhán Hoey for always supporting me in writing this book. I would also like to thank the Hoey family, particularly Ger's brothers, John and David.

Finally, I would like to thank everyone in the St Joseph's Doora-Barefield club, especially Patsy Fahey and Tommy Duggan, who gave me their blessing to go ahead with this project. To Darragh O'Driscoll as well, for his immense support in the early days. I won't mention the rest of the players and officials specifically but I just want to thank ye all for the best years of my life.

Hopefully, we will have plenty more. Both on and off the field.

Photo Credits